GW01607577

POST-IMPRESSIONISM

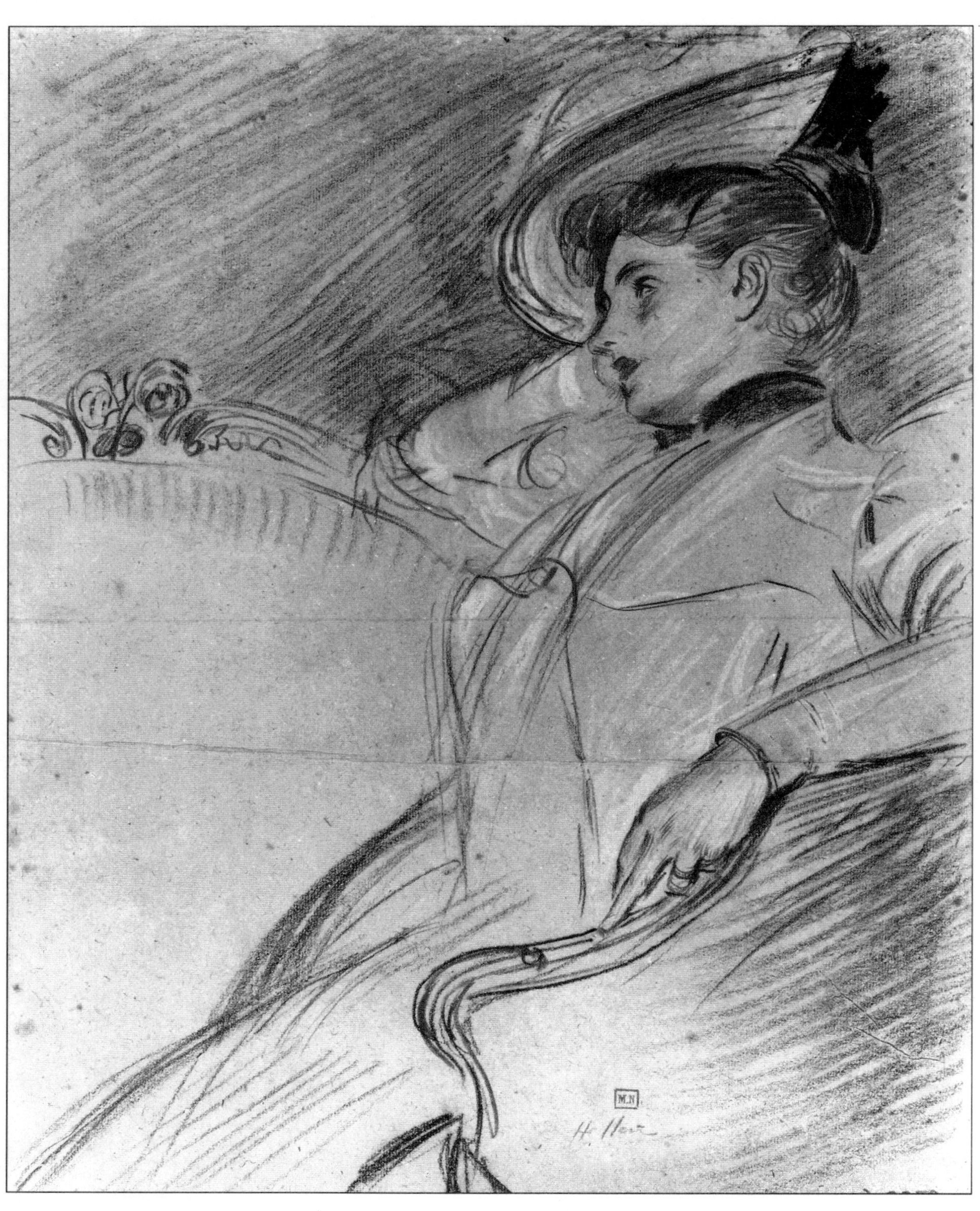

PER AMANN

POST-IMPRESSIONISM

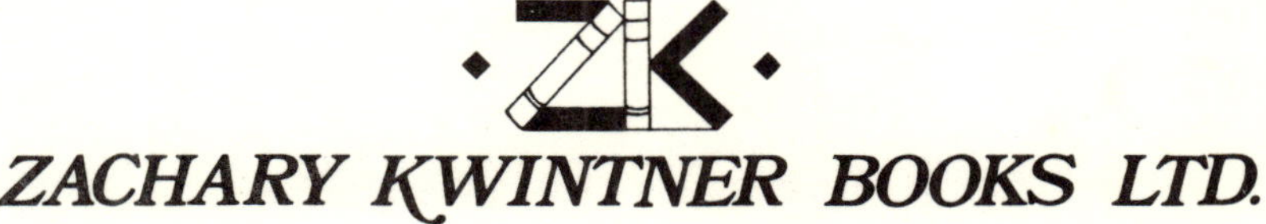

ZACHARY KWINTNER BOOKS LTD.

Cover motif:
Alphonse Quizet
Le Maquis de Montmartre (Detail). 1910
Oil on wood chipboard, 54 x 65 cm
Museé Petit Palais, Geneva

Translated by Stephen Gorman

This 1991 Edition published by
Zachary Kwintner Books Ltd.
6/7 Warren Mews, London W1P 5DJ
ISBN 1 872532 49 7
Printed in Germany – Imprimé en Allemagne

CONTENTS

A Historical Review

The history of western art shows that artistic creation is an area of human existence which is, to a great extent, subject to constant change and evolution. External influences and internal lines of development lead to a continual variation in art. Periods in which achievements ossified after having reached a peak, in which exaggerated abilities and repetition of subject matter kept the artists and the works of art at a mediocre level, were followed by epochs which produced great works never seen before, arising from new beginnings. The periods of profound artistic innovation gained a quick motion dynamism the closer they got to the present day. The Renaissance artists had almost a century to come to maturity with the change of generations, but already in Romanticism the artists only had several decades to reach their heyday. The main representative of German Romanticism, Caspar David Friedrich, was also its founder but he was already forgotten when he died, the period of Romanticism was already over. Within one lifetime the inner elements of art had changed. The attempts of Impressionism to make the perceptions of the overriding importance of colour, light and atmosphere the central point of a new style of painting were basically limited to the short space of time between 1850 and 1885. Admittedly the altered intentions were already evident in the works of many apprehending young artists before the middle of the century, but a systematic investigation of the new artistic terrain was only successful after 1850. Many like-minded artists who were becoming increasingly sure of themselves found themselves searching for something new to replace the stagnating interpretation of art.

We in the 20th century can see Impressionism as a great informative style. Even if there were many different sides to it, from plein-air painting to pointillism, it can still be seen as a complete movement. However, the artists at that time saw these years as an exciting epoch full of change: peaks, but also dangerous abysses were on the path for all of them. Very few Impressionist painters retained their original basic ideas into their late work. One of them was Claude Monet who created true Impressionist masterpieces well into this century. However, it was his individual talent which stood the test of time and kept a purity of heart and colourfulness of palette into a grand old age.

For most of the other friends from this circle the point came when they had to alter their art, so as not to rigidify – to struggle for new targets. "Around 1883, there was something like a break in my work", Auguste Renoir told his art dealer friend Ambroise Vollard, "I had reached the end of Impressionism and came to the conclusion that I could neither paint nor draw. To put it bluntly, I was at a dead-end ..."

Most of the other Impressionists were in the same situation as Renoir. They had to again leave the perception of their new painting behind them to find

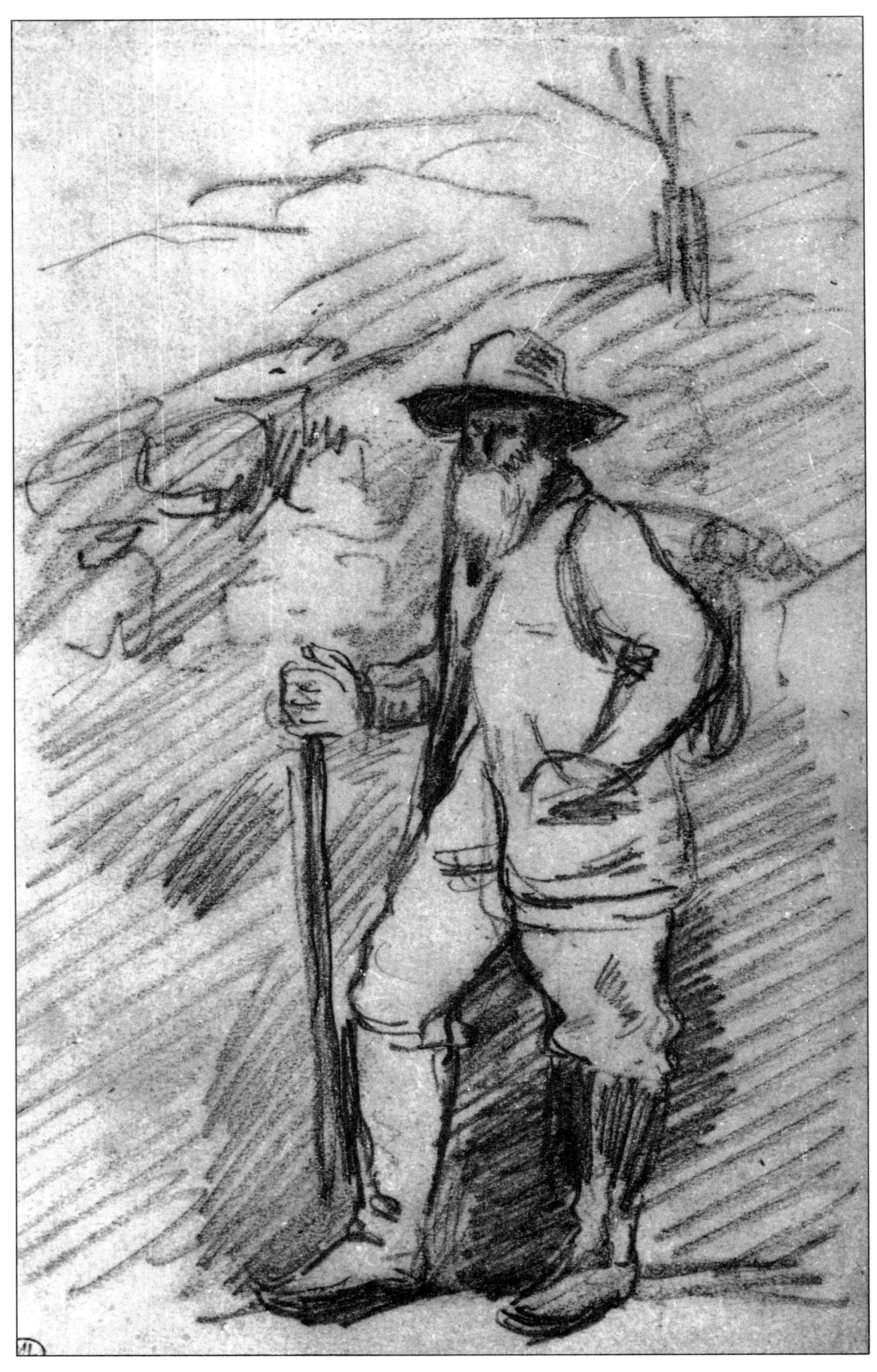

new artistic contents. Other younger colleagues were still concerned with reaching maturity in Impressionism, for example van Gogh, Gauguin, Seurat and Signac. They had all turned their backs on the sterile academy painting and turned to pure colour and the priority of light. In the colour values of their palette they were through and through Impressionists, however, in statement and composition they had developed further, they had found different artistic problems with which to occupy themselves. The horizon broadened out.

In recent times art historians have agreed on the term Post-Impressionism to describe the multifarious results of work done by the individual artistic personalities after 1880, work from those artists who had gained their main influences from Impressionism and had developed to new graphic statements in their individual careers. On the whole, Impressionism was a fluid development and its final notes and its fruitful transition to art in the 20th century is an especially fascinating aspect. Lasting values took shape from a continuous series of discoveries and perceptions which became a support for the following artistic generation.

The art lover looking at it from a historical point of view is used to seeing Impressionism as a homogeneous style epoch with distinct forms of expression and also as a style covering a longer period, beginning in 1850 and ending with the start of Expressionism in the first years of the 20th century. This view is only partly true. The style which presented itself so unified to the outside world had, as representatives, a number of highly individual artists with completely different views on many aspects of their painting. They worked together much more as a discussion and experimental group of friends than as a unified association orientated towards regimentation.

While the Impressionist artists were in no way an organized group with the same objectives, this was even more true for the following decades in which numerous movements of further development were formed independently of each other, together or even against each other. The poet Emile Verhaeren commented in those days, "There is no single school, hardly even single groups, as these are constantly splitting up. The many sided tendencies remind me of moving kaleidoscope-like, geometric patterns, which oppose each other only in the next minute to unite with each other, which one minute blend together, separate again and then disintegrate while still moving within a constant circle, that of the new art." This book presents movements which are a further development of Impressionism, although the reader has to realize that the complete complexity of artistic development in these years has an unending amount of correlations which cannot all be mentioned within this framework. From an incredibly interesting variety we can only pick out a number of guidelines which show a picture of the period without unfortunately doing justice to each of the individual ramifications. Behind every side shoot stands an artistic personality whose work would really be due a more explicit explanation.

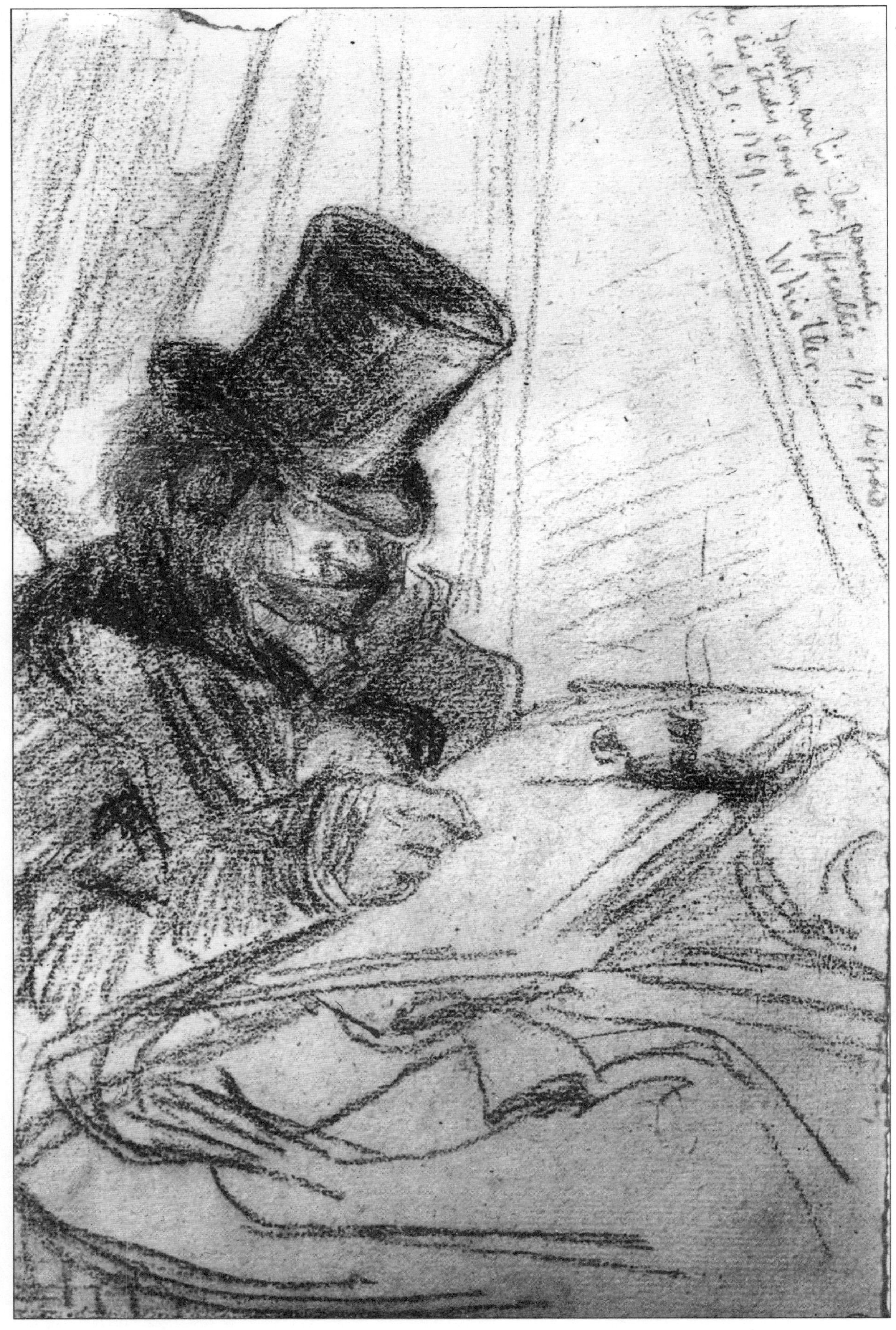

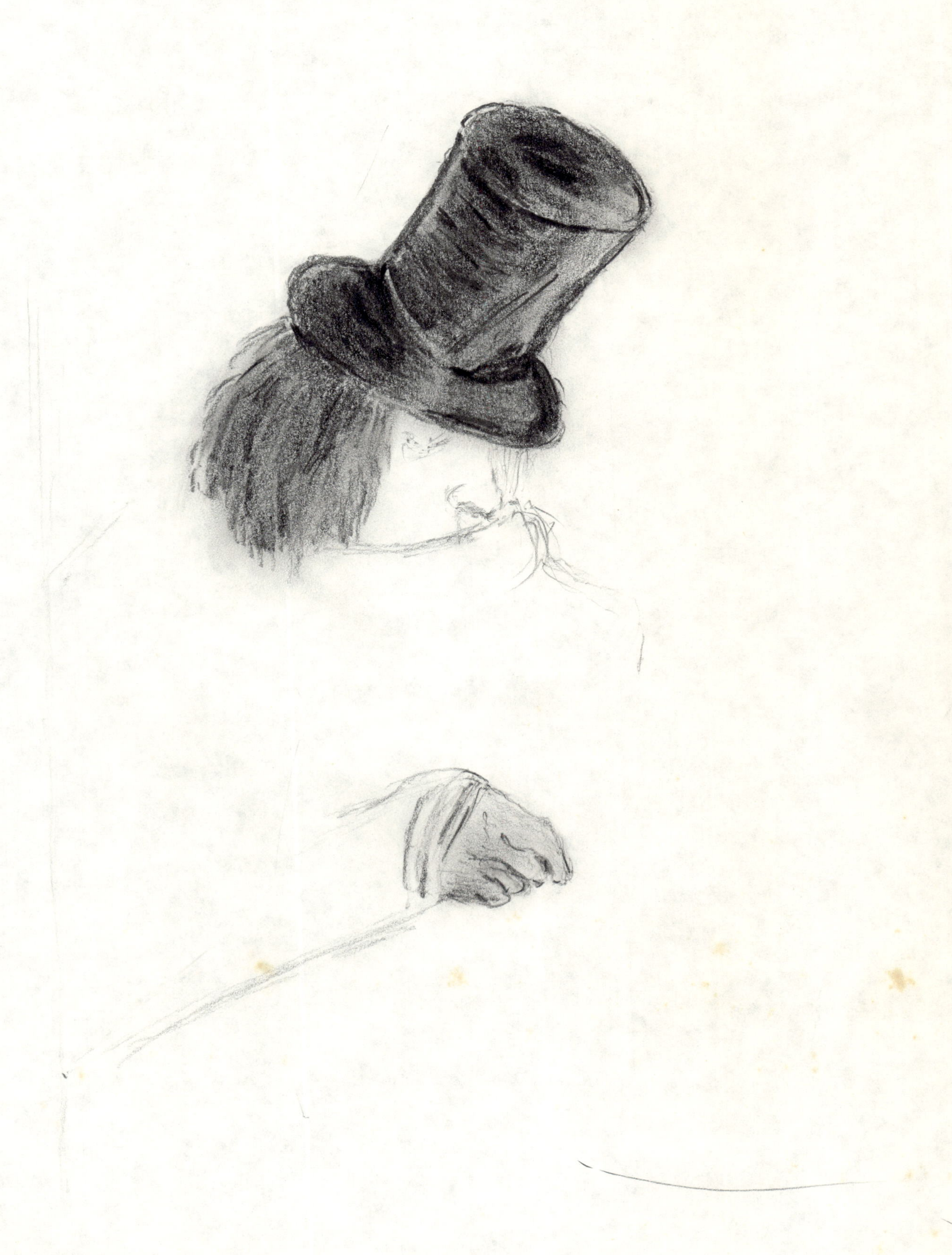

One point of view which has to be especially mentioned to allow an understanding of the epoch and the position of the artists in the social field is that almost all artists whose work occupies us in a historical review were more or less unknown during their lifetime, they were completely ignored by the general public or, at the best, they received only negative criticism. Their significance for art was only realized by a few people, mainly artists themselves with no influence, whose careers were also characterized by the same problem of a complete lack of recognition. No matter how much the artists, together or opposing each other, struggled for formal graphic solutions and the realizations of their artistic mission, in day-to-day life the lack of echo, the futility of trying to interest people for their art and of course attempting to sell their paintings was a crippling fate which developed like a red thread through the lives of several artistic generations. With the beginnings of Impressionism, art had freed itself from the society which supported it and from integration in academies. It was a step which was seen as a liberation by the artists themselves, however, they alone had to bear subsequent problems arising from this step.

The Impressionists and Their Intentions

The years around 1885, those years in which the already loose connections between the Impressionist painters disintegrated completely and when most of the companions turned their attention to new impulses, were years of great economic hardship for many people in France.

Revolutionary changes in the structure of society brought living conditions full of hardship for many people. The disintegration of traditional ties in the maelstrom of the period of promoterism unnerved the middle-class population. Unscrupulous speculators profiteered. Considerable fortunes accumulated in the hands of clever businessmen without an equal development in social conscience or the desire for cultural, i. e. promotional activities. The term nouveau riche, describing the economically saturated person with a considerable lack of culture, was first coined during this time.

With no real relationship to art, these circles had their houses furnished with artistic productions which were mainly representatively bombastic. The further a creator of art moved away from decorative ware to functionality, the more unlikely it was that he would sell his work or receive commissions. For the young artists, who mainly counted among the economically weak part of society anyway, the reticence of the state and the lack of understanding from other parts of the financially potent society meant for them an existence in destitution.

Art needs communication to have effect; the artist has to be able to present his work to the public in some way. Without a dialogue between painting and observer art cannot exist. Until the 19th century nobility and Church were always there to buy and commission works of art. With the decrease in commissions from the Church and wordly powers the newly arising middle class had to take their place as commissioner or buyer. However, with this democratization of the relationship between artist and purchaser there was at first no mediator, no instance which brought the interested party and the producer together on any social level. The academies only had a limited function, social alliances were more important. In France, the most influential institution which offered the best possibilities of exhibiting was the *Salon*, which was more or less a market place for the arts. However, before an artist could take part, he had to present himself to a jury of established artists, an omnipotent instance which preserved the habit of rejecting anything new, without consideration, if it strayed from the well-worn path of conventionality. In this way art was led by the nose in a highly conservative sense over many years. As every public recognition and also every financial success was linked to a participation in the Salon it is understandable that also the young artists struggled relentlessly to be able to use this single recognized forum. This is why, basically, the artists' work from the Impressionist period or the following Post-Impressionist decades was always created with the exhibitions in the Salon or in the laboriously self-organized substitute facilities in mind. Although the artists' working rhythm was determined by the changing of the seasons the constant problem of exhibition possibilities always remained in the background. For the annual Salon in May they painted, entered the paintings full of hope only to be overcome by deep disappointment and rage when they were not accepted. Once, in 1863, those whose work had been rejected organized in protest an extra *Salon des Refusés*, an "opposing Salon" in which the numerous rejected works were exhibited. Among these pictures were also works from Manet, Pissarro, Jongkind, Guillaumin, Whistler, Fantin-Latour and Cézanne. The art reviewer Castagnary wrote about their work, "The naturalistic school maintains that art is an expression of life in all stages of development; their only aim is to represent nature in all its power and forcefulness; it is truth which counterbalances knowledge. The naturalistic school rebuilds the destroyed relationship between man and nature. The artist in the middle of his epoch faced with the task of consideration has determined the true sense of the relationship and therefore the morality of art. Naturalism, which accepts all realities of a visible world, is not a school. Far removed from drawing a line, it removes all barriers. It does not force the artist to do anything, but instead liberates him. It does not place the artist's personality in chains, but gives it wings. It calls to the artist 'be free'!"

In 1874 the group which was loosely described as *Naturalists* eventually organized their first combined exhibition which brought them the derisive nickname *Impressionists*, a name which contained so much truth that it

Claude Monet lived for forty years after the disintegration of the group. Forty years of creative work in which a stirring late work was produced. He died at a time when the ideas which were at the root of his art had long belonged to the past. He was the first among the group of Impressionists to become successful. He had the privilege of celebrating triumphs in the public recognition, but eventually he was forced to realize that his personality led him to loneliness, that his consequential development of the once accepted methods exposed him to animosity from the young artists who only saw his work as a hindrance preventing enough attention being paid to their new ideas. "But Impressionism was not dead, just because those who created it had stopped being Impressionists. Even if this name was no longer a battle cry, it still remained a living inspiration for following generations. The forms of Impressionism had become common knowledge, the starting point for new discoveries. It is true that the young generation rejected most of the Impressionist principles, that the Fauves, Cubists, Expressionists, Futurists, Dadaists and Surrealists continuously opened new horizons; but in their struggles they had nourished themselves on works from Cézanne, Gauguin, van Gogh and Seurat who had all gone through an Impressionist phase. Even if the immediate influence of Impressionism on contemporary art sometimes seems insignificant, it was the art of Monet and his comrades which got rid of so many prejudices and opened the door to even more daring projects in technique, colour and abstraction." (John Rewald).

From the Impressionist circle it was above all Camille Pissarro who proved to be a true helping friend to his colleagues as well as to the young up and coming artists. The financial difficulties of the first years with which all young artists at that time had to struggle lasted especially long with Pissarro. He received no financial backing from his parents. He was also the oldest of the Impressionists and therefore experienced the desire to form a family before the others. But recognition and the corresponding remuneration for his paintings took a very long time in coming. However, that did not hinder him from looking at the artistic development problems of others with an open mind and sympathetic heart. Even such reserved characters as Paul Cézanne and Edgar Degas were close friends and can thank his advice and helpful tips for decisive steps on their way to artistic liberation. This was also true for Vincent van Gogh to whom he was a fatherly friend from his entry to the Parisian art scene right up to his tragic end.

Social consciousness was not just one of life's basics for Pissarro, he was a convinced socialist, very fond of political discussions. He was a good-natured, quiet artist with the heart of a lion. Full of conviction, he advocated an improvement in the situation of the artist in society, never tired in his struggle for better working conditions and above all fought that the general public should pay more attention to the artists' intentions. The burden of theoretical problems and technical experiments in his art seems to have weighed heavy on him in his creative processes. In spite of unending assiduity and great artistic strength he always ended up in difficulties when trying to realize his ideas, because theoretical consideration stood in his way. He sacrificed a great deal of time in mobilizing artists to achieve exhibition possibilities and present themselves to the public. The self-organized exhibitions from the Impressionists were probably the most convincing act in this direction. Pissarro was also the only one who showed pictures in all eight Impressionist presentations and in spite of all the changes in the constellation of personalities, he remained true to the original idea. Like Monet, Pissarro also clung to the once acquired principles in the Post-Impressionist period of his work, apart from the odd deviation.

One of Pissarro's colleagues, Edgar Degas, also tended, like Pissarro, to give his painting a strictly theoretical base. He thought out a large number of unusual themes, and in his mind he explored his environment for unusual perspectives. "No one ever painted monuments and houses seen from below, close up as you see them when you walk through the streets" or a series on smoke, "cigarette smoke and smoke from locomotives, chimneys, steam-ships etc." And "dancers where you only notice the bare legs, observed in full motion … and cafés in the evening with gas lamps shining with different intensities and their light reflected in mirrors …" Admittedly, as opposed to Pissarro, Degas never allowed himself to be harassed by his theoretical problems. If the ideas did not fit in with his intuition at the time, he let them fall without another thought. Degas became the masterly arranger of the flimmering play of colour. However, he did not find his fulfillment in the landscape, it was much more the human field which captured his attention. The atmosphere of the racetrack and the horses whose existence was concentrated on rapid movement, the tightness of the stage experience in the theatre, the extreme concentration on precise movement in ballet: in all these things he was completely given to Impressionism. Degas sought the unusual perspective, the odd view of an event. When he had found an inspiration, he directed his attention towards observing exactly and placing the scenery in the right light. His character tended more towards the quick sketch, but he forced himself to work on his paintings in his studio in an almost Old Master like fashion: with no other artist is the difference between a quickly executed sketch and a thoroughly composed painting as great as with Degas. Degas became one of the main representatives of Post-Impressionism, and although he belonged to the artists from the first hour of Impressionism, this style remained remarkably strange to him. In his work it looks as if he only used the painting media of Impressionism when the respective painting demanded the use of this style. He incessantly watched the young dancers practising, sketching them quickly so that he could paint them in his studio from memory, adding the details which were the charm of the particular work. While Degas' friends became more convinced that they should only paint what they had in front of their eyes and what was present while they were working, Degas maintained the opposing principle. He observed without painting and painted without observing.

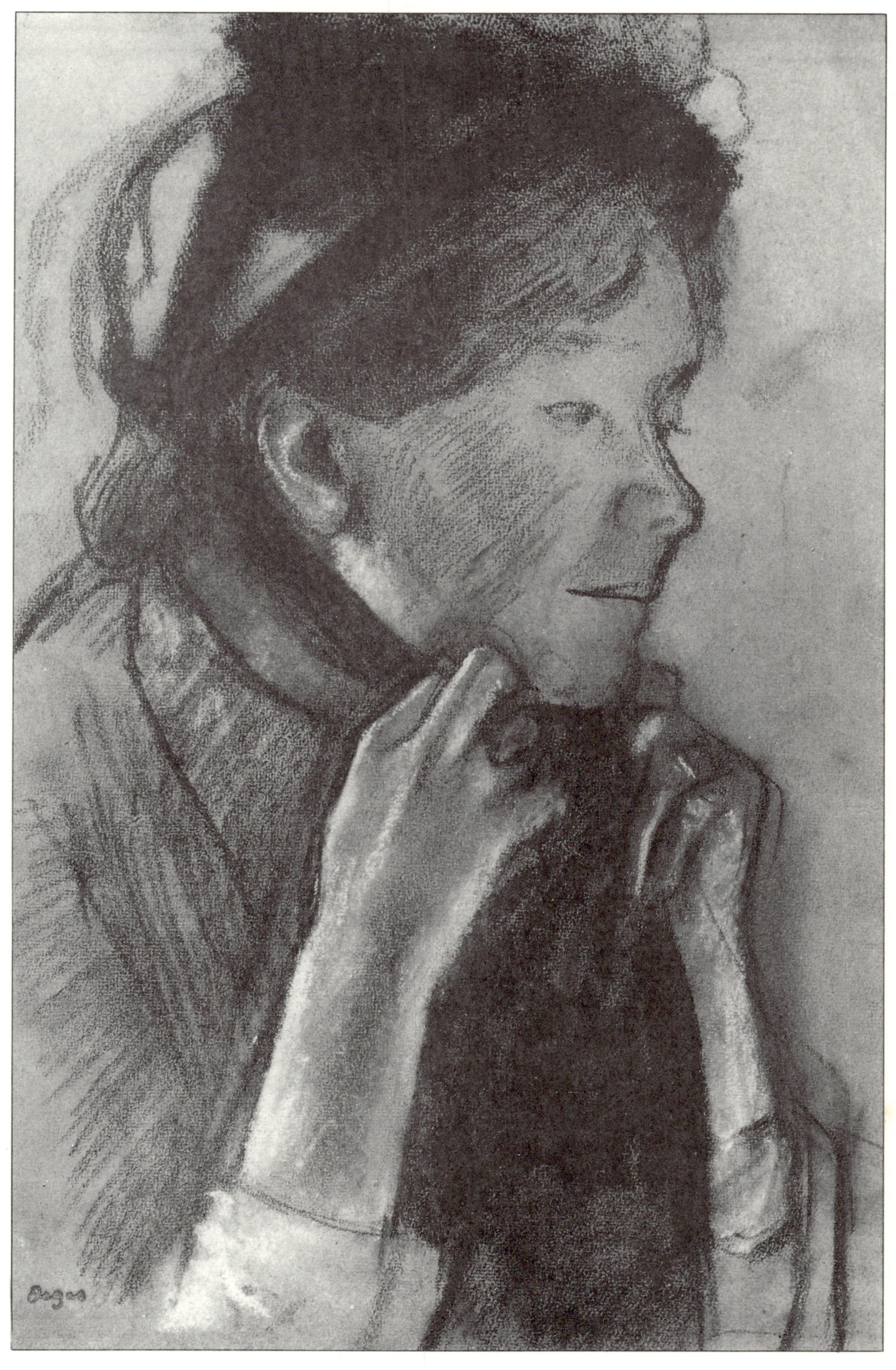

that he was also reacting for all the other artists who had been rejected, "Monsieur, I had the honour of writing to you recently about the two pictures which were returned to me by your jury. As you have not replied allow me to come back to the contents of my letter. You have most certainly received my letter, therefore I do not have to repeat the arguments which I have already presented to you. I would only like to say again that I cannot accept the unfair judgement of your colleagues who did not have my permission to assess me. I am writing to you again to stress my wish. I would like to turn to the public and, in spite of my rejection, to be exhibited. My wish does not seem exaggerated; and if you asked all painters in my position you would receive the answer that they all renounce the jury and would like to take part in one way or another in an exhibition which should be available, without obligation, to anyone working seriously. The Salon of rejected artists should be introduced again. Even if I am there alone, it is my most ardent desire to show everyone that I am as anxious not to be mistaken for the members of the jury who seem just as anxious not to be mistaken for me. I imagine, Monsieur, that you will not continue to remain silent. I think that every decent letter earns a reply."

Apart from the occasional discovery which he made, Cézanne was respected by the other painters of the time without being especially popular, only a few were able to understand his work. He had a few artists as friends, like Renoir. Pissarro concerned himself with Cézanne's artistic development and the younger van Gogh was a great admirer, although this love was rather one-sided. He himself, because of his rather taciturn nature, was not made to be the centre of a circle of artists which his significance for the history of art would have earned him. As said before, following generations found the key to modern art in Cézanne's work. It was his work which made Post-Impressionist art important for the progresses of 20th century art.

Further Developments from Impressionism

Three years after the death of Edouard Manet who had rightly been described as the father of Impressionism, the Dutchman Vincent van Gogh entered the Parisian art scene. He was thirty-three years old and his life up to that point had shown him almost all the downs in life. His brother worked at that time as an art dealer in Paris and was his first mainstay in the new surroundings. Van Gogh had taught himself to paint in the Netherlands with an unyielding will, and as an autodidact he had reached an inner condition which was like a time-bomb just waiting to be triggered. Paris was the first occasion for the artist to paint a true flood of paintings in a frenzy of enthusiasm. In Holland he had already shown himself to be a significant and novel painter of an unbelievable intensity. But when he came into contact with the Impressionists, a stunning colourfulness came to light with such a power and sureness, from the very first day, that it was clear that everything inside him was prepared, matured through a long development. Van Gogh with his moving compositions and brilliant palette of colour was like a shining star in the art heavens. It is the great tragedy of his life that the age was not yet mature enough for his genius. No one noticed that such a work of genius was in the offing, no one could see the exceptional greatness of this artist. Even Vincent's brother, who was convinced that he would one day be an important artist, looked for excuses why his brother painted so wildly. He thought that Vincent just still had to calm down.

In Paris, van Gogh took in everything that he could learn from the Impressionist painters, and he felt that he was one of them. Looking back at his work it has to be mentioned that Vincent only painted very few of his pictures in the style and spirit of the Impressionists. He was much too loaded with tension to be able to absorb the atmosphere with no emotion, too much of a fighter to consider moods in a detached manner and make them transparent. It was as if he was forced to throw everything that he had to express onto the canvas. Colour was not a means of expression for him. Colour was for him a hard, real material with which he sought a physical intercourse. As a common style, Impressionism was already at an end at the time of van Gogh's entrance to the scene. A variety of different developments had taken up the perceptions of the earlier years and changed and developed them. Van Gogh entered this constantly changing process of change seeking. He had enough contact to the other artists. At first he worked in Studio Cormon where he became a friend of Toulouse-Lautrec, Anquetin and Bernard. Through his brother Theo he got to know Pissarro, Degas, Guillaumin and Renoir, and later also Seurat and Gauguin. He took an active part in the friends' discussions. They talked well into the night, they argued and attempted to realize new things in common work. Vincent's life has been compared to a candle which has been lit at both ends, and which consumes itself at an incredible rate. He did actually come to Paris in a physically desolate state and life in the city was not really suitable for improving his health. The concentrated atmosphere of the city had brought about his creative breakthrough but the daily life and the extensive intercourse with the other artists underminded his health and weakened his nerves. As well as this, the natural surroundings which van Gogh was used to living with and which were very important for his work were missing. In spite of all the inspiration which the city offered, the artist felt drawn to the countryside. After living in Paris for two years he decided to move to southern France and eventually landed in Arles. There the light of the south and the completely different atmosphere put him into a condition of frenzy. In Paris he had been used to living and working with complete disregard to his health, but in the south this became worse so that he worked even more furiously, "Today I worked again from seven o'clock in the morning till six o'clock in the evening without a pause apart from occasionally walking a

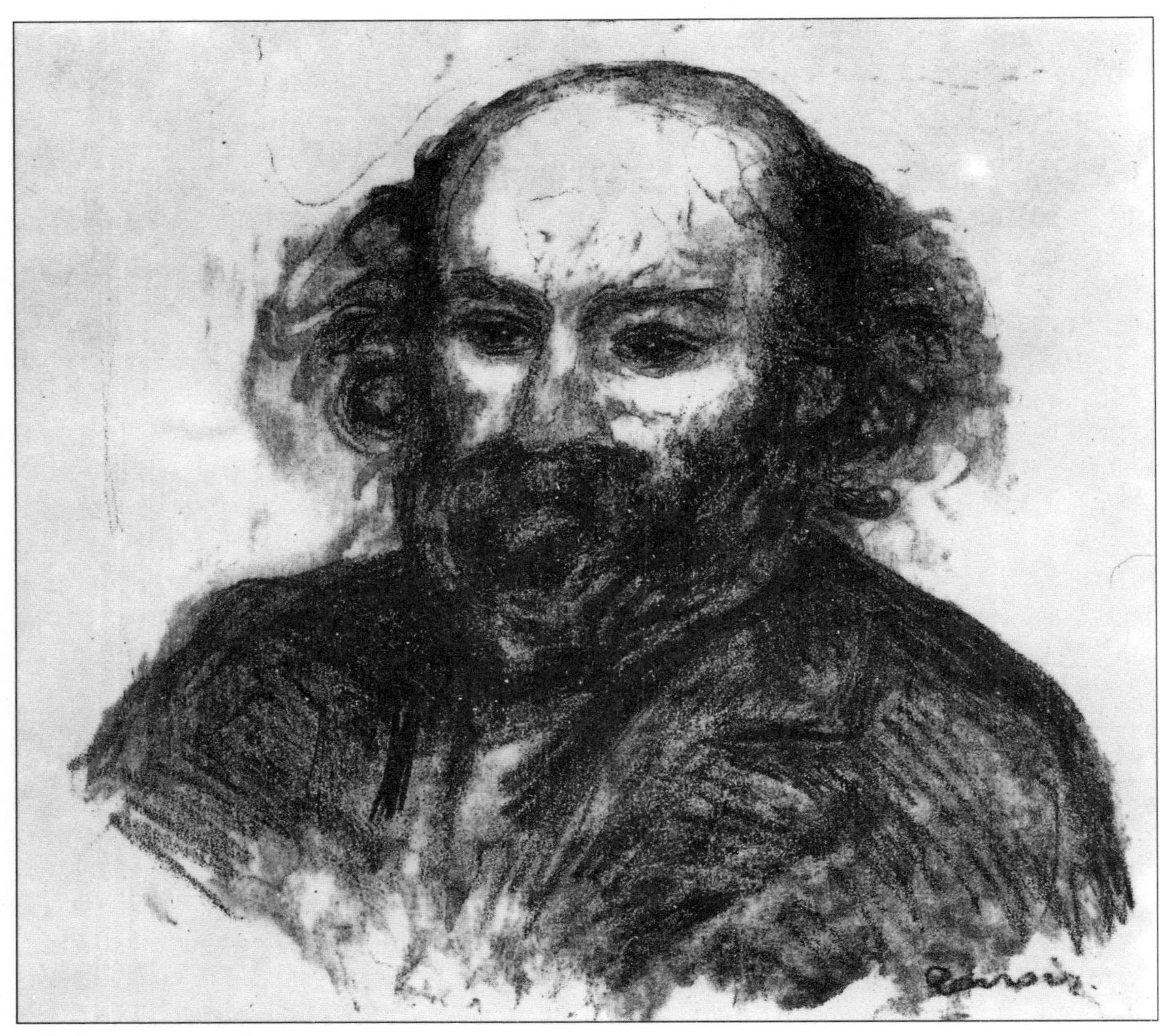

few steps away from the easel to take a bite to eat. I feel absolutely no sense of weariness; tonight I will paint another picture and I will manage it."

There was probably no other artist who created such an amount of intensive works as van Gogh did. In the short period he spent in Arles, he produced an almost immeasurable series of brilliant paintings. The painter must have been under an enormous creative pressure. The result was physical and mental fatigue. Van Gogh had to enter a sanatorium where, although he was able to carry on working, he suffered repeated breakdowns. His and his brother's complete lack of success in their attempts to find some echo from art lovers would also have worn him down. Friends and colleagues recognized that van Gogh would some day become a significant painter but none of his contemporaries realized the true quality of his creations. He was too far ahead of his time. Towards the end of Vincent's life the young art reviewer G. Albert Aurier anticipated the artist's greatness. "The speciality of all these works is the excess, excess of strength, excess of sensitivity, of the power of expression ... In his often individual simplification of composition, in his presumptiousness in painting the sun face to face he shows himself to be a person full of strength, boldness and masculinity, often brutal and sometimes unbelievably gentle, a sort of intoxicated giant, who is more successful in shifting mountains than in his association with knick-knacks, an erupting brain which pours its lava irresistably in all abysses of art, a frightening mad genius, often sublime, often grotesque, almost always on the border of the pathological. His colours are unimaginably brilliant. He is, as far as I know, the only painter who observes the colourfulness of things with such an intensity."

Van Gogh did not found a school and had no followers during his lifetime who would have been associated with his work. However, in the posthumous exhibition of his work many young artists, when confronted with his paintings, were deeply moved and sought to learn from his art. On the whole, the effect of van Gogh's œuvre had an enormous significance on the further development of modern art.

Many of the Impressionists and Post-Impressionists first turned to art after having had other careers. For example, Pissarro was originally a merchant and Degas was a solicitor. Van Gogh can also be regarded as having a late calling. However, in Paul Gauguin's case the beginning of his artistic career can be seen more as a break in his life. Gauguin was a successful banker, a renowned broker with the corresponding middle-class ambience, with a family and a promising career in the French world of finance. It would have surely been a great shock for Madame Gauguin when her husband began to turn his whole attention to art. For a normal middle-class thinking person it seems completely unimaginable that a successful, wealthy financier could end his career so abruptly, that within a few months he and his family were faced with financial ruin or that his dislike of his previous career and the concentration on his work made him forget to think about any financial safeguard. Paul Gauguin suddenly knew that he had to become an artist and that every diversion from this one aim would be detrimental to his work as an artist. With his typical stubborness he ignored all good advice from his friends, let his wife down and invited the reproach on his conscience that he had left his family with no money, living on the generosity of her relations, only to chase after the phantom of an artistry which he was the only one convinced existed at all. He angrily struggled to be accepted as a painter, grabbed at every straw which offered a handhold, but the idea never entered his head that he should reactivate his financial knowledge to secure an economic basis and at least save himself the worse reproaches from his wife and family. An inner compulsion commanded him to realize the ideas of his new artistry undisturbed by all resistance. He did not even fall back upon his earlier abilities when money was not just lacking for the simplest necessities of life but he did not even have enough money to buy paint, canvas and paintbrushes.

Influenced by Pissarro's Impressionism, from which he had received his first practical knowledge, Gauguin soon began painting in exciting flat colour.

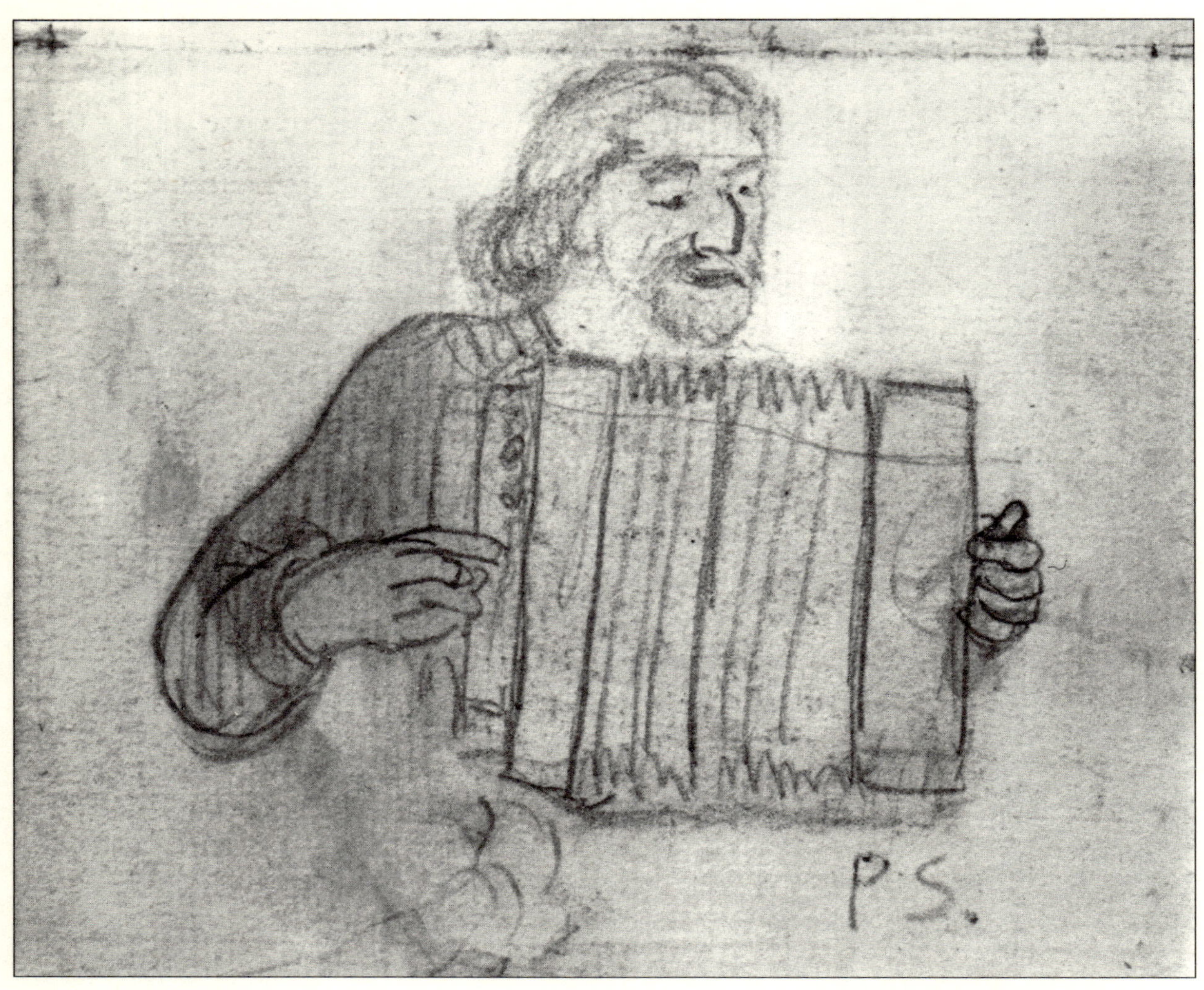

Together with his colleague Bernard in Brittany, he developed a technique called Cloisonnism, characterized by dark lines enclosing areas of bright flat colour as in Cloisonné work, the melting technique in which metal crosspieces separate colours and in stained glass windows with their lead framework. In later years there was a dispute as to the origins of the Cloisonné pictures as both Bernard and Gauguin claimed the invention of the technique to be his. It seems that it was actually Anquetin who was the first to make experiments in this direction. Bernard attempted to express the notional background of the new style of painting in words. Strangely enough his formulation conveys above all a rejection of Impressionism as an essential element of the new style. But that is exactly what these experiments were not: the technique lived from the colourfulness of Impressionism, from its new perception of area, from its priority of light. A contemporary, Edouard Dujardin, found a clearer valid formulation of the first new side-shoot of Post-Impressionism, "At a first glance these pictures give the impression of a decorative painting; clear-cut contours and lively colourfulness are suggestive of folk art and Japanese woodcuts. Under the overriding character of drawing and colour you discover an unheard of truth of feeling which frees itself of any romantic passion. But above all it is the intentional, well-founded, intellectual and systematic construction which invites us to analyse it. The painter draws with closed lines between which he places various colours, whose contrast is meant to bring out the desired general colour effect. In this way the colour emphasizes the drawing and vice versa. This work has something of painting in separate sections like the old Cloisonné technique." Bernard's tendency to support all of his steps in painting with philosophical thoughts made a great impression on Gauguin. Although Gauguin had a clear desire to do something new in art, it came more from his hand than his head. He therefore watched in fascination when his young friend Bernard accompanied every new experiment with soul-searching discussions. Gauguin, together with Bernard, in his experiment in synthesis, as he called it, succeeded in not just using it in practical painting but also in formulating the theory. "The path of synthesis is, of course, full of dangers; I have taken the first step, but it is the way which corresponds to my nature and you should always follow your temperament. I know that I will be understood less and less. But what does it matter if I detach myself from the others? For the masses I will be a puzzle, for some a poet, and sooner or later something which is good will succeed ..."

In spring 1889 under the sign of the iron Eiffel Tower the large World's Fair was opened. The art section contained an exhibition of the century which included several of the latest works from Manet, Monet and Pissarro. For Gauguin and his friends there was absolutely no chance of being able to exhibit within the official sphere of the World's Fair. However, Emile Schuffenecker, one of the artists from the circle of friends, found a solution. The large hall of a café in the fair was without the mirror decoration which had been ordered, due to a delay on the supplier's side. Schuffenecker persuaded the owner of the café, an Italian called Volpini, to allow the *Synthesists*, as they called themselves after much consideration, to use the walls for an art exhibition. The show went down in history as the famous Volpini exhibition. On posters the group were described as *Groupe Impressioniste et Synthétiste*. This double description came from the problem on the one hand of not wanting to dispense with the term 'Impressionists' which the public had just begun to recognize; on the other hand using the name 'Synthesists' they wished to document a certain distance to another group which had formed in the meantime calling themselves *Neo-Impressionists* who felt themselves to be the successors of the Impressionists. Gauguin and his friends did not want to be confused with this group.

These Neo-Impressionists, whose choice of name caused such problems for the group of friends around Paul Gauguin, who were, as already mentioned, originally called Cloisonnists, went down in history as the Pointillists. Their leader was Georges Seurat. The eloquent mouthpiece and unremitting mentor of the group was, however, Paul Signac. Seurat was a quiet reserved person. Everyone, including van Gogh was convinced that he was the leader among the painters of the young generation. His cool intellect shared this view. With an enormous straightness he followed the aim which he had once decided was right to go beyond Impressionism and to give a rational scientific basis to the art which developed from this advancement. Even in his younger years, during his time at the academy, he turned his attention to experiments in the theory of colour from leading physicists and after he had begun his painting career he endeavoured to realize these theoretical perceptions in his work. Through a well-balanced division of horizontal and vertical elements and through a detailed elaboration which he had worked out in innumerable preliminary studies, he achieved a methodical separation of the elements: light, shadow, local colour, interaction of colours as well as their balance and harmonic proportion. As a mixing of the colours necessary for a complete colour nuancing was not possible on the palette (too many pigments mixed together give black), it was not a great step in achieving the complete colour nuance by optical means, i.e. on the canvas, by placing small touches of pure colour next to each other. The painter who has placed the individual colour elements on his canvas leaves it to the retina of the human eye to mix them again.

Seurat's central work in this technique was *Sunday Afternoon on the Island of La Grande Jatte* which had a tremendous effect on the painters of that period. Other artists attempted Pointillist paintings, but their method of working was not suitable for the over-exact and careful technique, for example Anquetin or van Gogh who soon realized that his spontaneity suffered under the technique. Camille Pissarro was also impressed and convinced that Seurat and Signac had been successful in corroborating Impressionism with the means of modern science. Pissarro, who at that time was very dissatisfied with the results of his work, who found his painting too coarse, was especially receptive for the constructive element in Seurat's theories. He eagerly took up the new technique and was even able to give his two young colleagues many hints and tips from his long experience. In the last Impressionist exhibition Pissarro introduced Seurat and Signac and had them accepted. However, the participation of the *Neo-Impressionists* as they allowed themselves to be called in honour of the masters and to document the similar sources of their art, was also the reason for Monet, Renoir and Sisley being absent.

After many attempts in the new technique, Pissarro realized that his creativity suffered under the much too strict regularization and that his need for a more powerful form could not be satisfactorily fulfilled. After a long phase of interesting work in the Pointillist technique he again returned to his own mature style. The perceptions which were embodied in the new style, however, still had a great influence on artists in France and in other countries. It was Félix Fénéon, a young art reviewer who made himself the convinced spokesman of the new technique and spoke of Neo-Impressionism. Seurat would have preferred the term *Chromoluminarism*, however, this could not assert itself. The term *Pointillism* became valid, a name which was strictly rejected by the artists around Seurat. Fénéon undertook to explain the different attitudes of the Impressionists and the followers of the new style, "The phenomena heaven, water, bushes etc. vary from second to second according to the view of the original Impressionists. Their aim is to capture one of these fleeting moments on the canvas. This causes the necessity of capturing a landscape in one sitting and from this comes the tendency to distort nature to prove convincingly that this moment is unique, that it will never return again. The intention of the Neo-Impressionists is to give the landscape a final aspect which gives its impression duration. In addition to this their process makes haste impossible and requires a lot of work in the studio. The objective reality is for them just a starting point to a higher, more sublimate reality into which their personalities are poured."

While Impressionism flowed into international art as a style element and united harmonically with traditional and existing movements without a true break being necessary, the working methods of the Neo-Impressionists took a completely new line in the œuvre of many artists. In several cases the technique has an almost put-on effect. Giovanni Segantini from Italy and Ferdinand Hodler from Switzerland found interesting formal solutions. They led their indigenous art, which resulted from strong folkish powers, through the Pointillistic style of painting to a great transparence and lightness. In Belgium and the Netherlands contact to the group *Les Vingts* which was founded in Brussels in 1884 and which had supported the Impressionists from the very beginning led especially to a propagation of the new art direction. The group's journal printed a debate on the last Impressionist exhibition which went into the details of Seurat's work. Because of this the artist was invited to participate in the group's exhibition in the following year, together with Pissarro and Berthe Morisot. Henri van de Velde and Theo van Rysselberghe were the most important Netherlandish Pointillists, the author Fénéon their very eloquent protagonist.

Literature and Painting: Symbolism

Literature began to have an especially strong effect on painting. This was true for the Pointillists but took on a special intensity for the emerging form of *Symbolism* which came completely from literature. The desire of the poets to reform modern life by giving inspiration, dreams and hallucinations an important role in life led to a new level of consciousness in literature with an immediate influence on painting. Gustav Kahn, Felix Fénéon's friend, formulated, "We have become tired of the humdrum, the obvious and the inevitably modern. We wish to be able to place the development of the symbol in some period, even in the landscape of dreams as a dream cannot be distinguished from real life. We want to replace the struggle for individuality with the struggle of feelings and ideas."

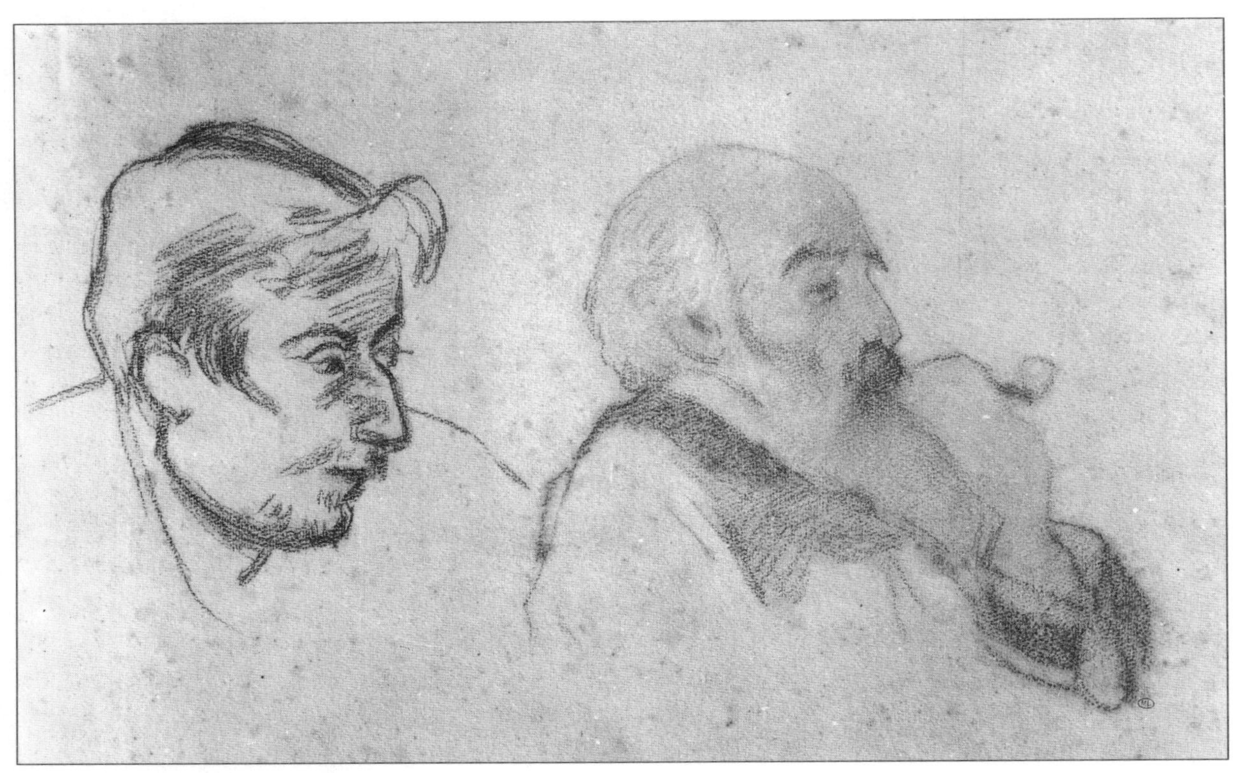

Symbolism was soon cultivated in the respectable Parisian salons. The poets Stephane Mallarmé and Paul Verlaine became the protagonists of the new style. Mallarmé's house was the place to be seen in. "Mallarmé sat on the rocking chair which rocked beside the faience oven or he stood with his red or white clay pipe in his hand. The other visitors moved their chairs around the table in the middle which was dominated by the hanging lamp. On the table, beside the grog glasses, was the Chinese clay pot in which he kept his tobacco. This room which served the poet as dining room and in which Lilith, his black cat, lithely moved around, was furnished with a sideboard of polished wood with peasant pottery on top of it. In the corner, on a pedestal, was a sort of Tahitan idol which Gauguin had carved. On the walls a few pictures: Manet's portrait of Mallarmé and – also from Manet – a pastel which represented a scene from *Hamlet*. This pastel from Manet hung for a long time above the small settee; then it was replaced by a landscape from Claude Monet and a charming beach sketch from Berthe Morisot ..." (H. de Régnier)

The magical musical world of Richard Wagner was venerated and among the painters it was Odilon Redon who hit the exact note with his puzzling surrealistic works. The spiritual centre point was Gustave Kahn's journal *Le Symboliste*. "In painting and literature the representation of nature is a delusion." E. Dujardin formulated, "in fact, it is the aim of painting and literature to represent the perception of things with the means of art. What should be expressed is not a duplicate, but instead the character which is concealed inside: Why should the thousand meaningless details which the eye sees be drawn? One has to search for the essential and reproduce it, or better, produce it. A contour is enough to represent a face. The painter will capture the intimate reality, the essence of characteristic lines and colour ..."

Gauguin, Bernard and Meyer de Haan from the Netherlands had also approached Symbolistic thought trails in Brittany. They made contact with Odilon Redon who had always attempted to realize medial dreams in his art. Gauguin returned to Paris and through Redon's good offices he soon found himself a friend of the circle of Symbolistic poets, although Gauguin had actually given up his domicile in Brittany for Paris only because he urgently needed financial means so that he could realize his plans for travelling to the South Seas and he assumed that this would be easier in Paris. But he felt rather flattered when he was received in the circle of Symbolists as an important and respected painter. The poet Charles Morice wrote about Gauguin, "A wide bony face; a small forehead, a nose which, although not broken, appeared bent; a small-lipped straight mouth; heavy eyelids which lifted above slightly protruding eyes whose bluish pupils circled in their sockets, looking to the right and to the left while his head and the top half of his body remained almost motionless. This foreigner did not have much appeal but still he was attractive due to his personal charm, a mixture of proud, inborn nobility and a simplicity bordering on triviality: Aristocracy soaked in proletariate. His head was truly beautiful ... He spoke with a deep, slightly husky voice, 'Primitive art comes from the spirit and avails itself of nature. The so-called sophisticated art comes from sensuality and serves nature. Nature is the servant of one art and the ruler of another art. But the ruler cannot forget her origins and she degrades the artist by allowing her adoration. We have declined to the abominable error of naturalism which began with the Greeks and Pericles. Since then only those artists who in one way or another went against this mistake were more or less great. Truth lies alone in a spiritual art, in a primitive art. In our present misery there is no other rescue apart from a prudent and open return to the basis. This return is the necessary feat which has to be accomplished by Symbolism in art and poetry.'"

At that time Gauguin struggled to acquire a financial possibility for an artistic life in the Tropics. He believed that he would find his well-being in a primitive existence, living together with simple folk. His dream was the paradisiacal condition of people living on the best of terms with their lavishly sumptuous nature. He worked to participate in this life, to choose his models from the simple, naturally naked natives. A few years later he actually realized his dreams, although the outer conditions were far from ideal. But until he was so far, he still had to do a lot to be able to realize his travel plans.

In Paris, a group of young painters showed a lot of interest and admiration for Gauguin. A small picture indirectly had a great deal of effect. The painter Paul Sérusier once spent a summer in Brittany where he was intensely interested in the work of Gauguin and his friends, although he did not dare approach the group. But one day before his journey back to Paris he plucked up courage and went to Gauguin. Gauguin looked at the young man's work and spent the day teaching him. They went out of doors and under Gauguin's instruction Sérusier painted a small autumn landscape. Gauguin pointed out that the trees looked yellow, therefore Sérusier should paint them yellow. The shadows were blue, the leaves red. Gauguin explained that the natural impression and aesthetic feelings had to be balanced, that the artist chooses, arranges, simplifies and through this creates the synthesis. He explained that the painter had to create a work from his power of imagination, from the bond between his spirit and reality. Gauguin insisted on a logical construction of the composition, a well-balanced distribution of light and dark areas of colour, a simplification of form and proportion to give the contours strong, eloquent expression. After this exclusive tutorial Sérusier was very happy and returned to Paris where he was studying at the Académie Julian. He showed his painting to his colleagues at the academy and reported about his meeting with Gauguin and everything he had said. These fellow students were Pierre Bonnard, Edouard Vuillard, Maurice Denis, Félix Vallotton and Paul Ranson. The young artists were deeply impressed by Gauguin's suggestions as they had been conveyed by Sérusier. They formed a group which was also joined by Aristide Maillol who was still a painter at that time. The group called themselves *Nabis*, which comes from Hebrew and means 'prophets'. When Gauguin returned to Paris he found himself honoured as mentor by this group of artists although he had never even heard of their existence before. However, it is probable that he felt flattered by this "discipleship".

The actual great influence which the Nabis had on the further development of art came about through a magazine in which works from the group were presented: *La Revue Blanche*. This name stands for a programme which led graphic art to an unimagined height. At the same time the magazine stands on the threshold of Post-Impressionism to other modern styles: Art Nouveau began to germinate and Expressionism developed with the Fauves whose first works were published in this periodical. However, in the centre were the Nabis who had found in Revue Blanche a publication platform which could be seen from a great distance, where they could publicize, theoretically and practically, their symbolical opinions and their new graphic attempts at expression. A completely new style of illustration developed, the symbolic united more and more with the decorative. The Belgian Henri van de Velde joined the group, but above all it was the brilliant Henri de Toulouse-Lautrec with his graphic works who linked the early days of Impressionism to the threshold of Expressionism.

Lautrec came together with van Gogh and Emile Bernard in Studio Cormon, through them he had immediate contact to the Impressionists and for many years he was the central figure in the Bohemian life of the artists. He was interested in the Parisian demi-monde. He was fascinated by the figures in the nightclubs and found his stimulus in the milieu of grisettes, chanson singers, dancers and actors. His eccentric lifestyle stood in direct contrast to the strength of his sick body. But still he created an enormous œuvre in the years between 1884 and 1894. It was many-sided and unique in the fullness of its social background. From 1894 he was the declared master of lithography of a high artistic standard. In this technique he was the rival of Jules Chéret who was admittedly superior to him in a technical sense; however, in the artistic quality it was undoubtedly Lautrec's work which allowed him to remain the artistic personality in posters and graphic illustrations. Lautrec became one of the leading contributors to Revue Blanche. The enormous quality of this publication is certainly due to him as he was also a great stimulation for the other artists.

The art historical period of Post-Impressionism ends with Toulouse-Lautrec and the artists from the circle around the Nabis. The impulses which developed from the art of those years became more numerous, initial approaches were consolidated, new directions grew onto it. Even in works from Vincent van Gogh and Gauguin trends towards Expressionism could already be seen, which in France was propagated as the shining beacon of the 20th century through the Fauves with their pure colours, freed of everything close to nature. But the colour dispersion of Pointillism and the rhythmic staccato stroke of van Gogh's brush lived on in their work, too.

Art Nouveau, which was to inundate Europe in the following years, was ushered in in numerous works by other Post-Impressionists – Toulouse-Lautrec is mentioned as an example. Everywhere new elements and new talents entered the arena of art development, they learned from the existing, took in inspiration from Impressionists as well as from consecutive developments and found their way to a new art. Matisse, Picasso, Munch, the young Expressionists in Dresden and Munich all rightly felt themselves to be innovators in art and all had the art of a great era as a basis. Maurice Denis described this inference very clearly, "In this way we liberated our sensitivity, and art, instead of being a copy, became a 'subjective deformation' of nature. From an objective point of view the decorative aesthetic and rational composition – which the Impressionists did not consider because it went against their preference for improvisation – became the counterposition, the necessary corrective of the theory of equivalents. All of this, considering the expression, justifies self-caricaturing transformation and exaggeration of the characteristic. To put it in a nutshell: The expressive unit, the symbol for a feeling has to be an eloquent translation and at the same time a composition to please the eyes."

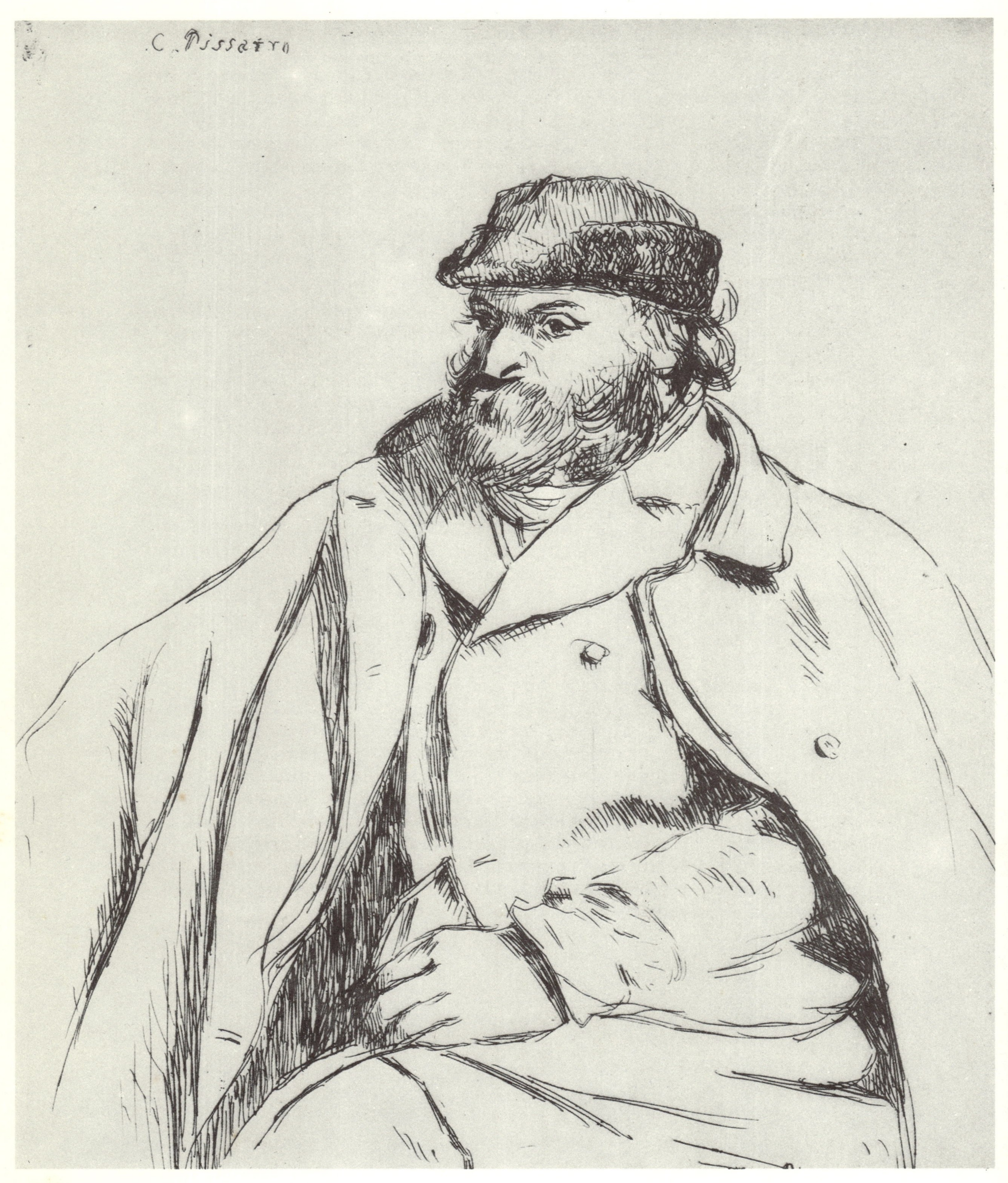
C. Pissarro

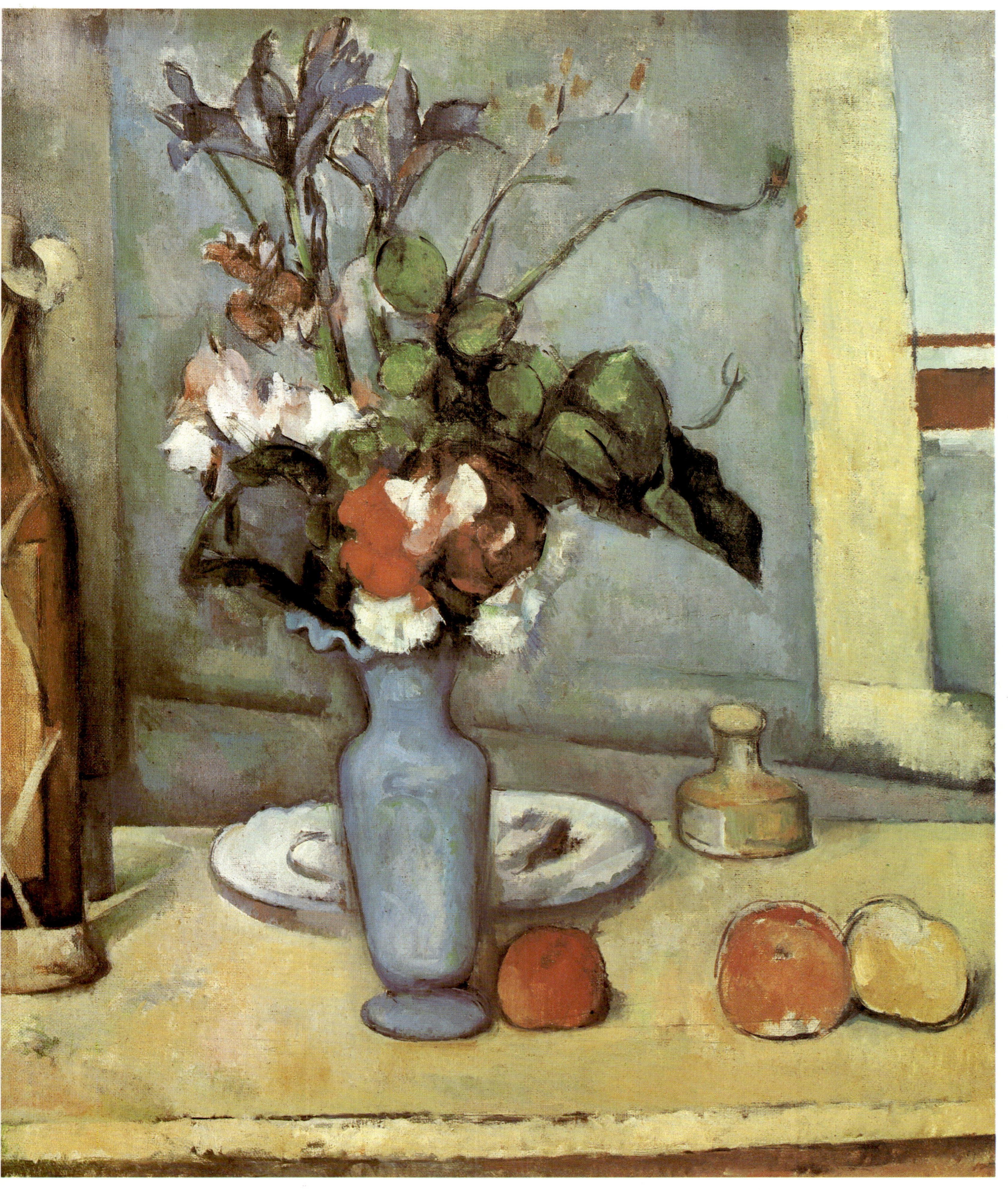

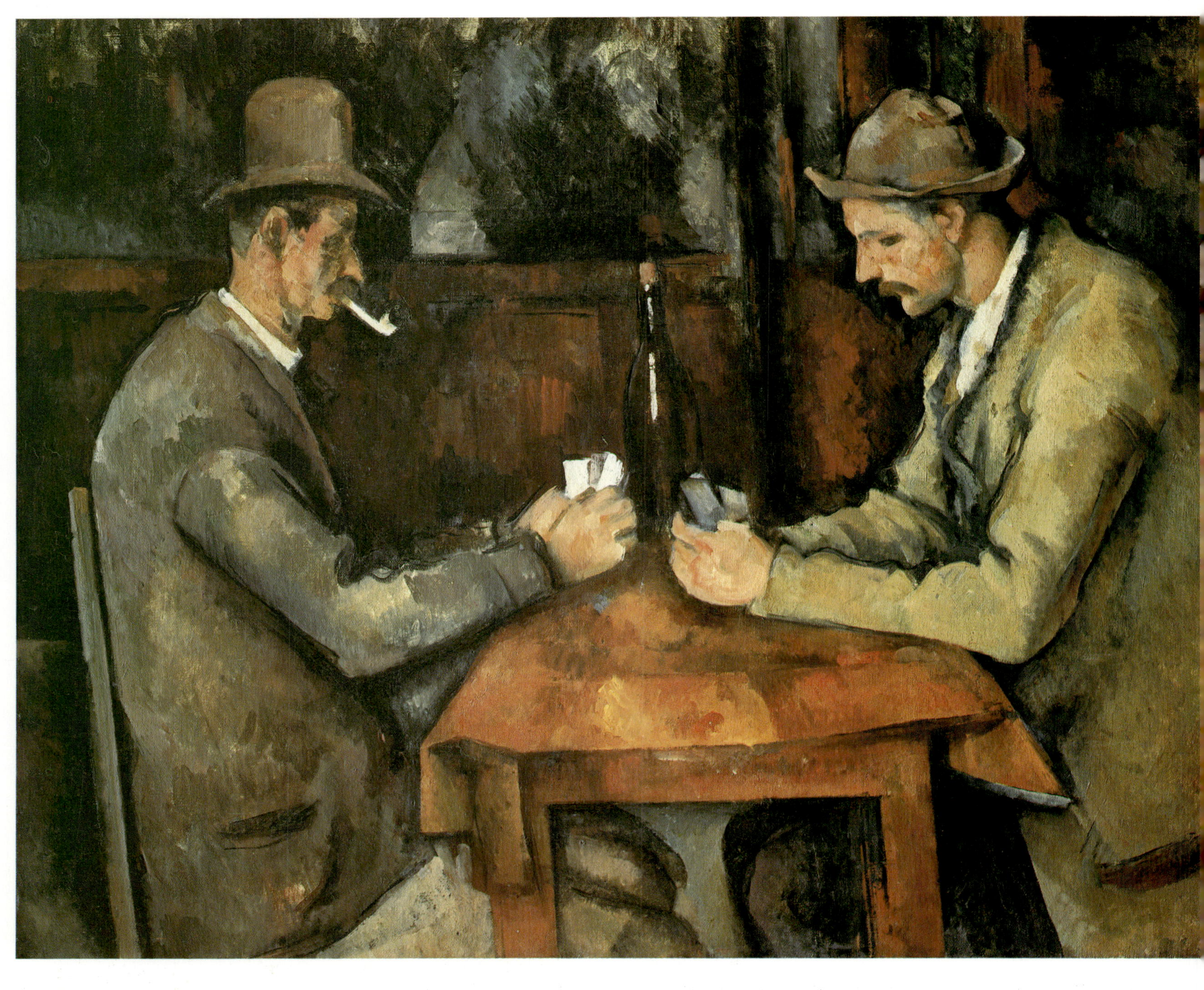

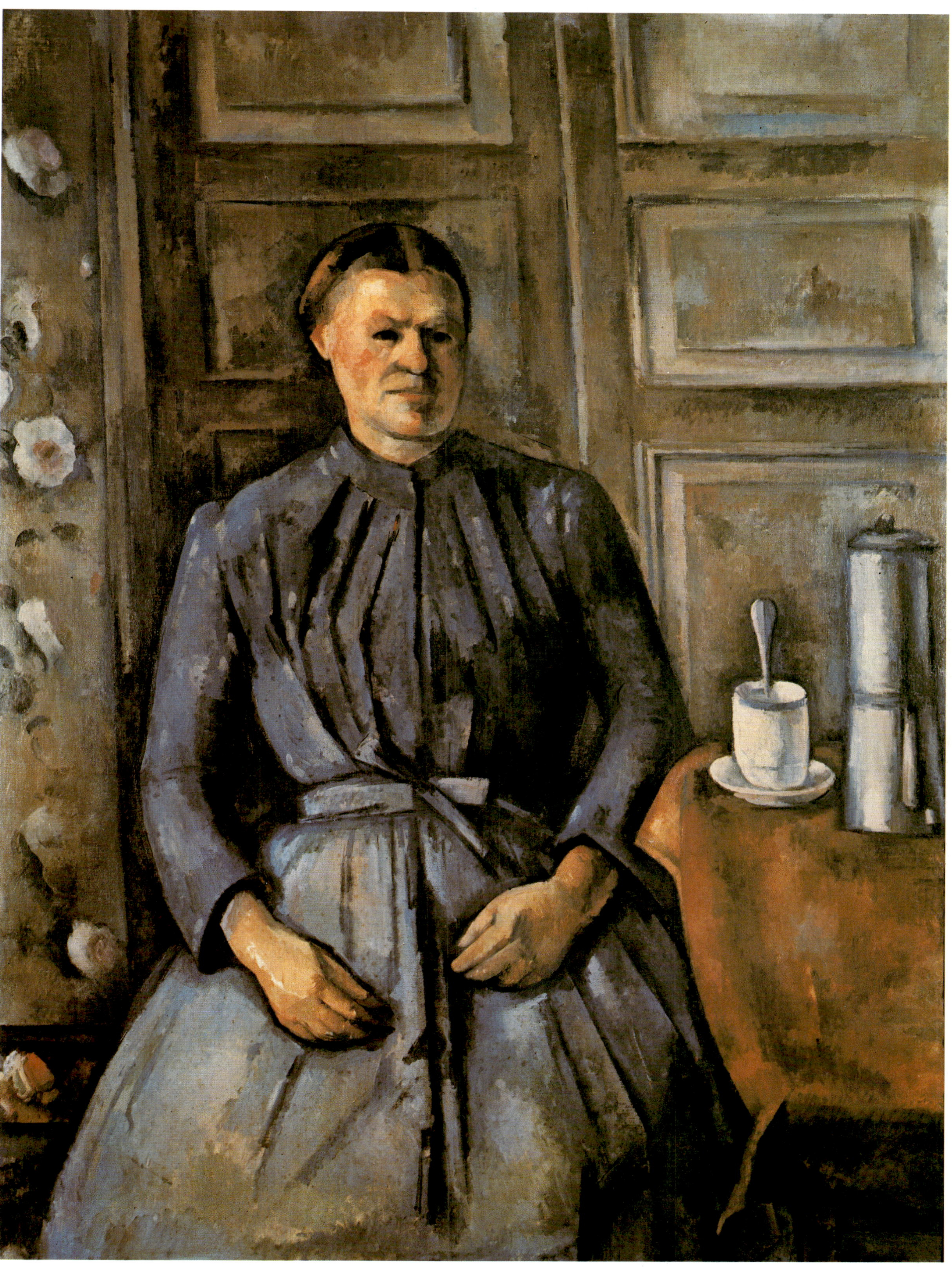

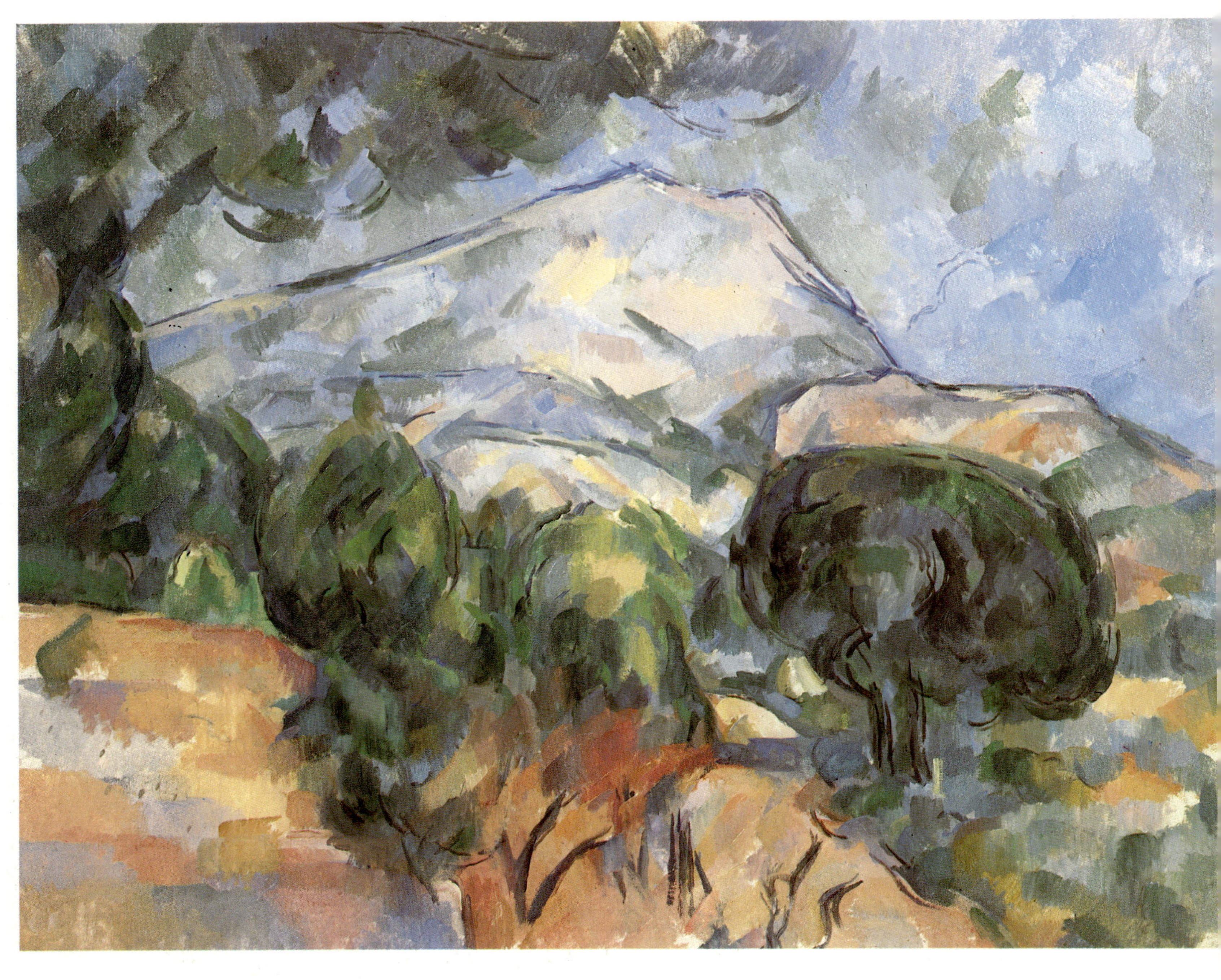

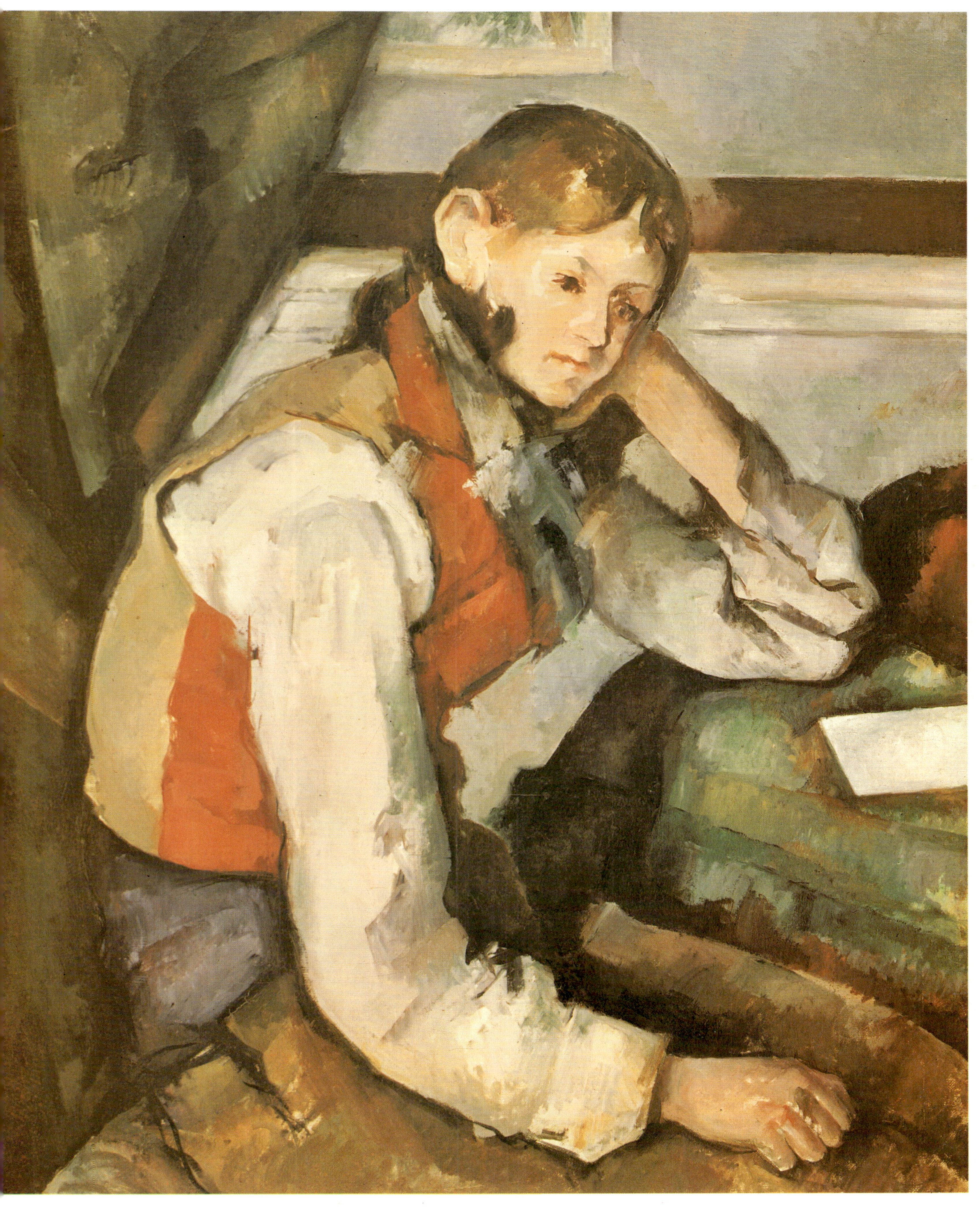

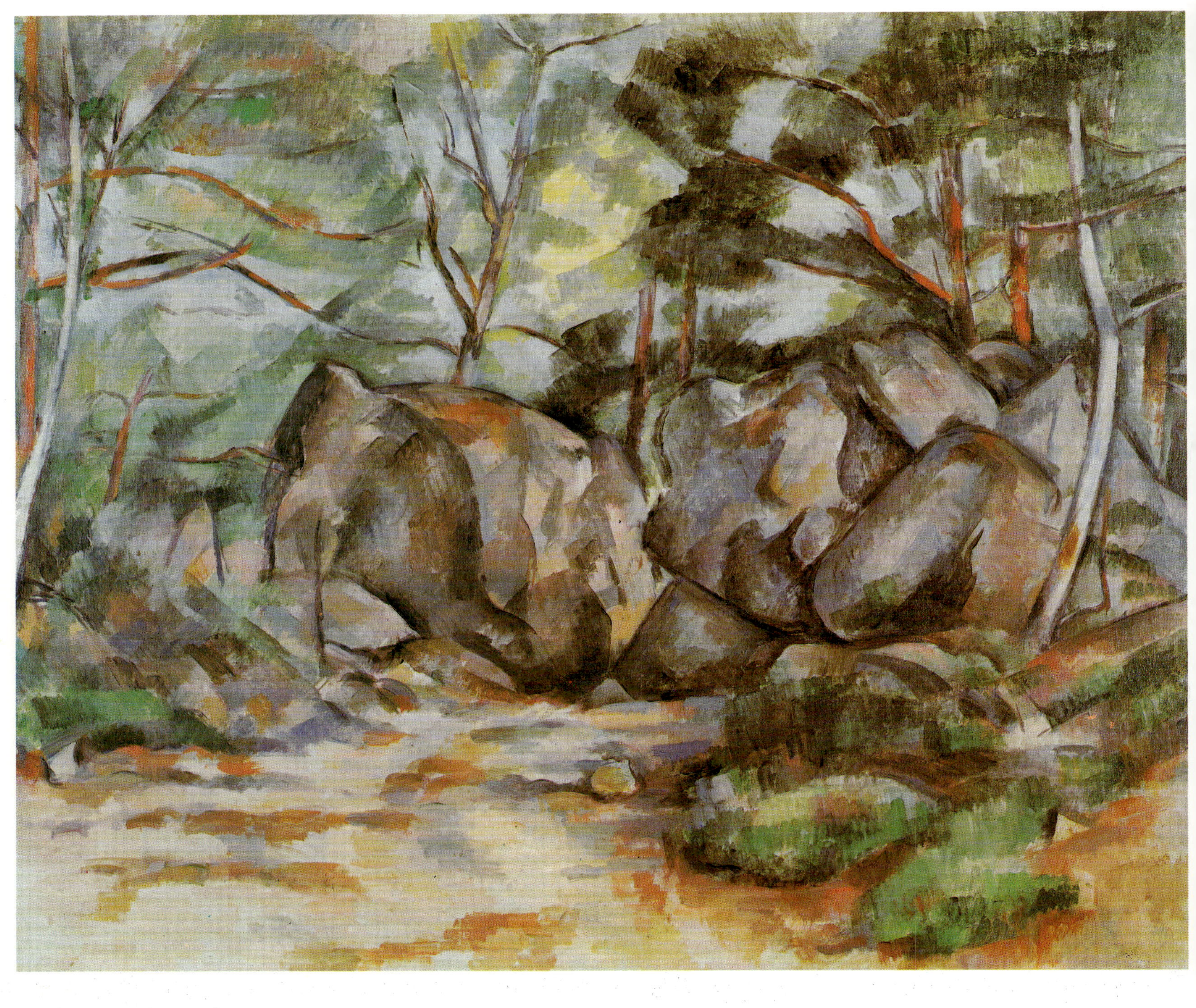

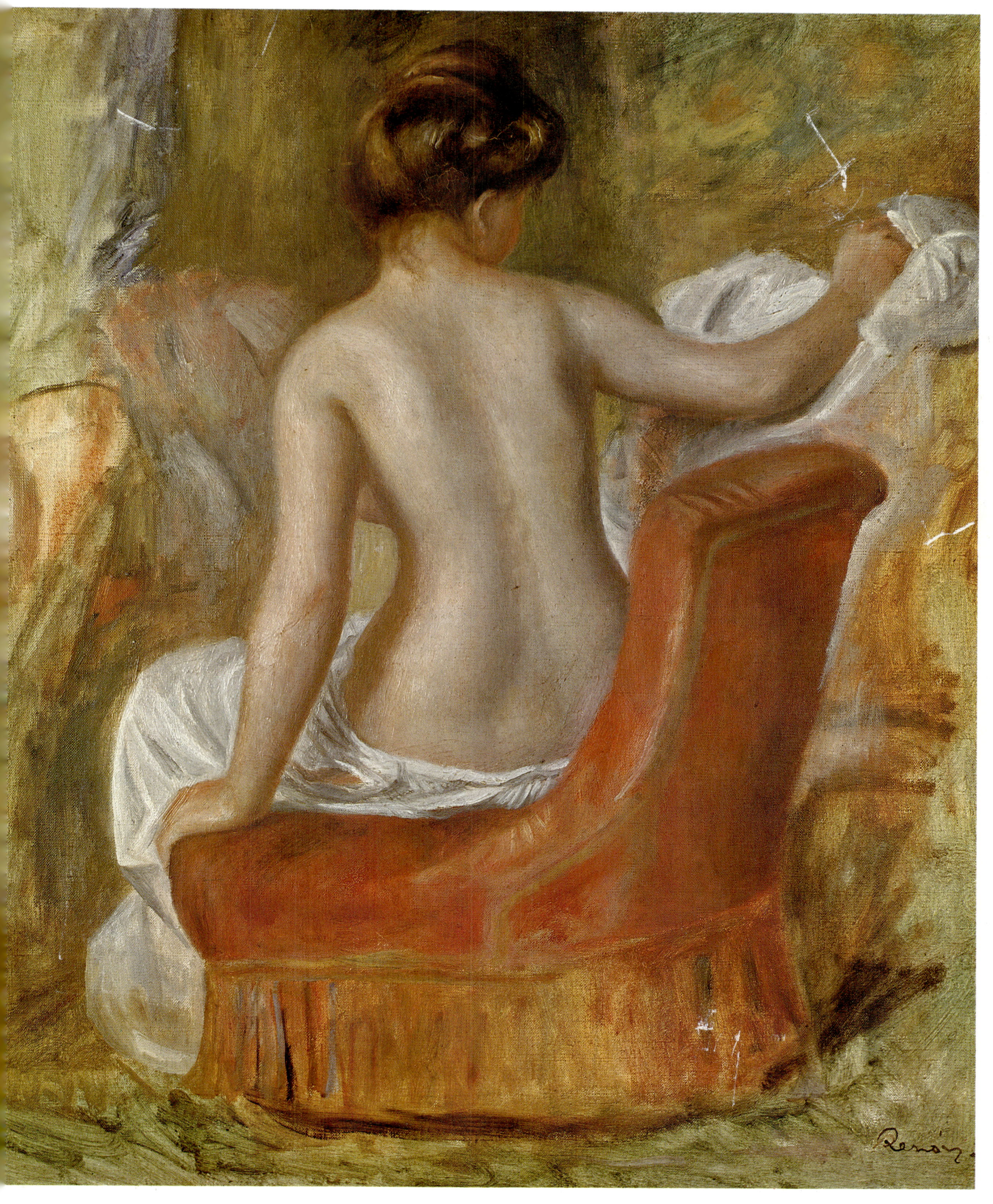

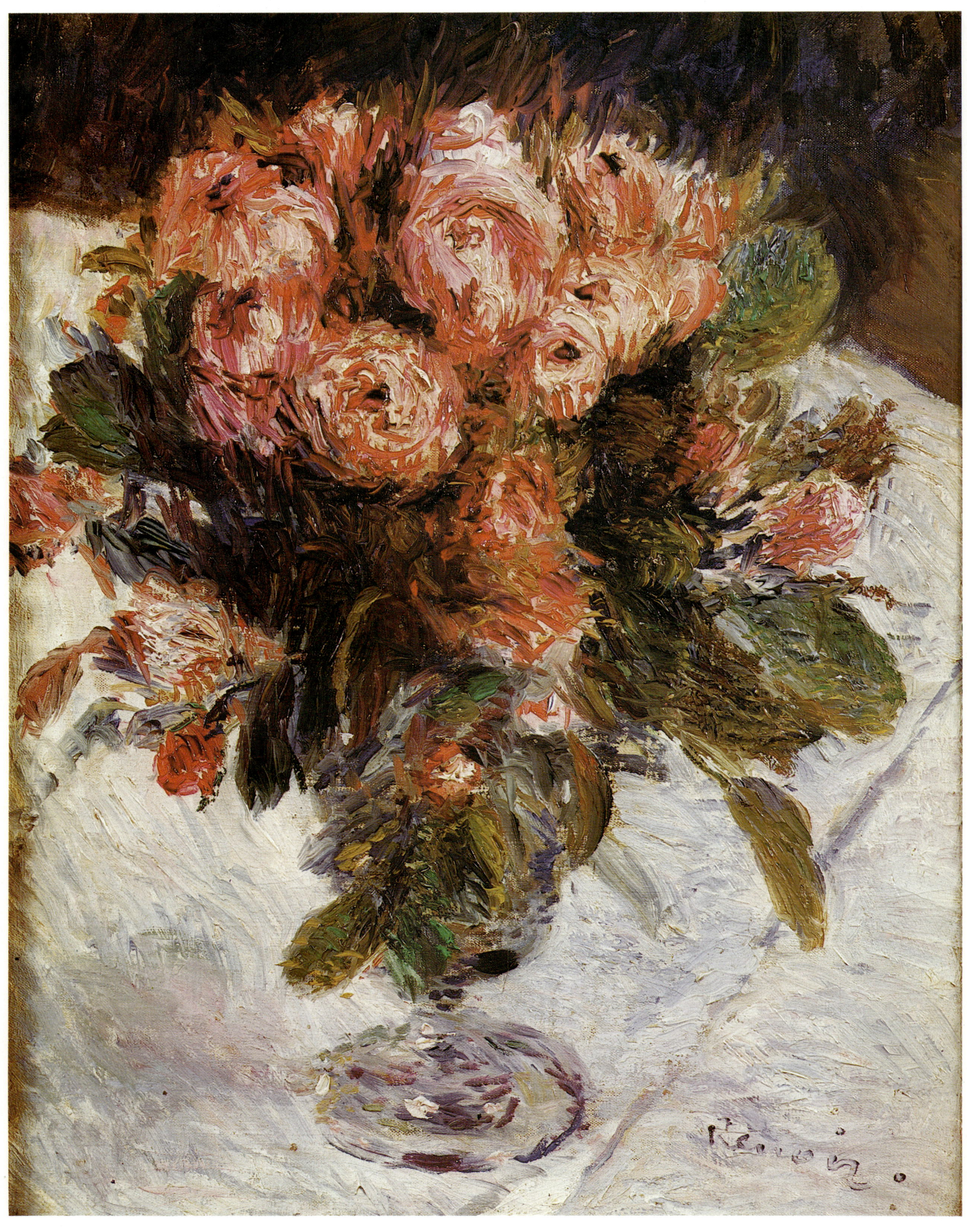

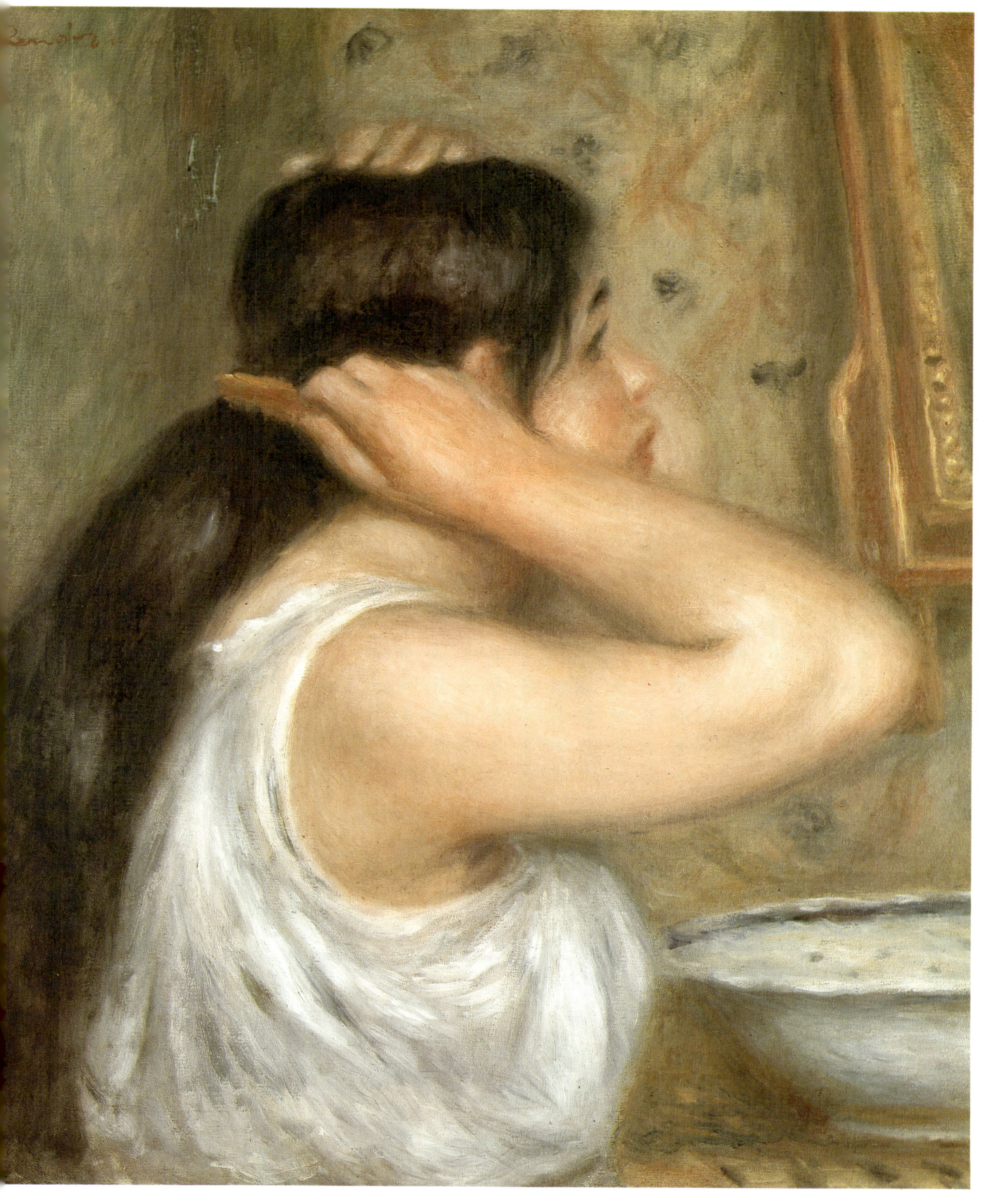

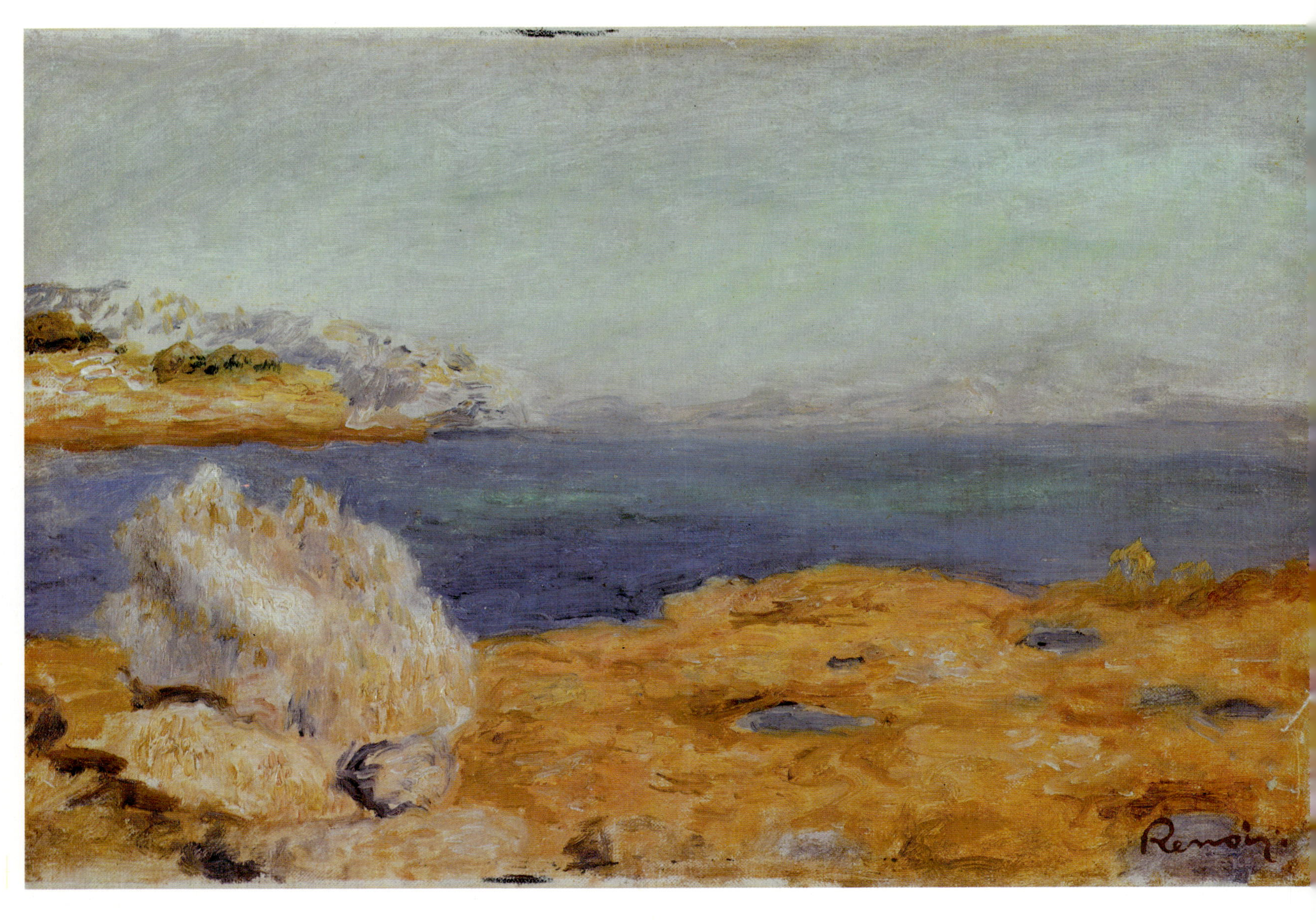
Renoir.

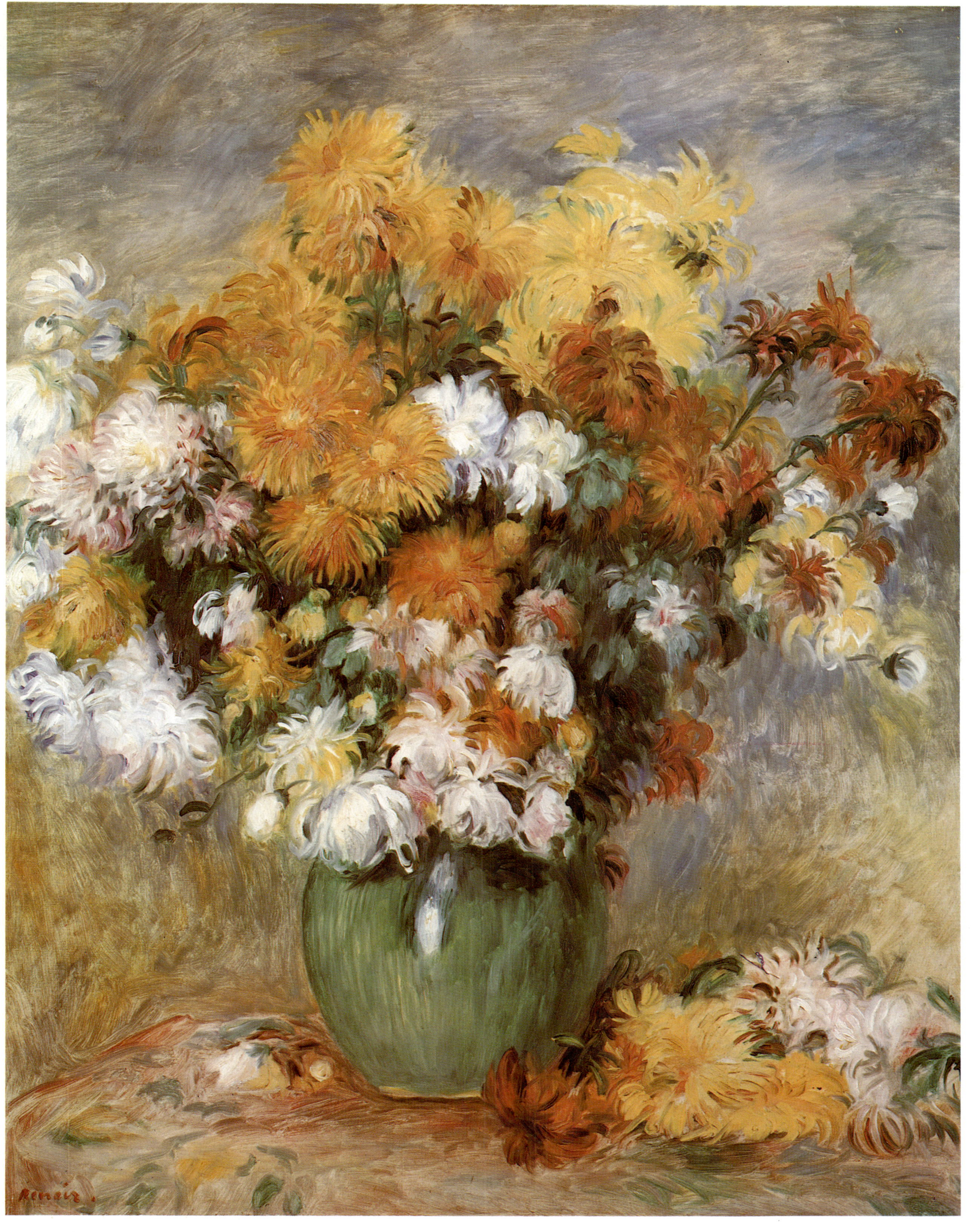

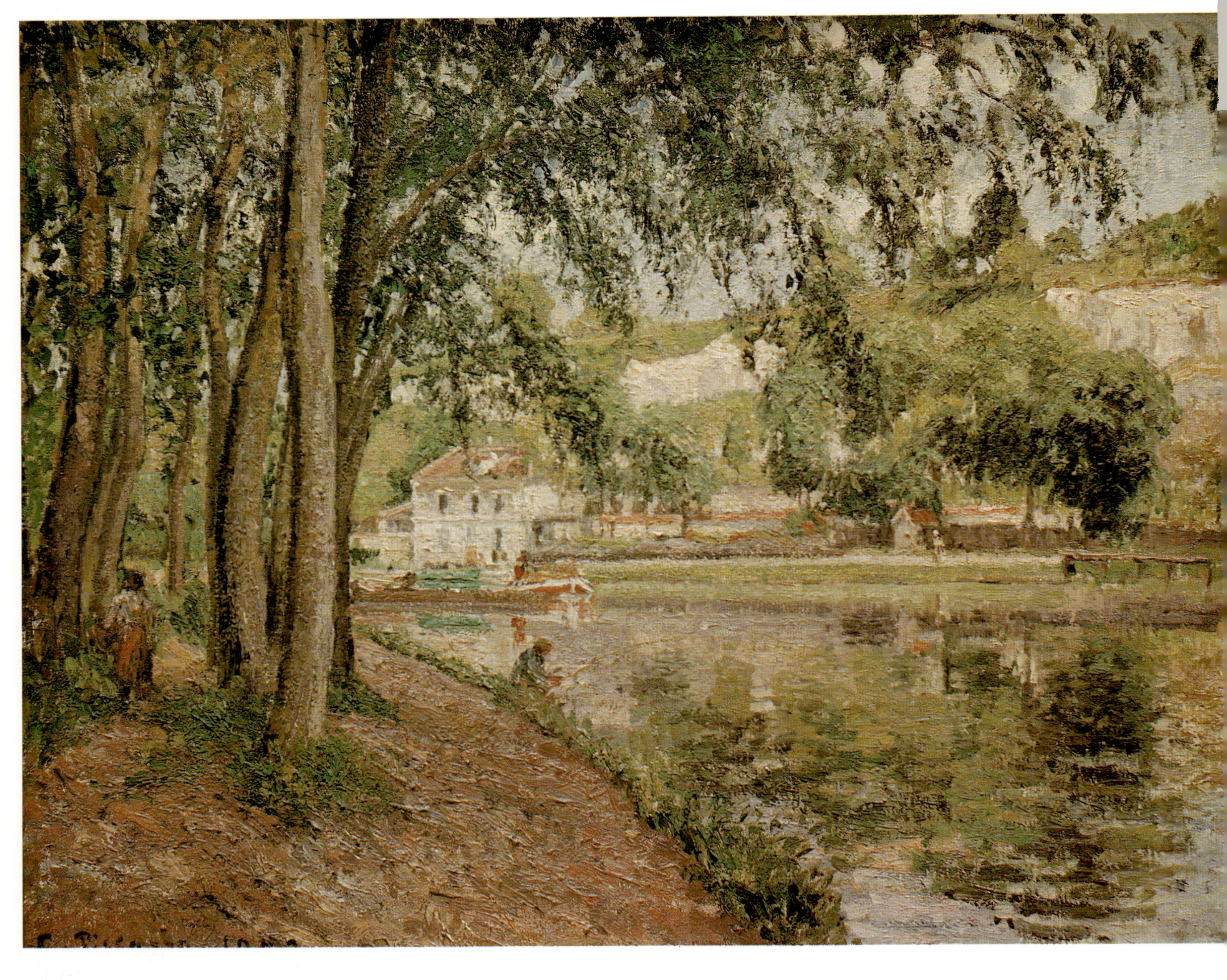

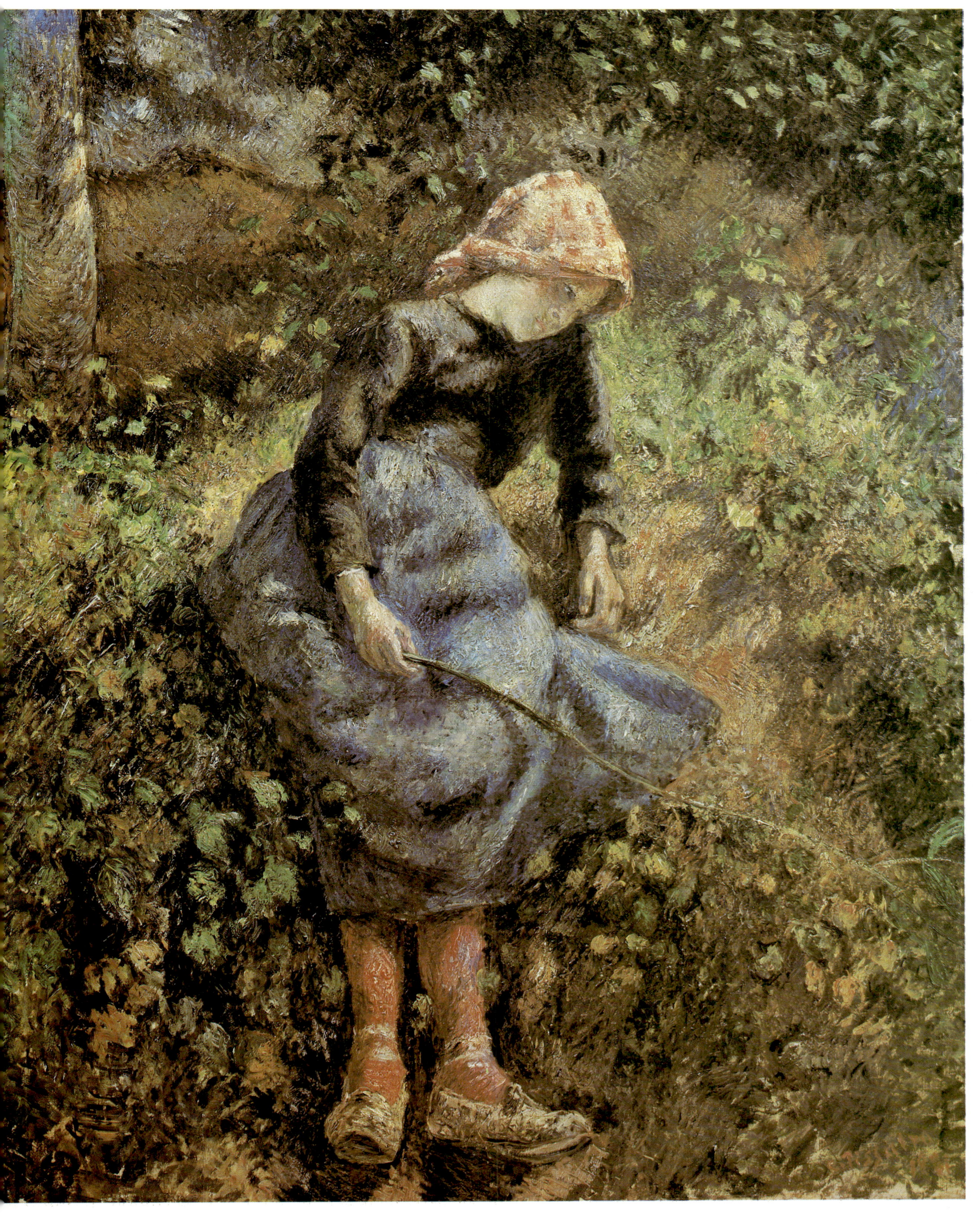

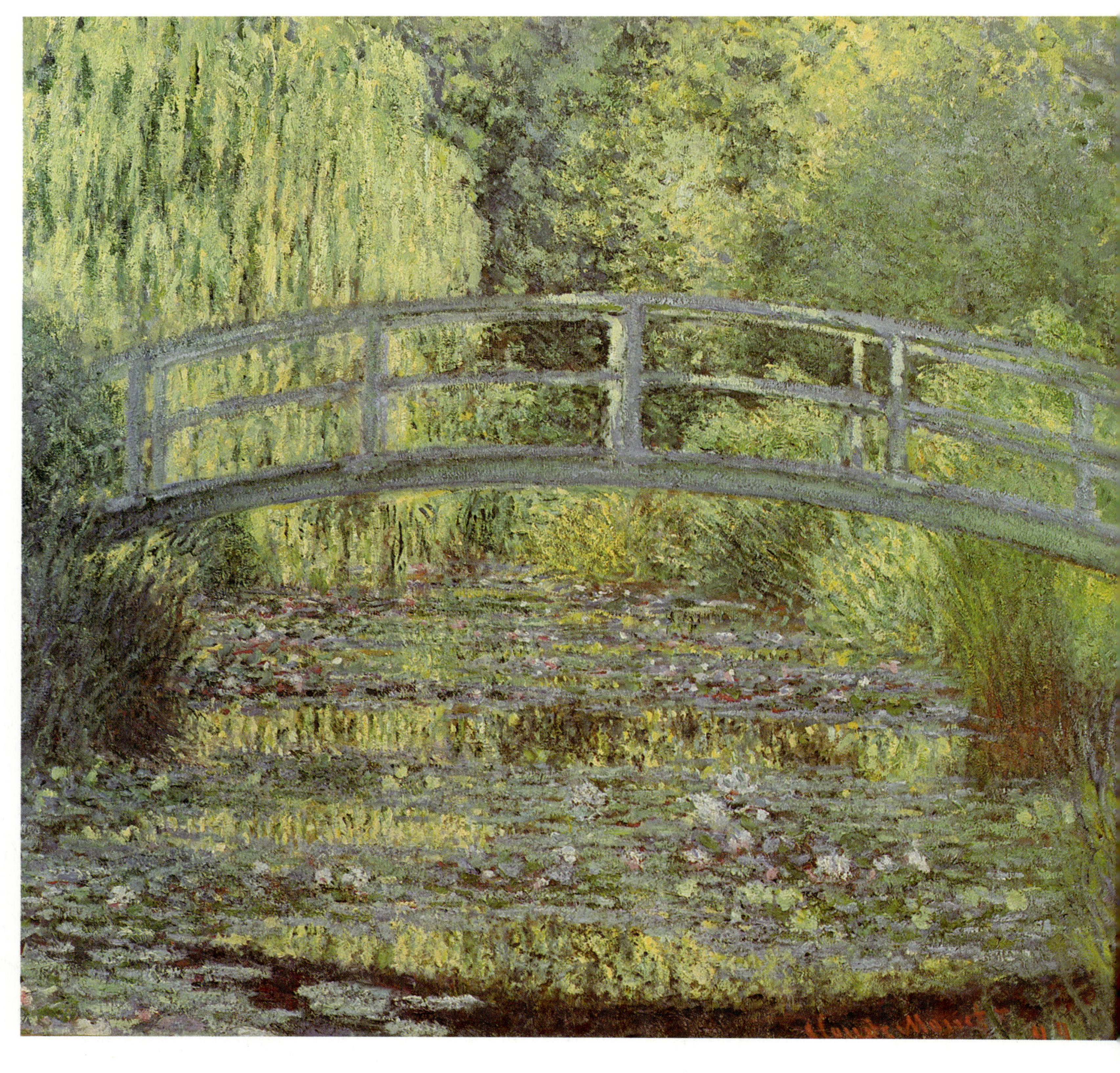

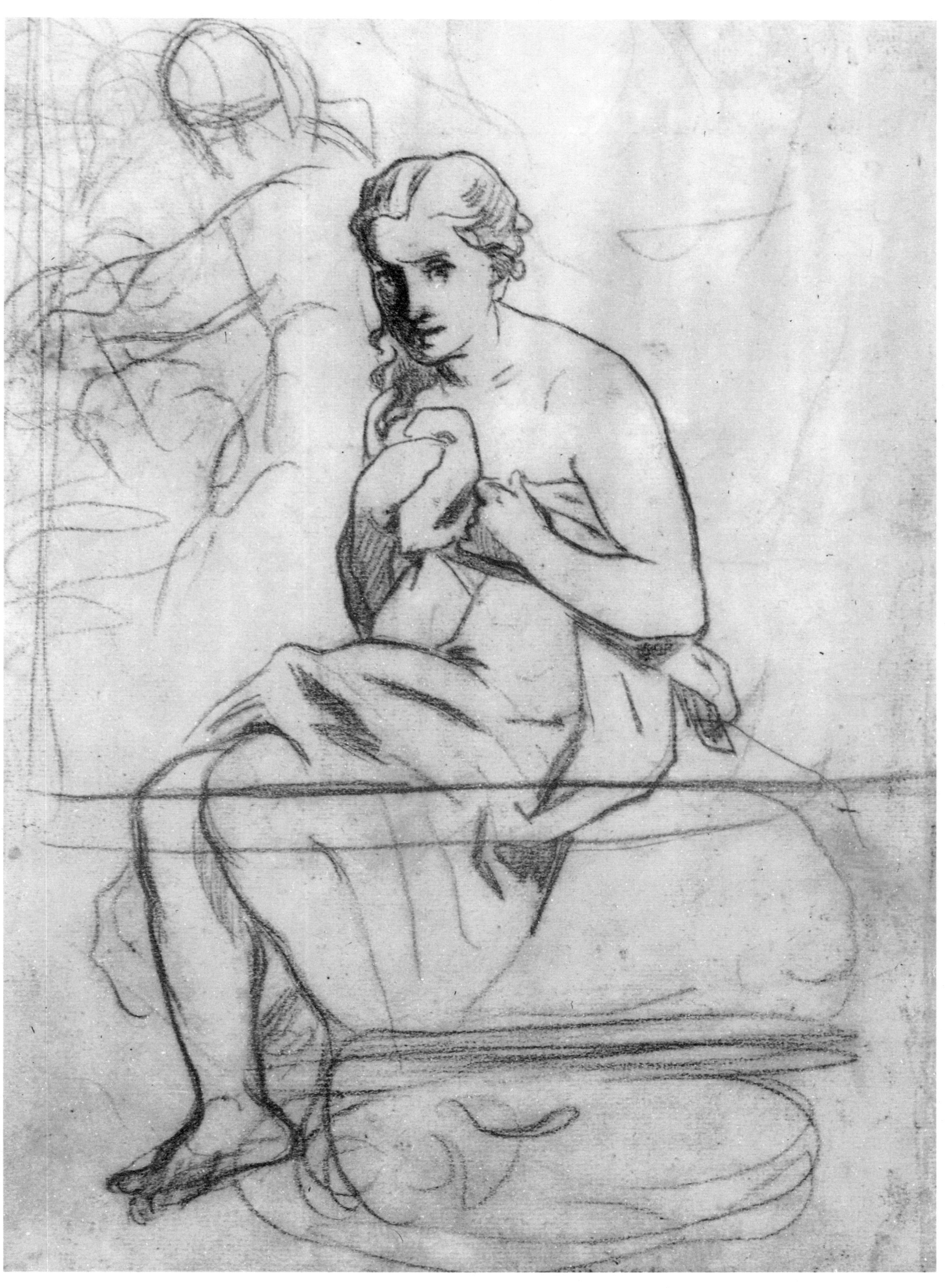

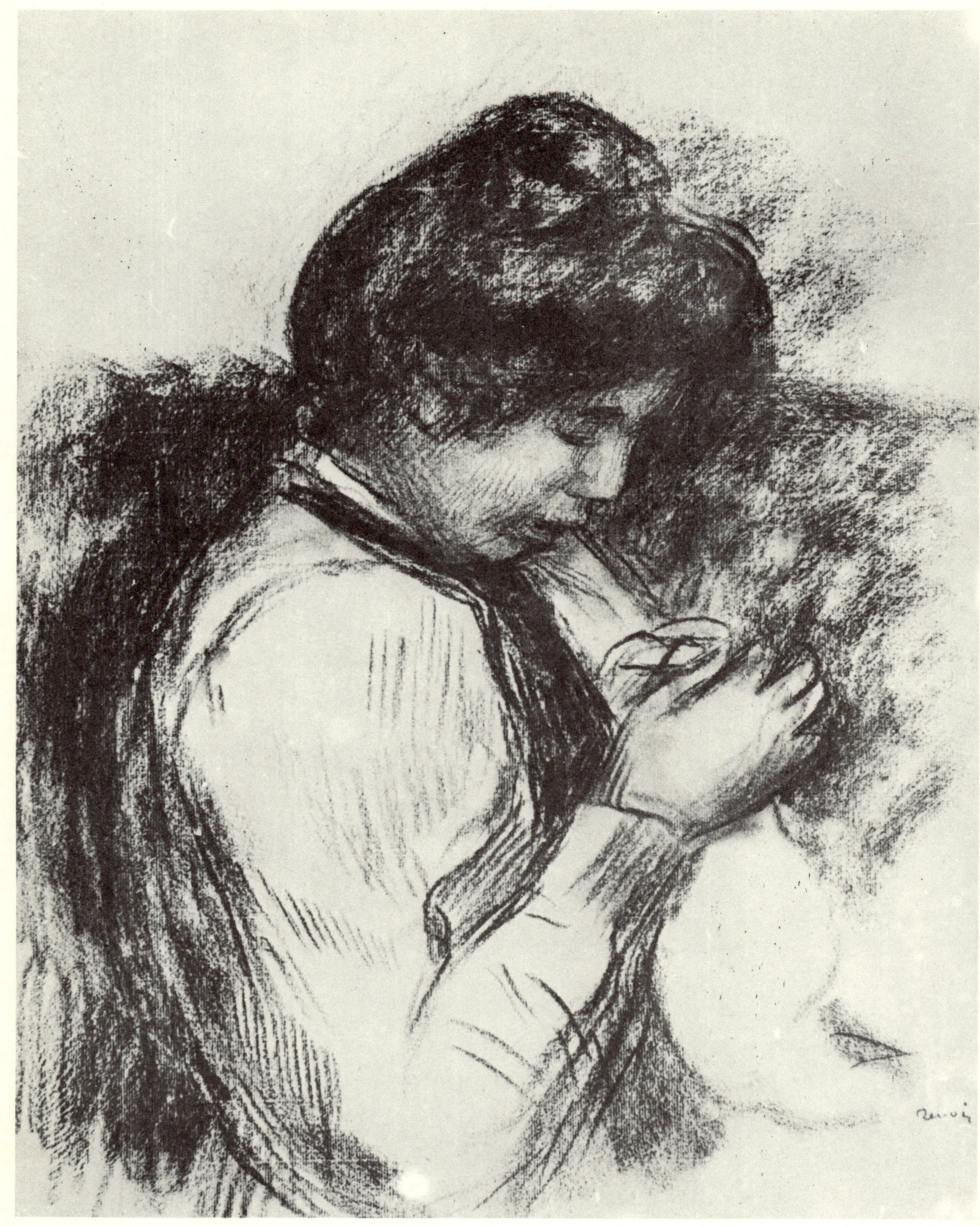

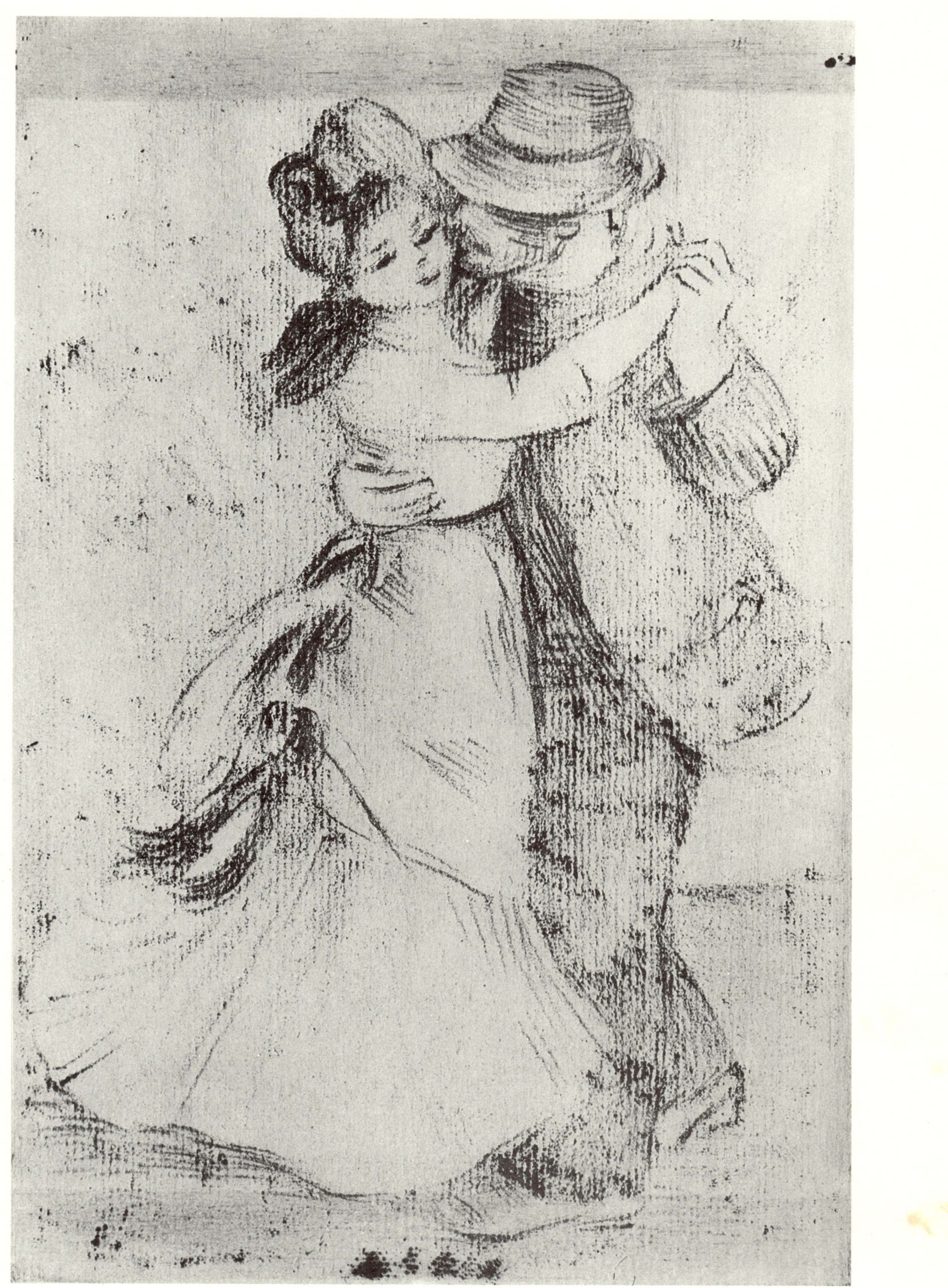

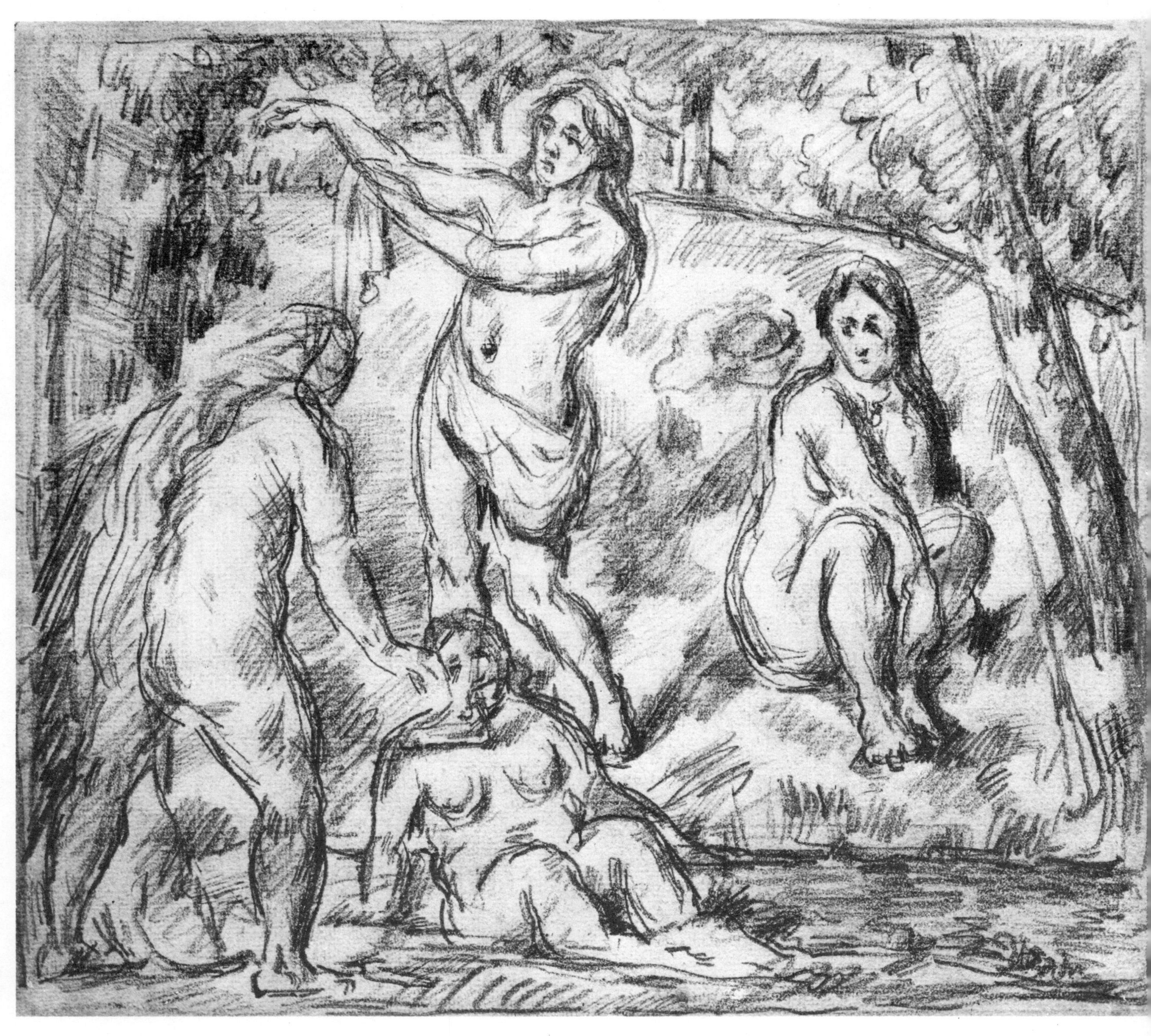

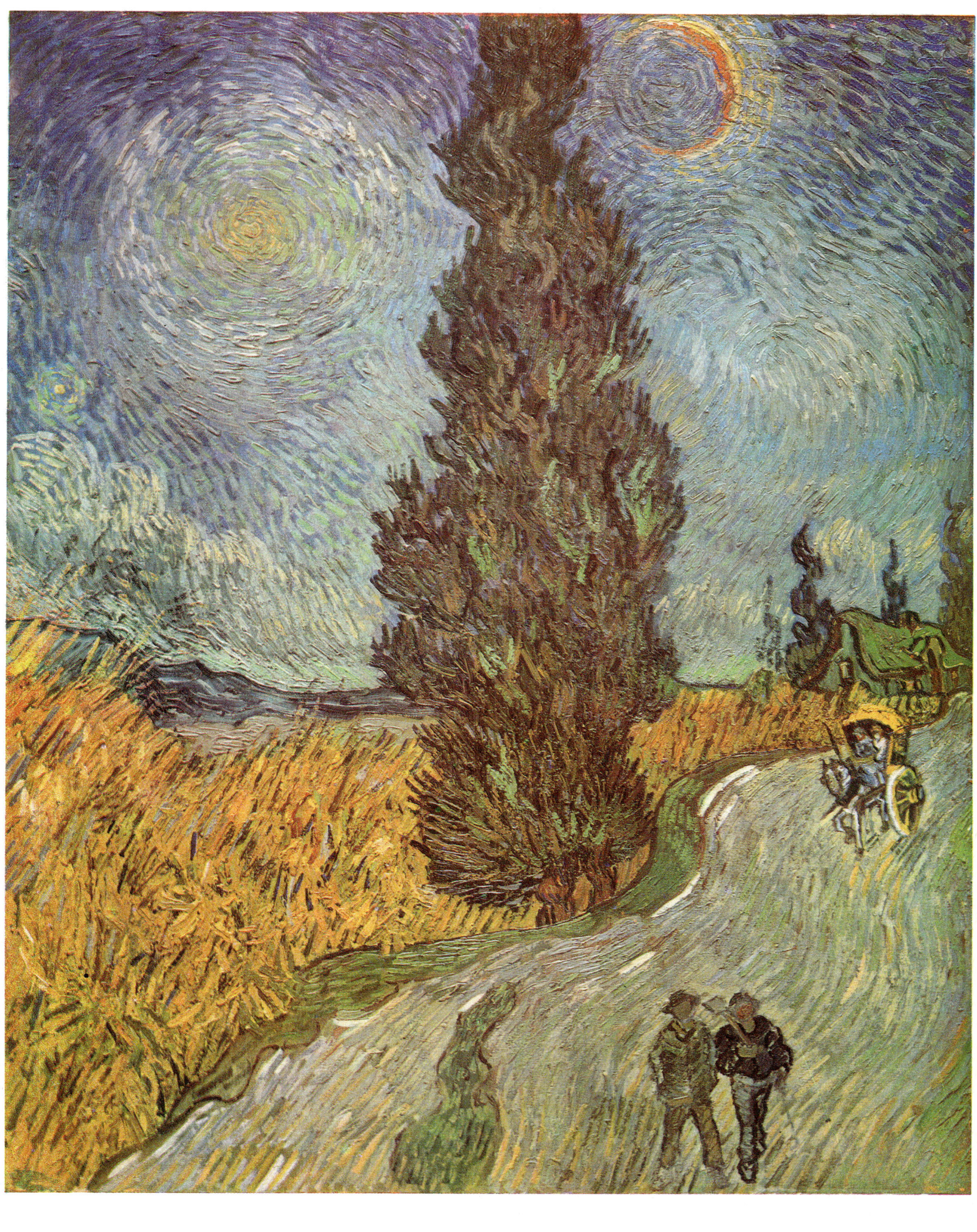

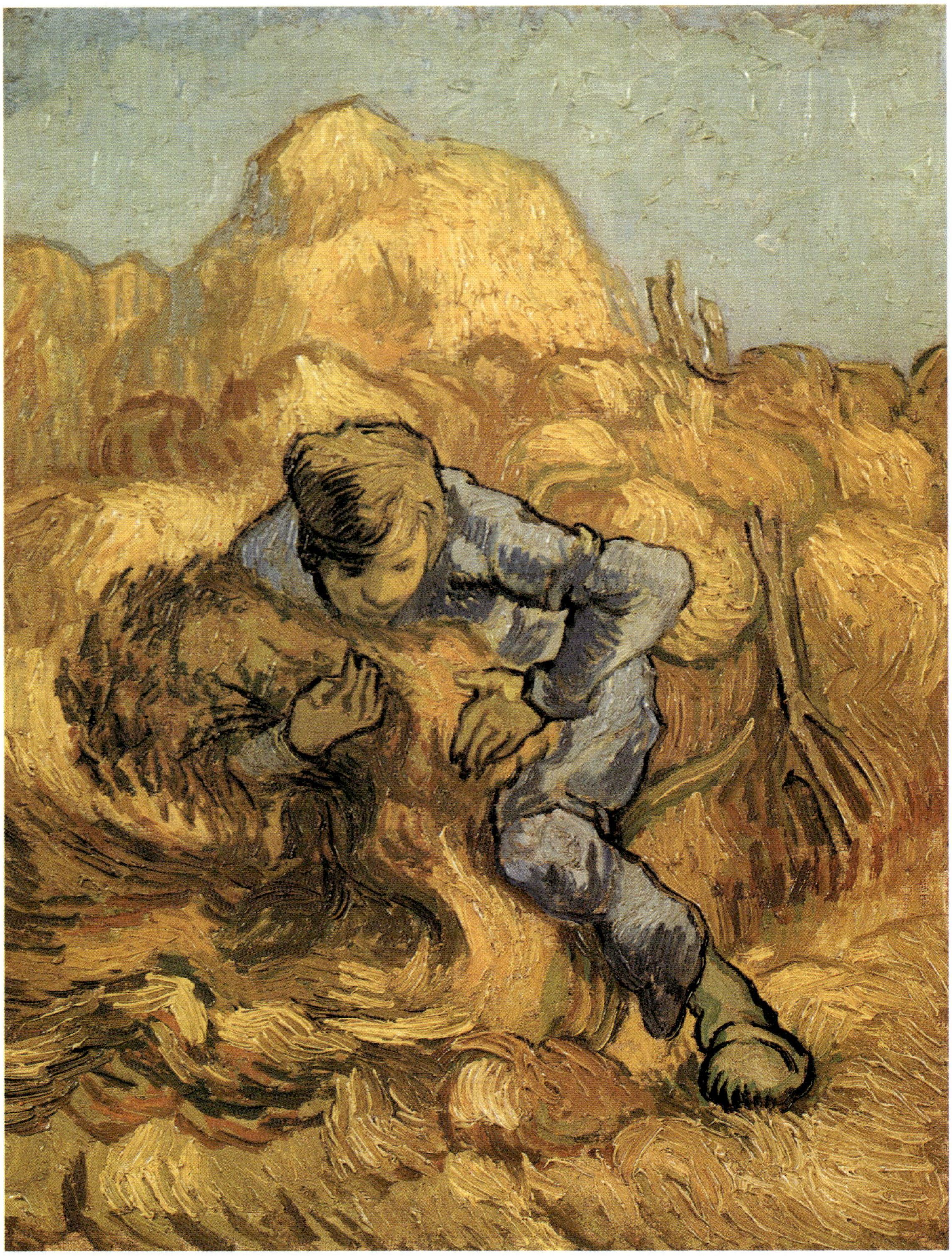

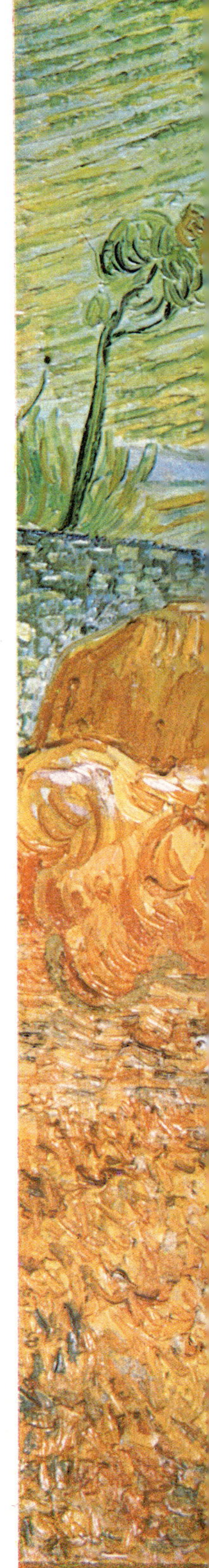

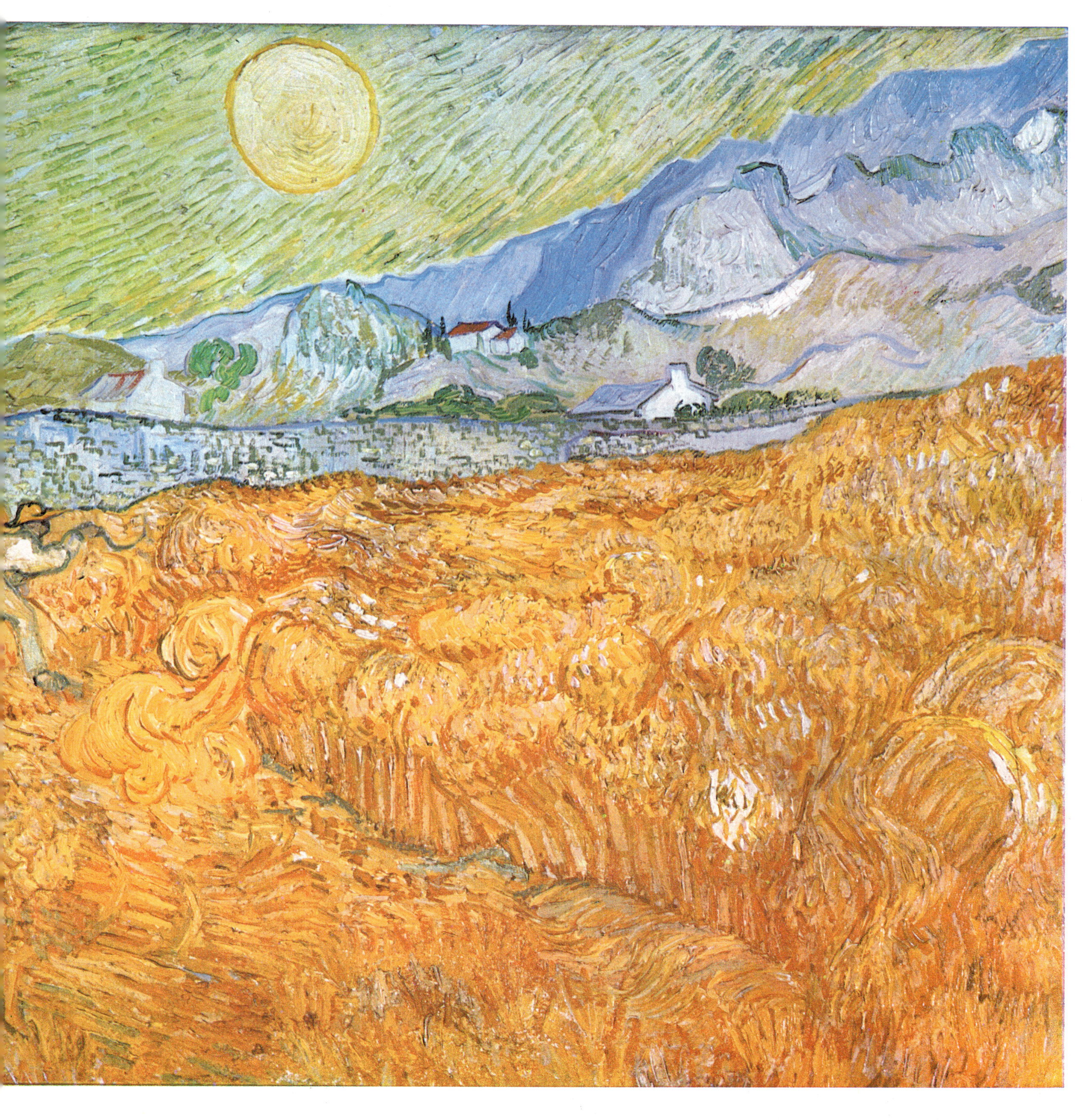

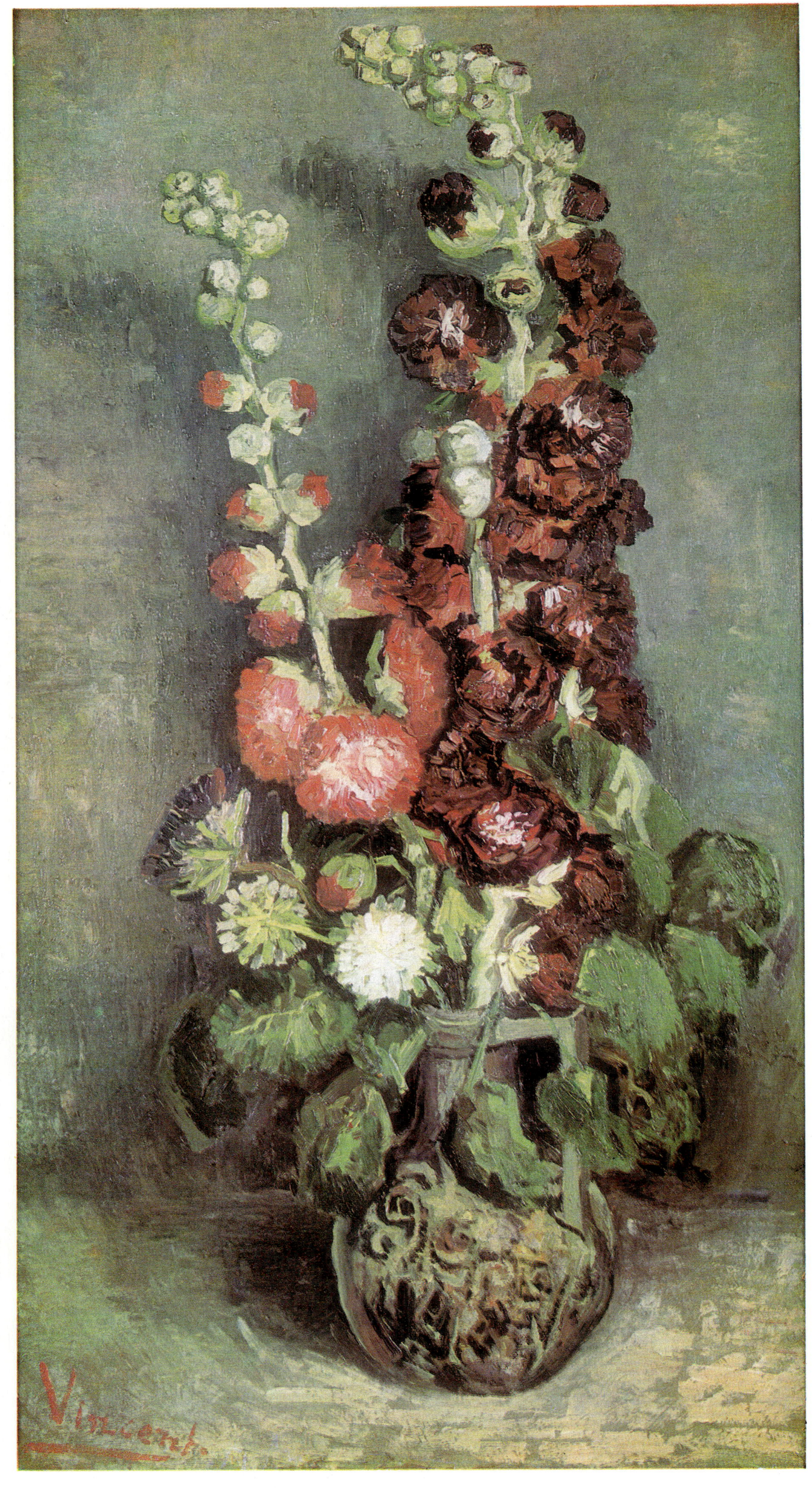
Vincent.

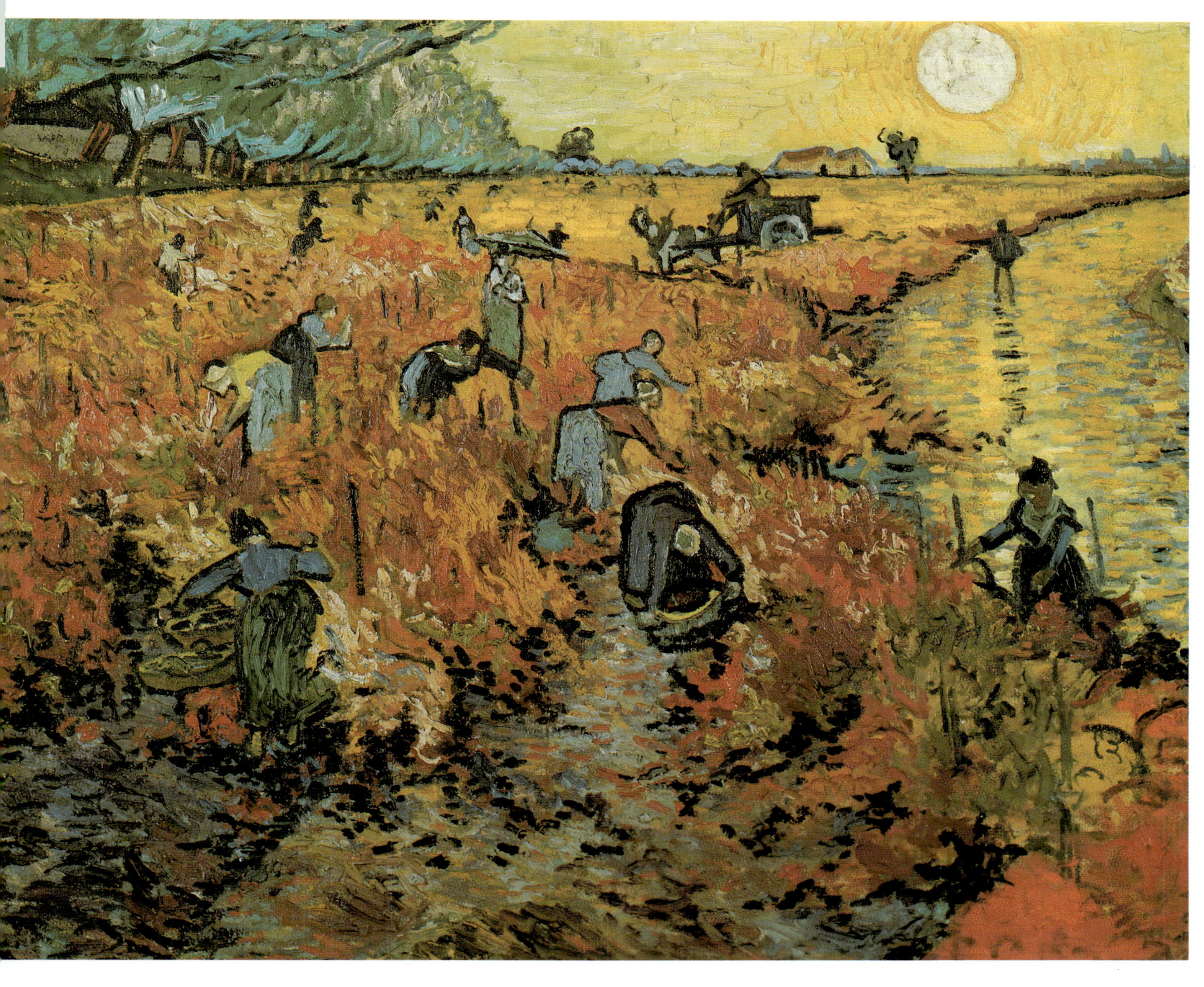

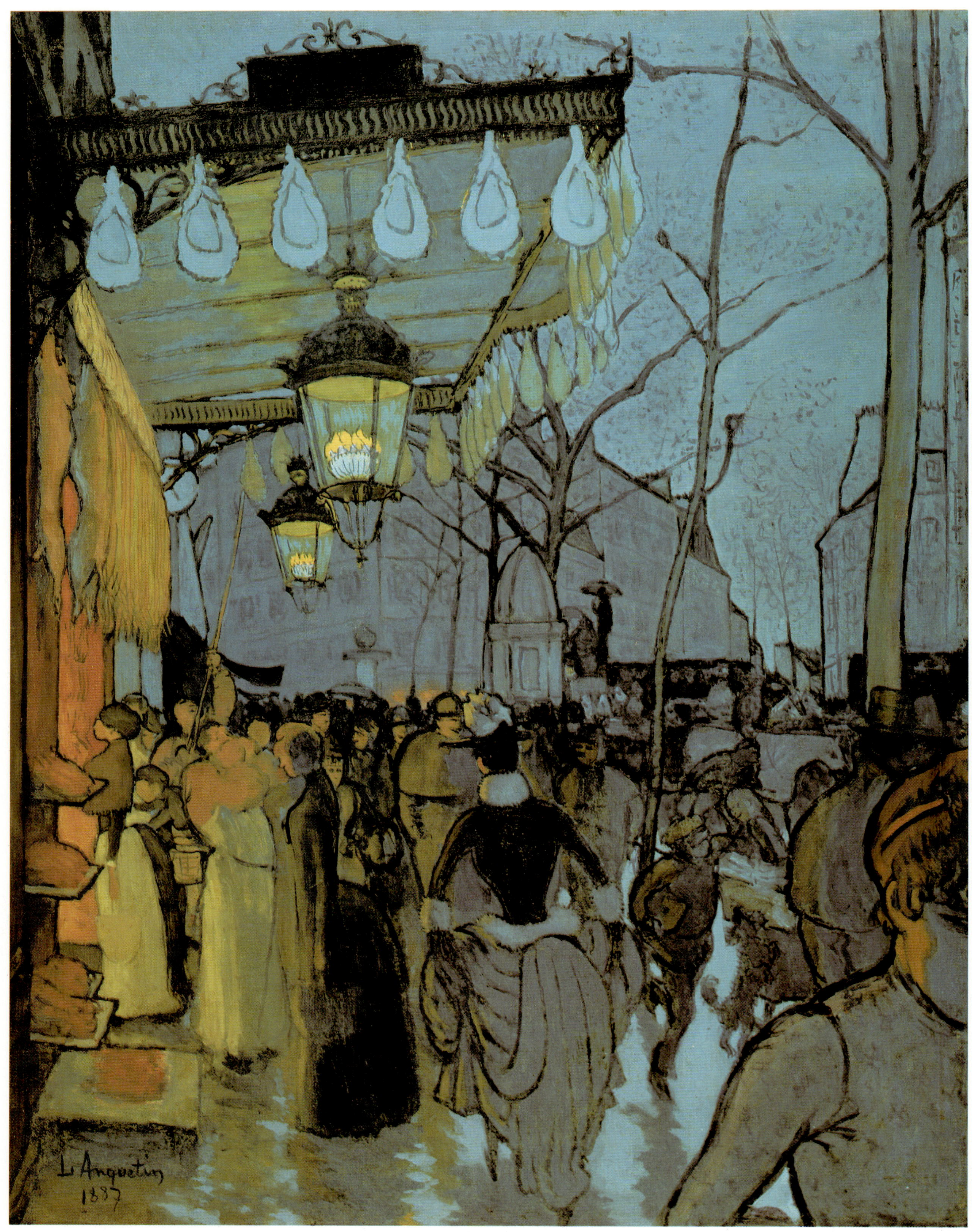
L. Anquetin
1887

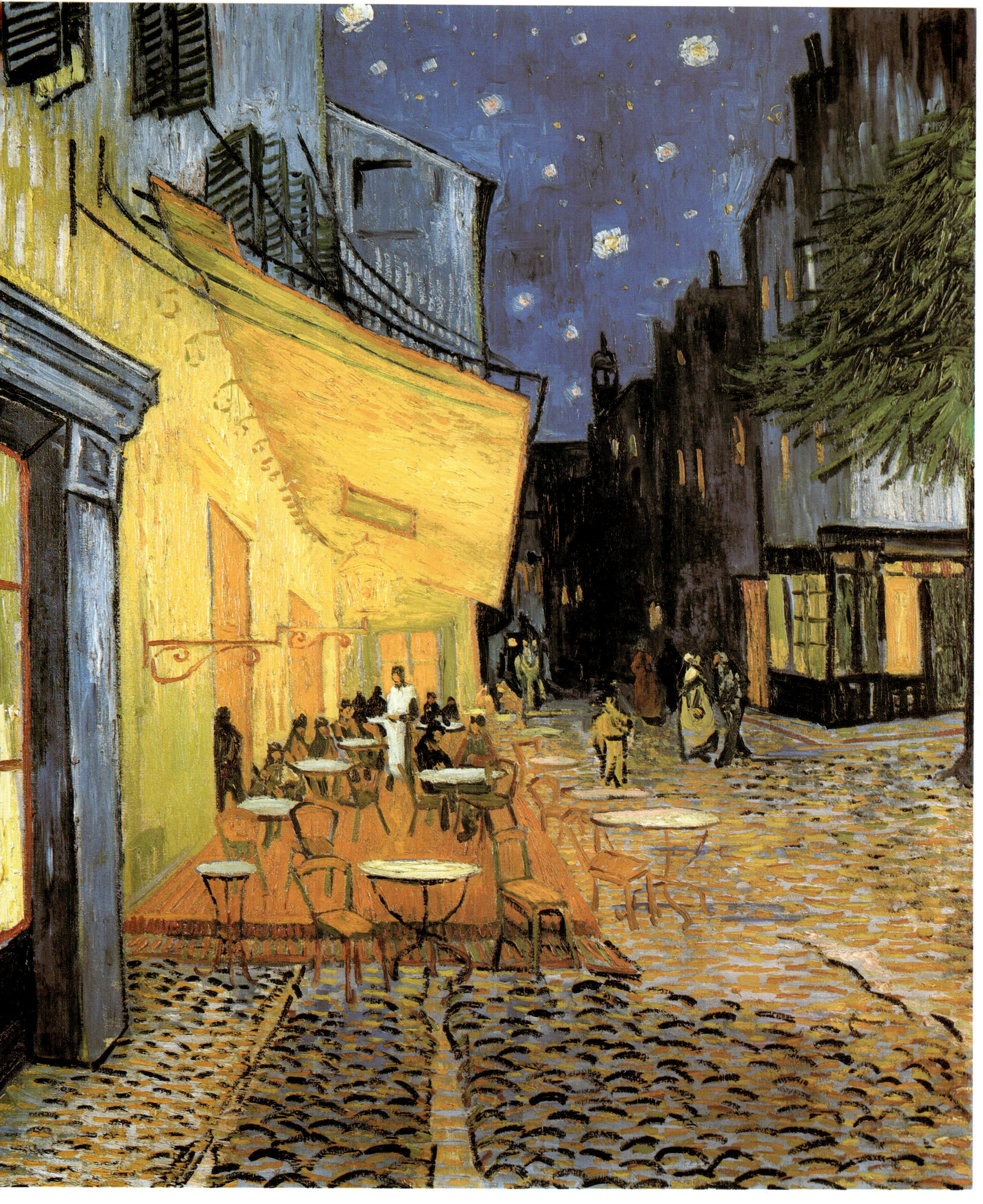

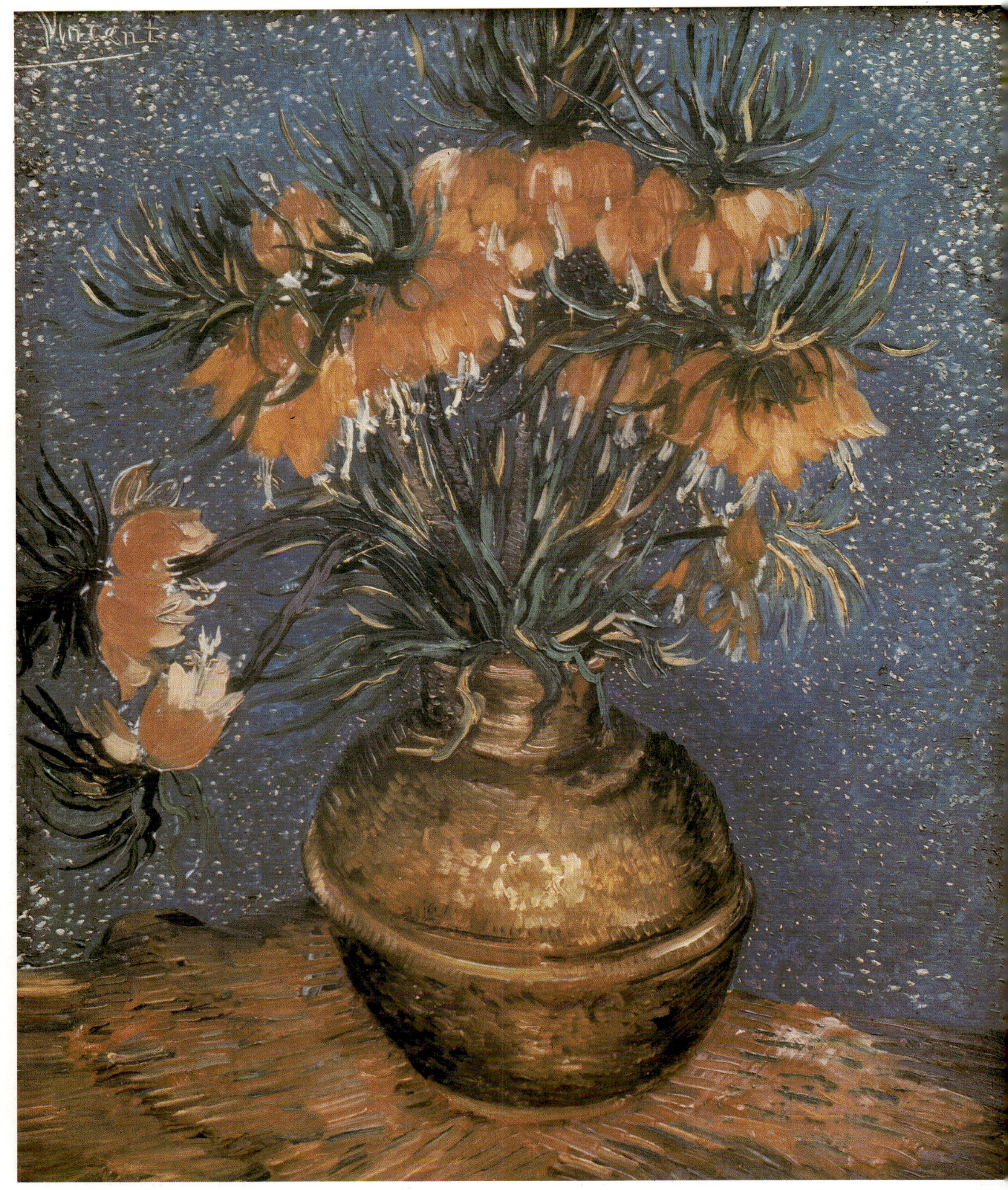
Vincent

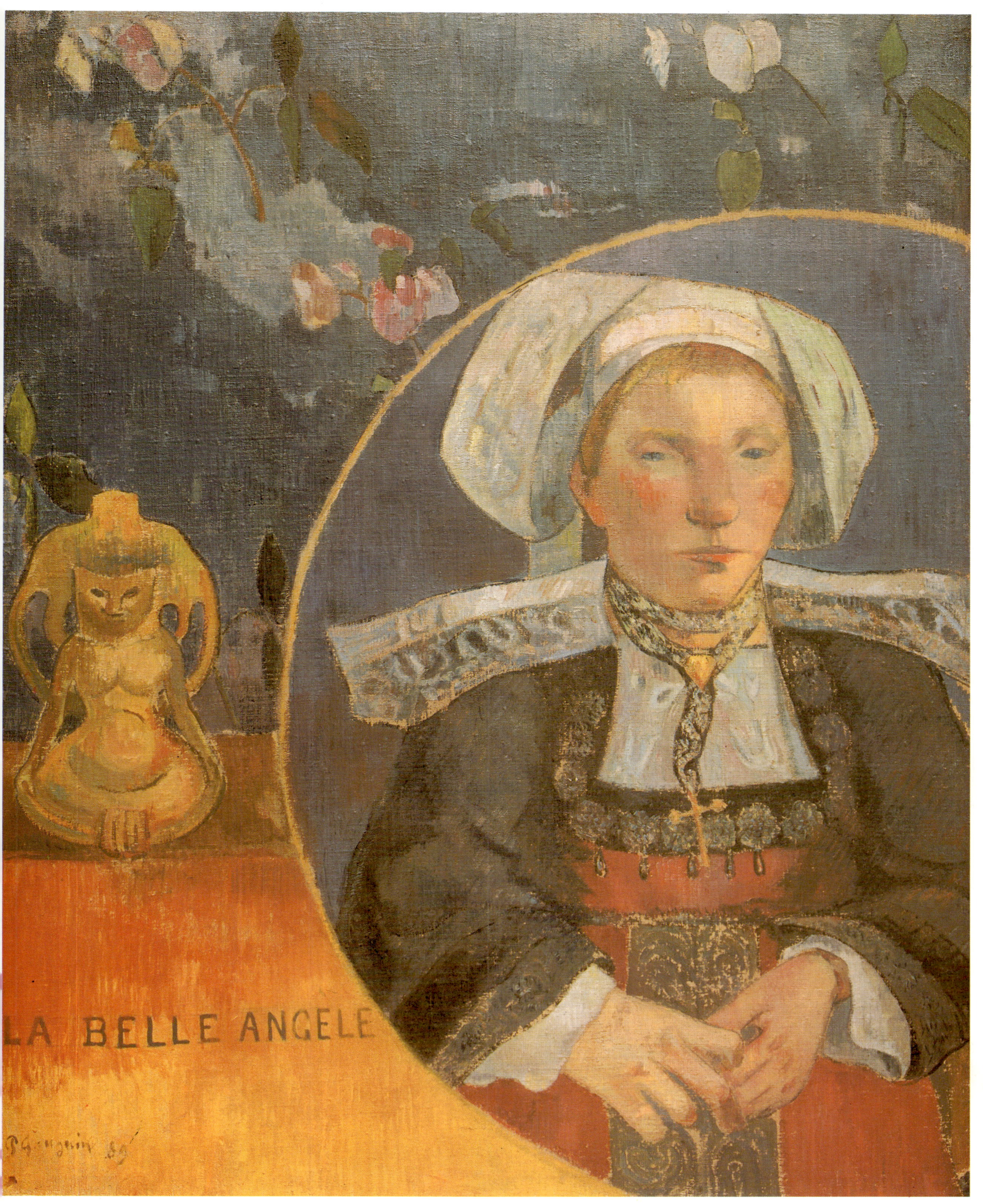
LA BELLE ANGELE
P Gauguin 89

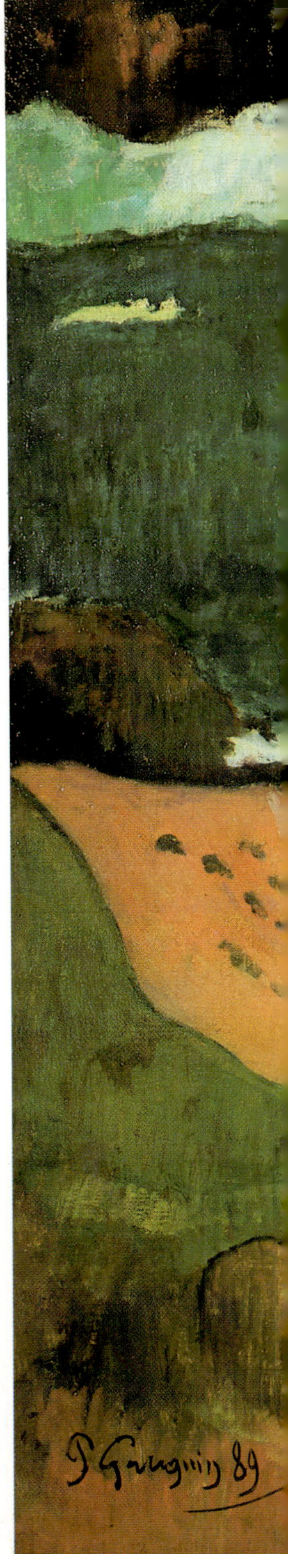

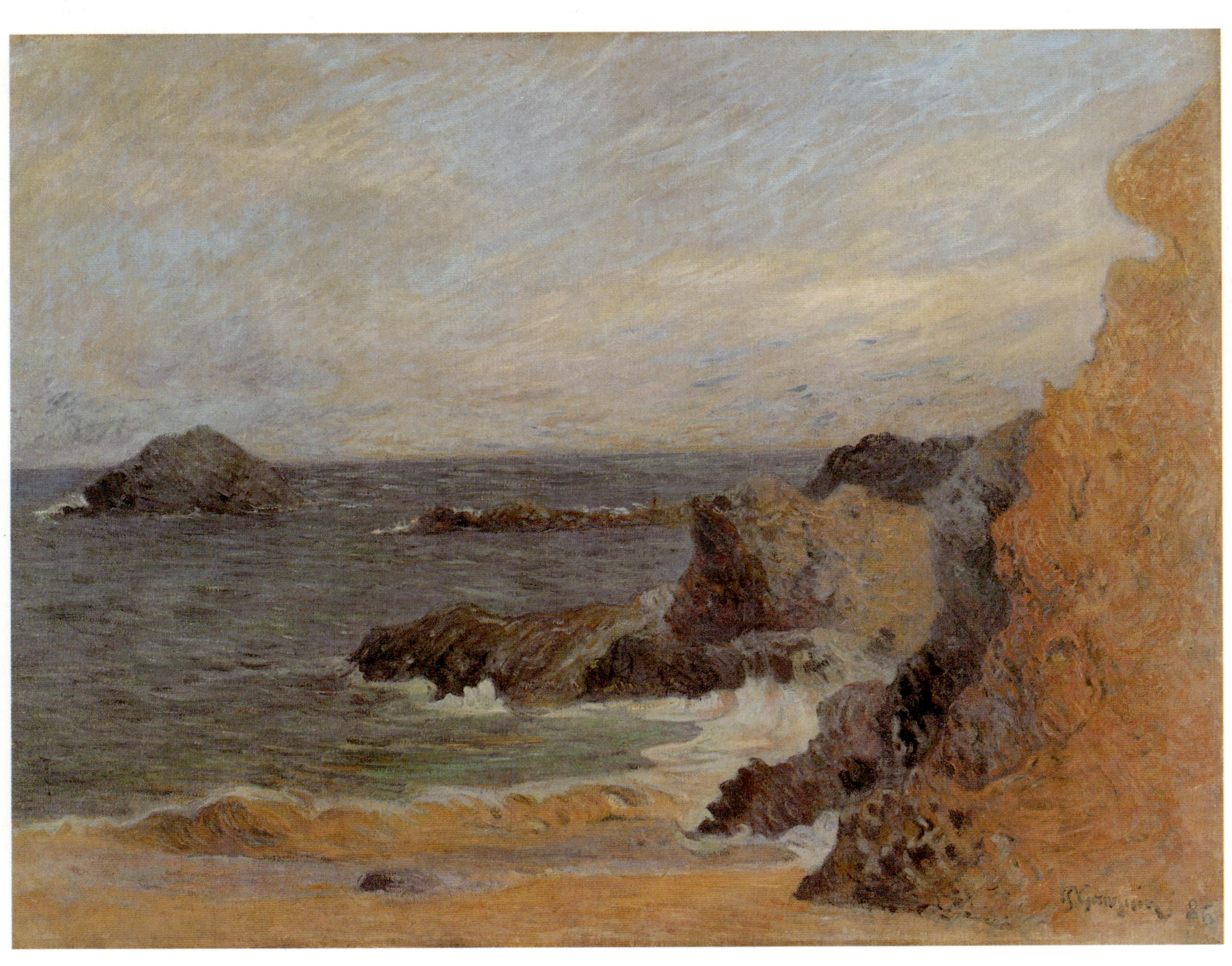

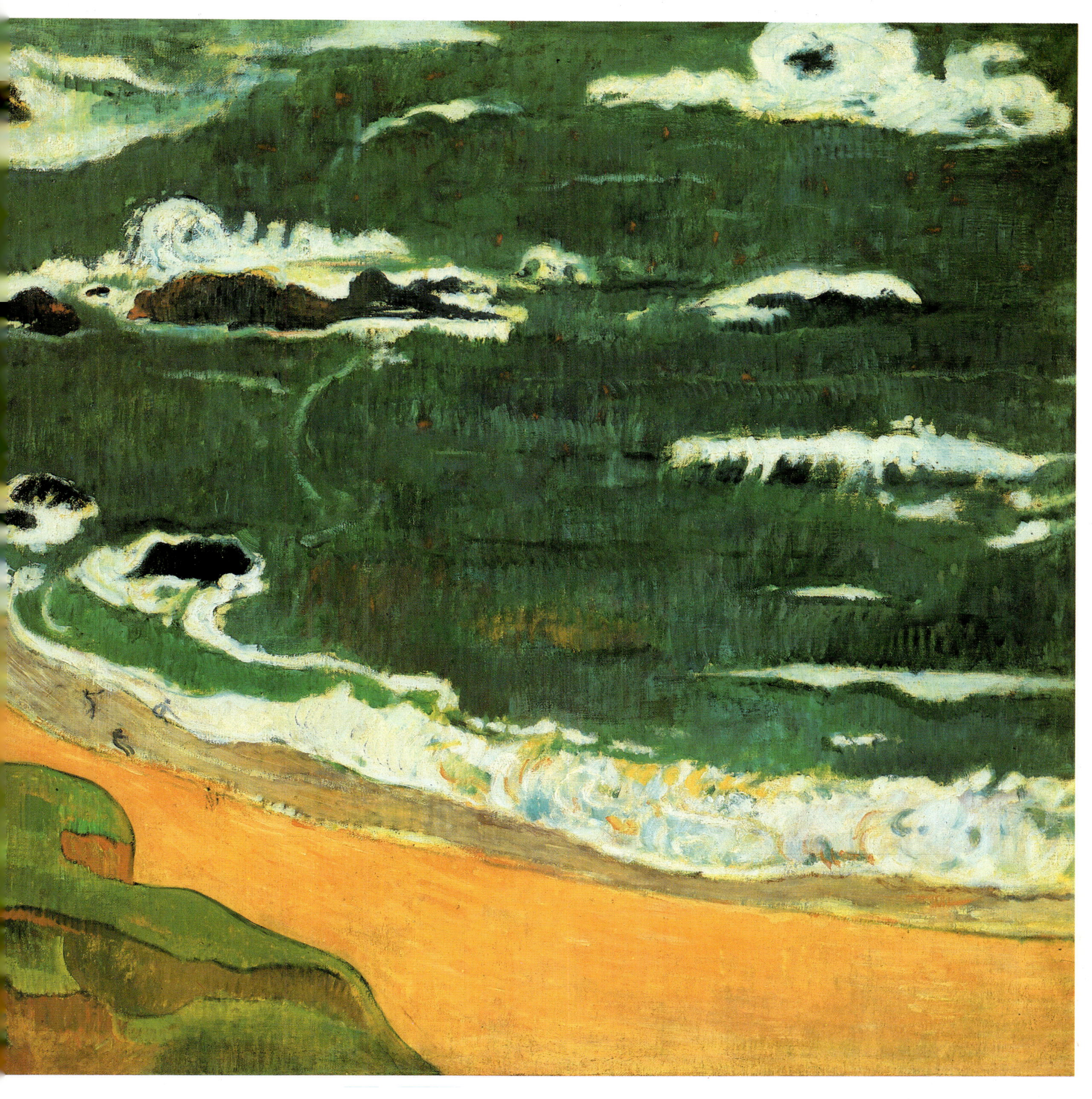

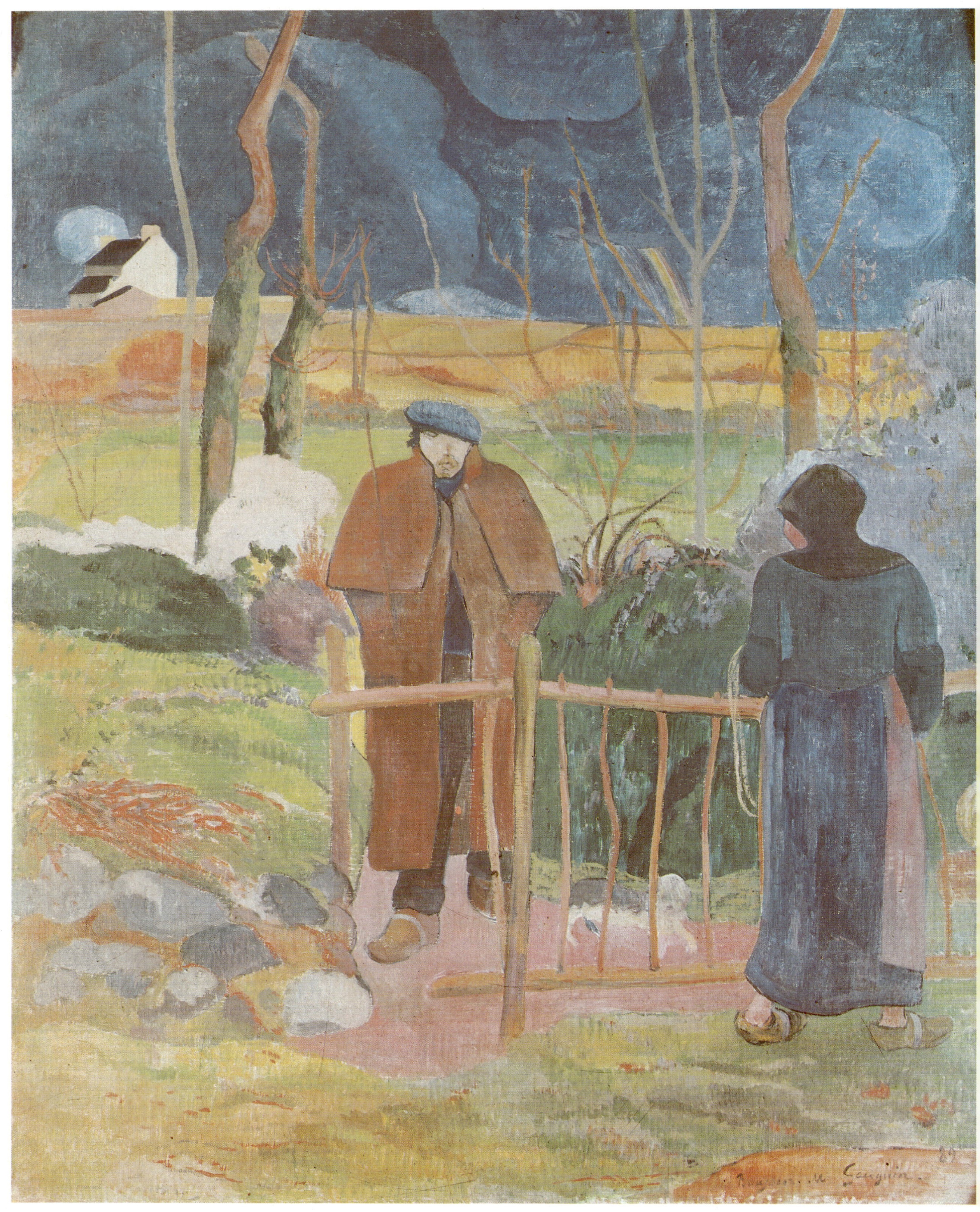

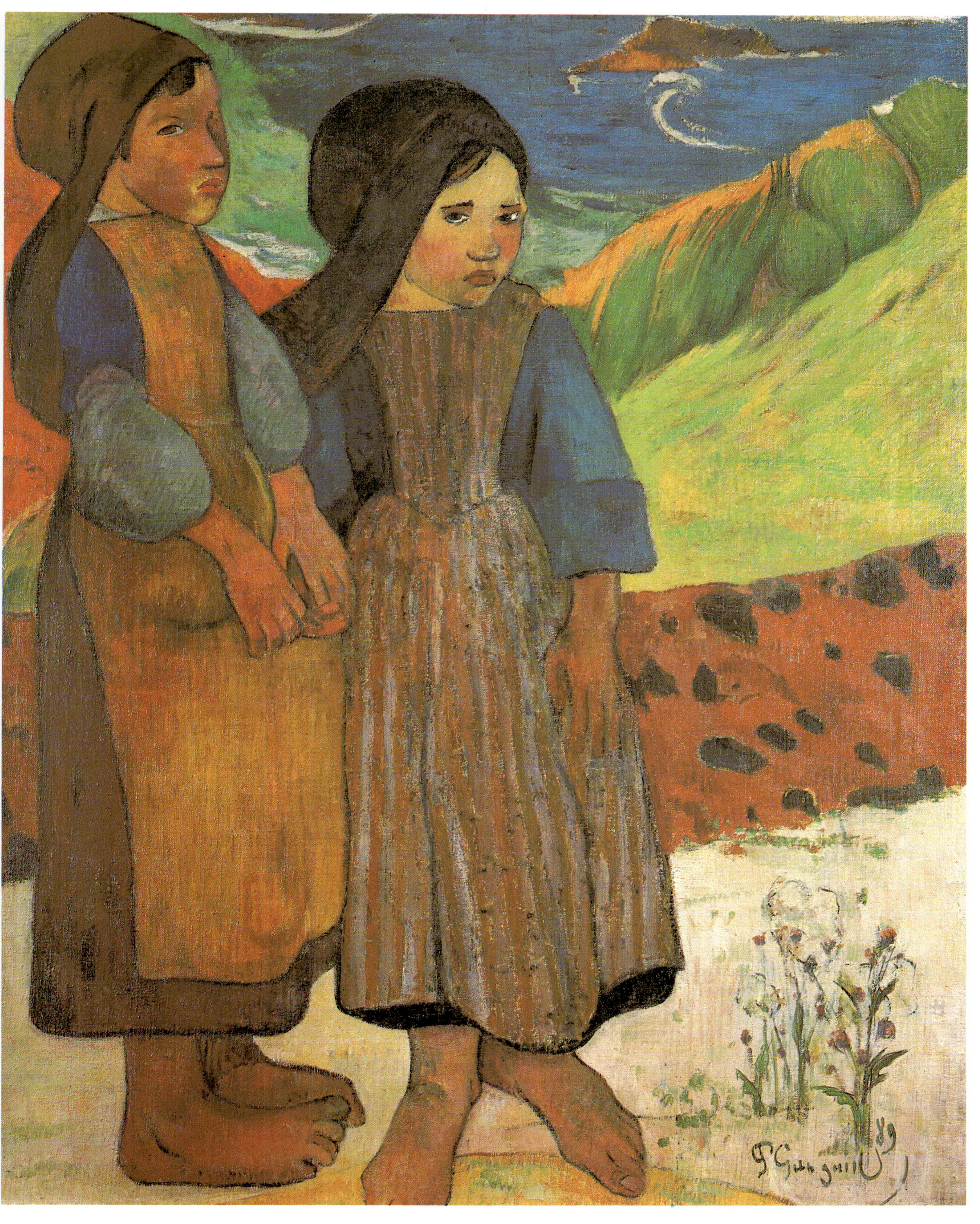

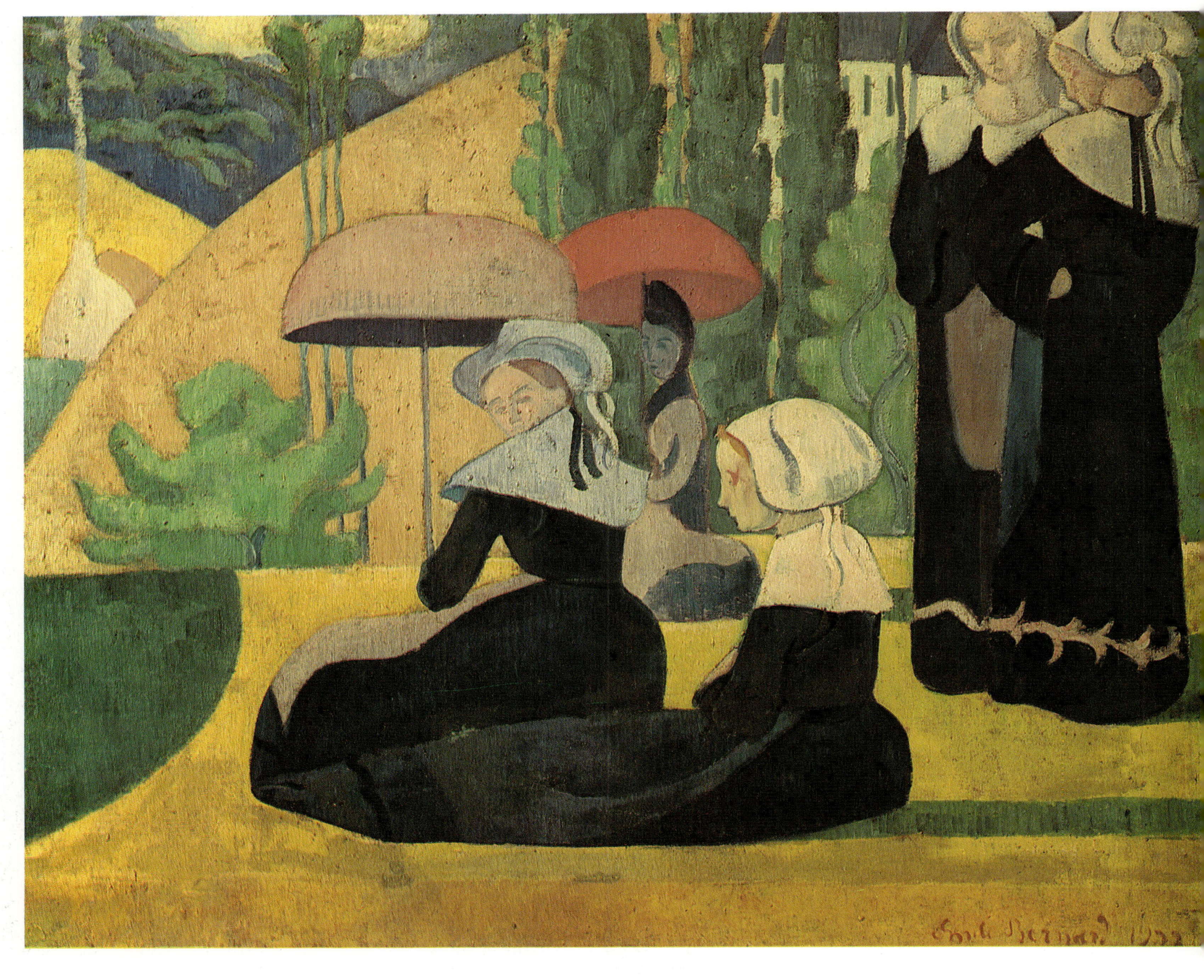

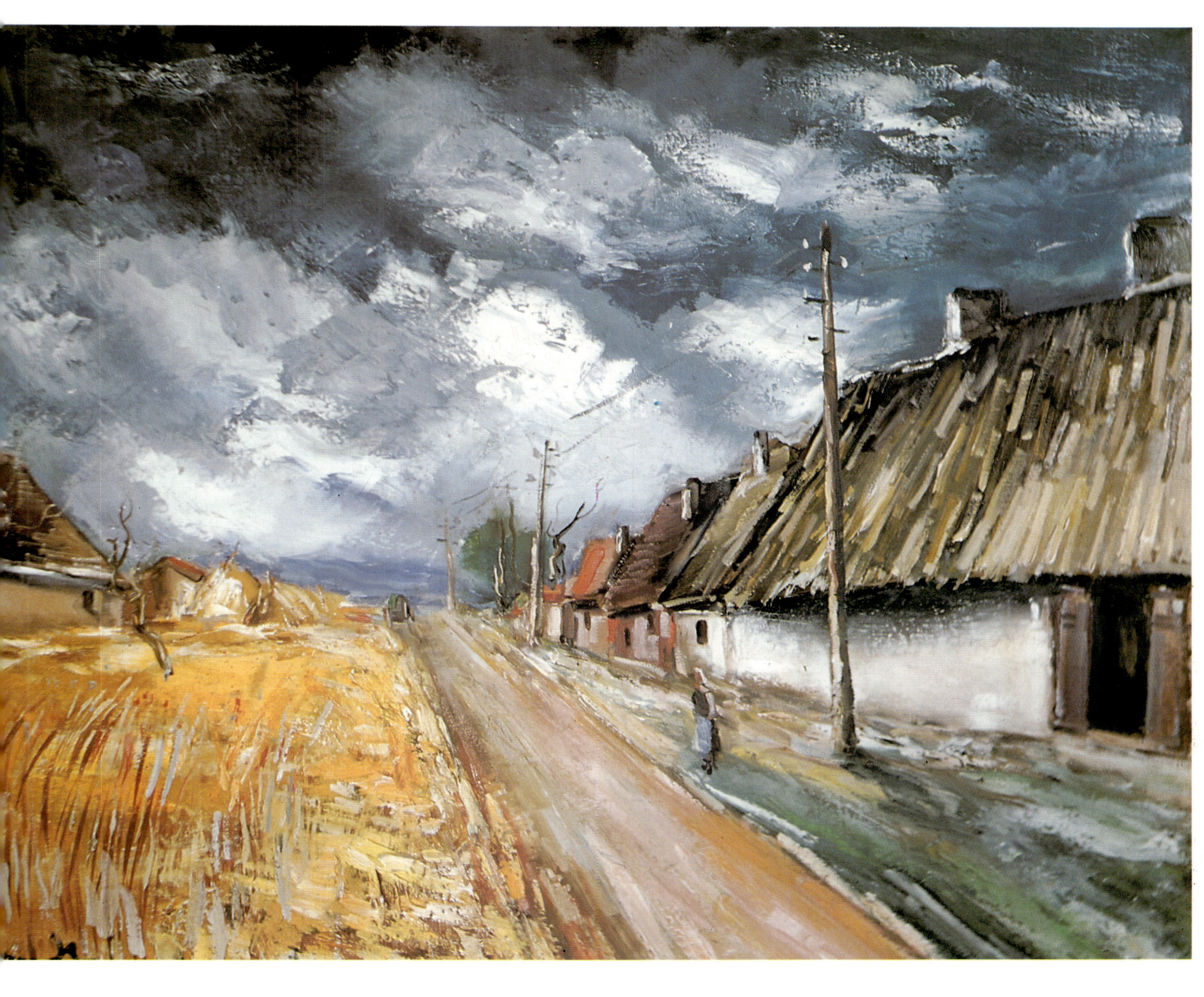

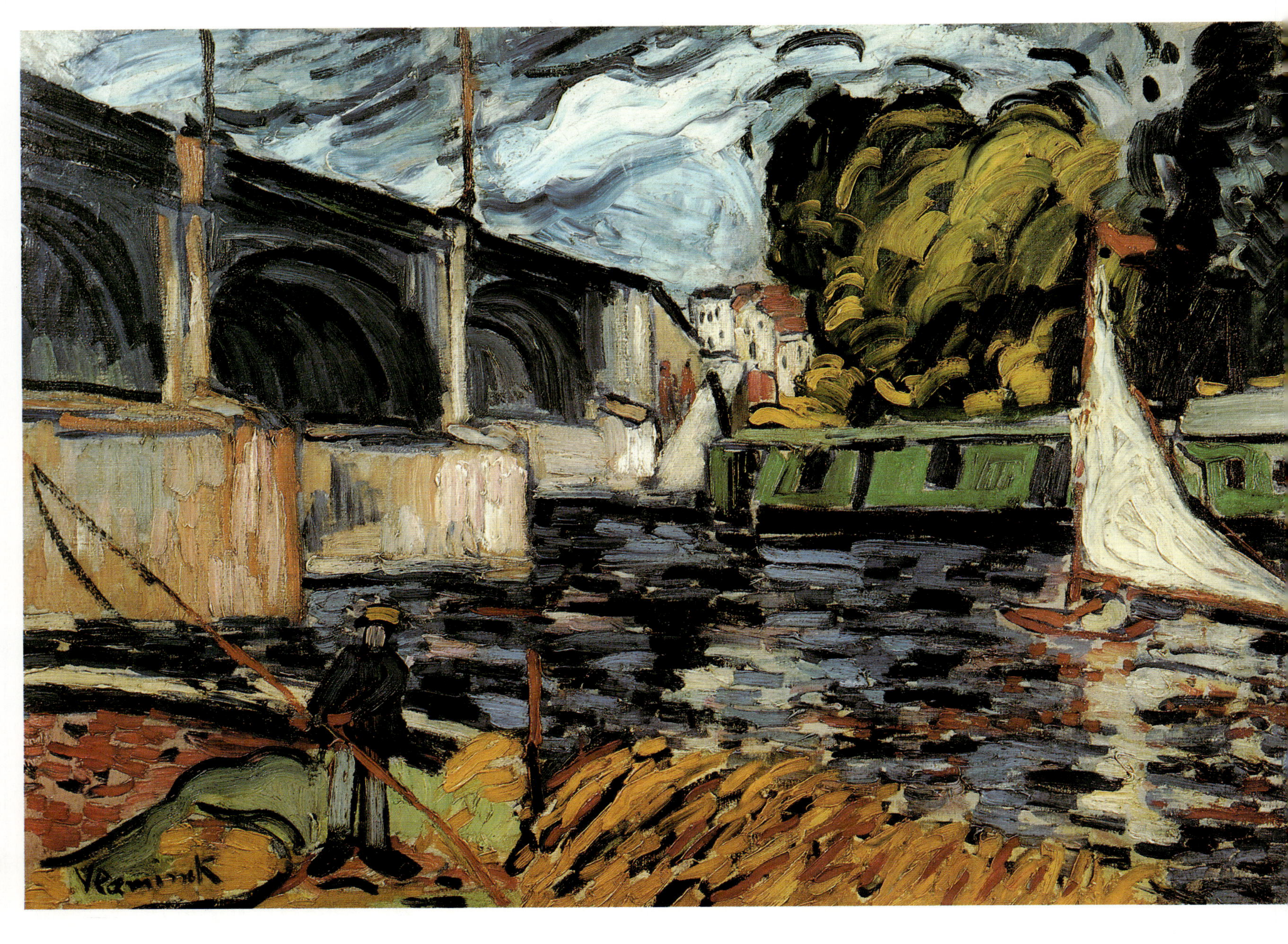
Vlaminck

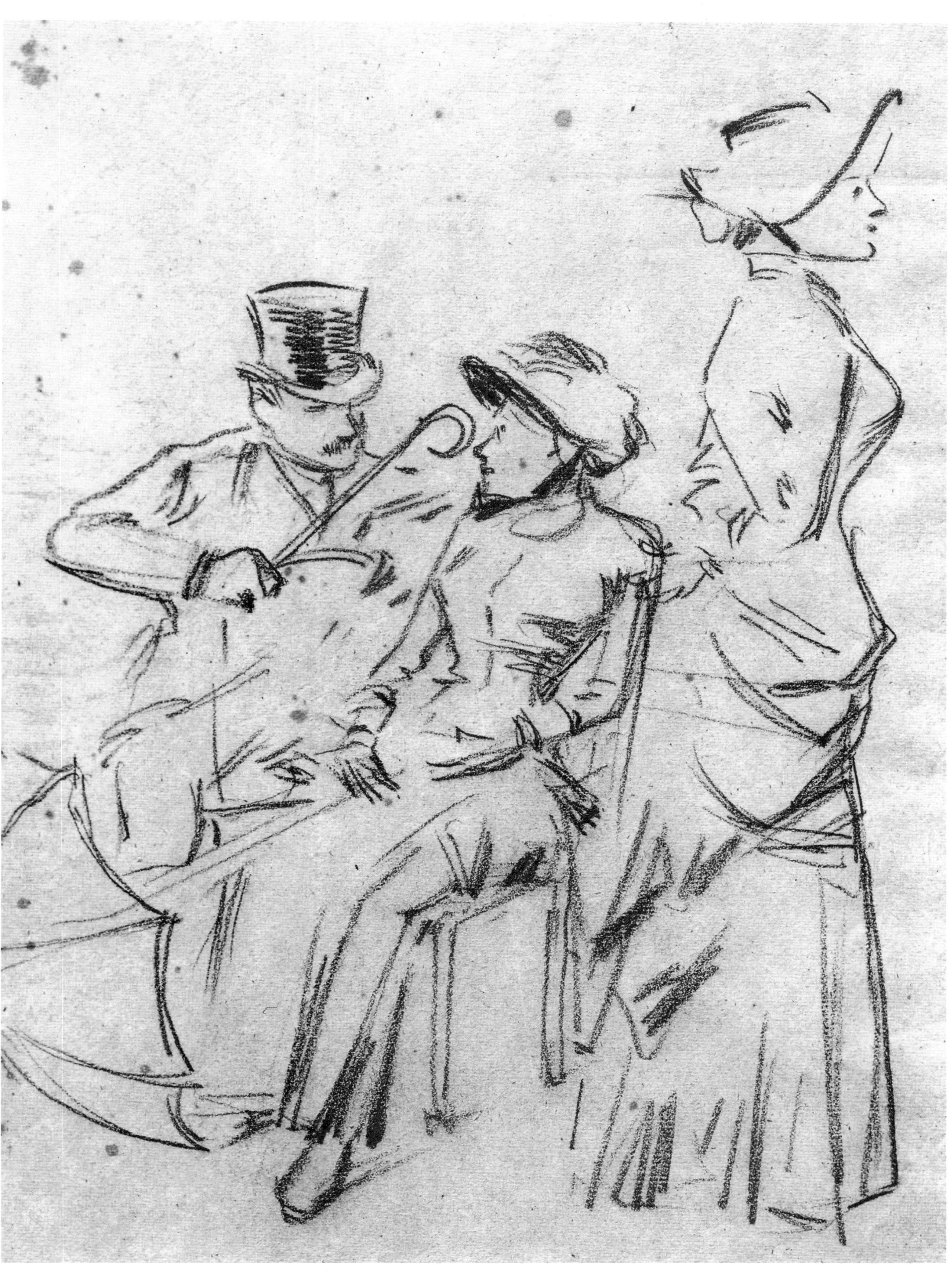

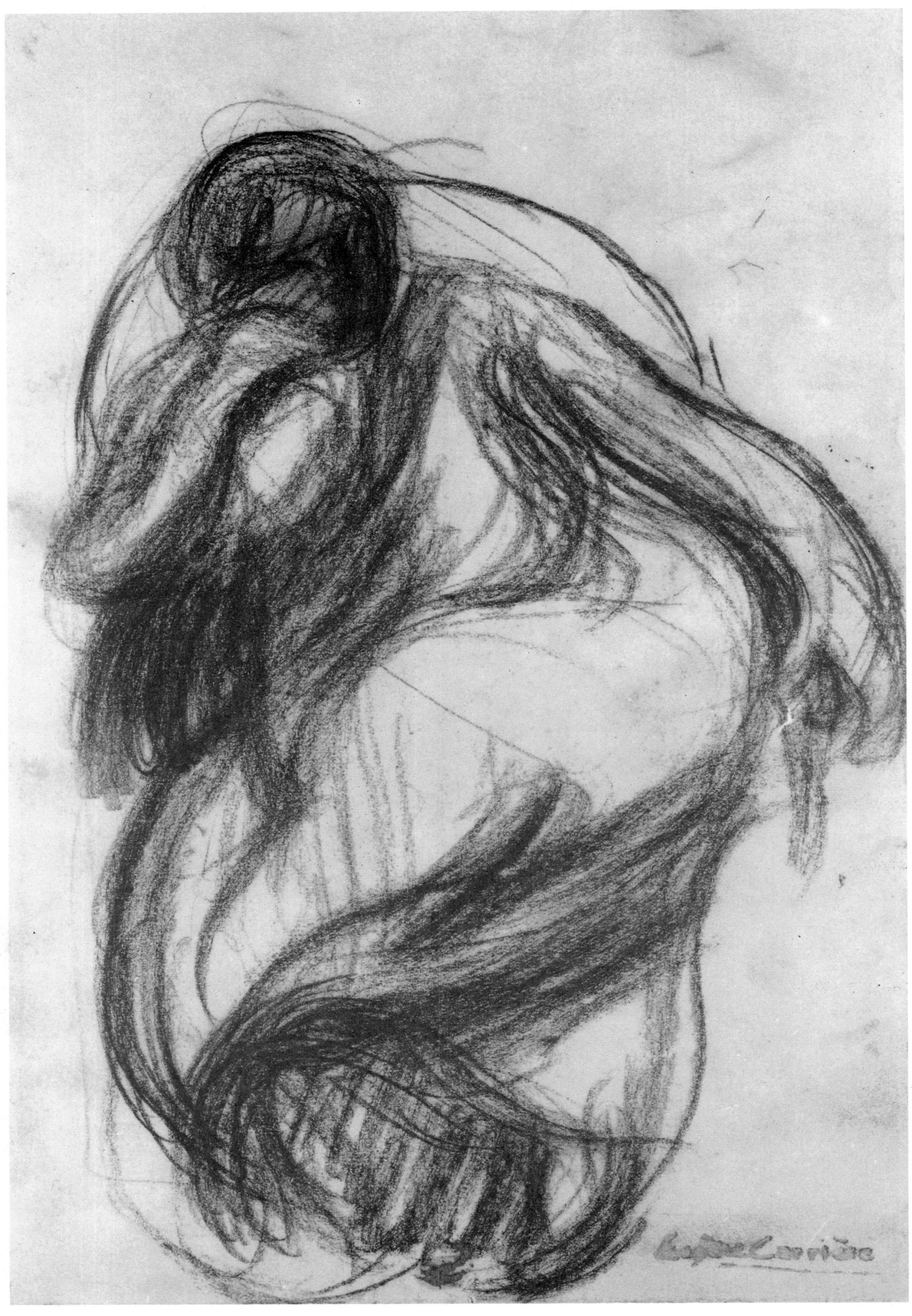

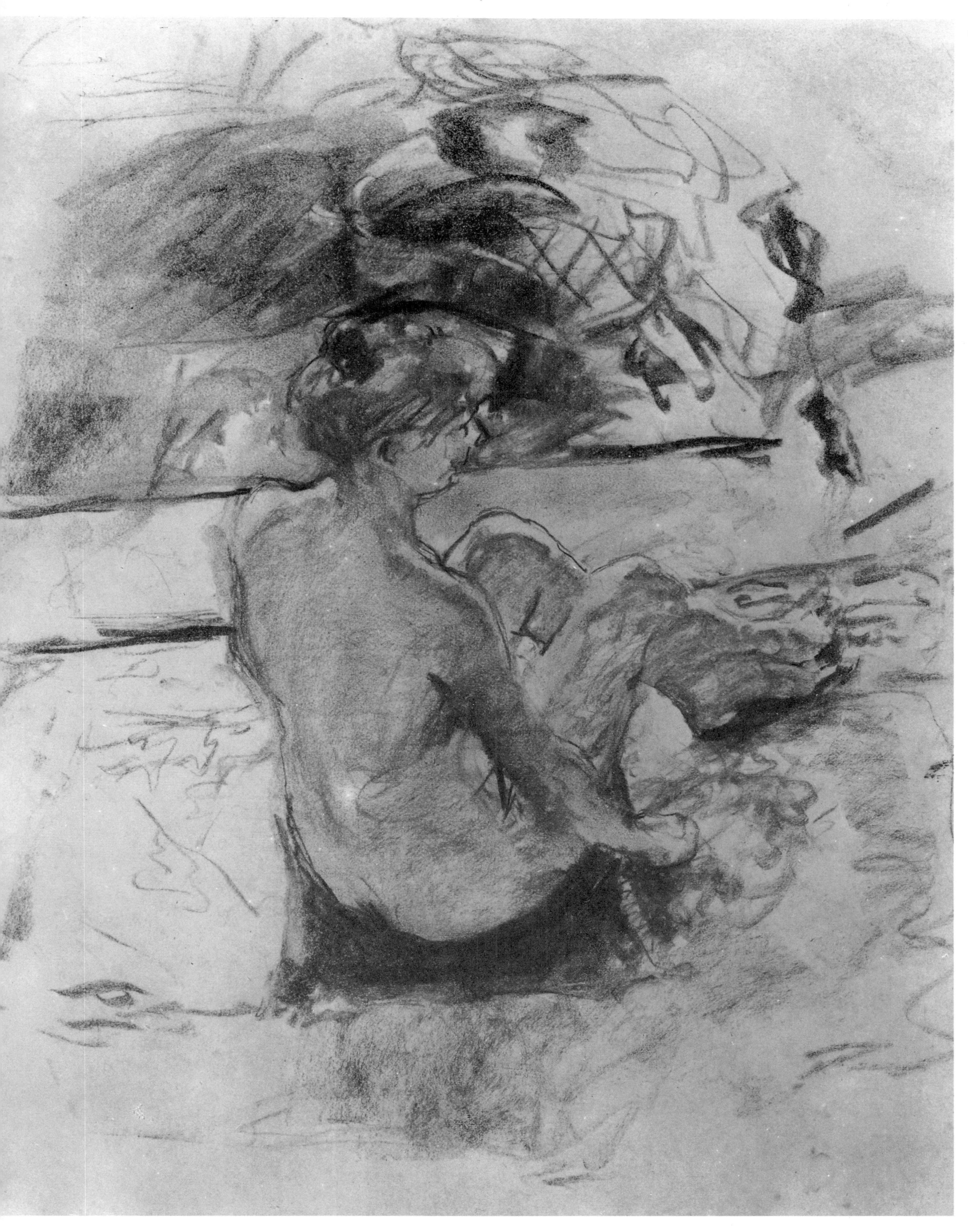

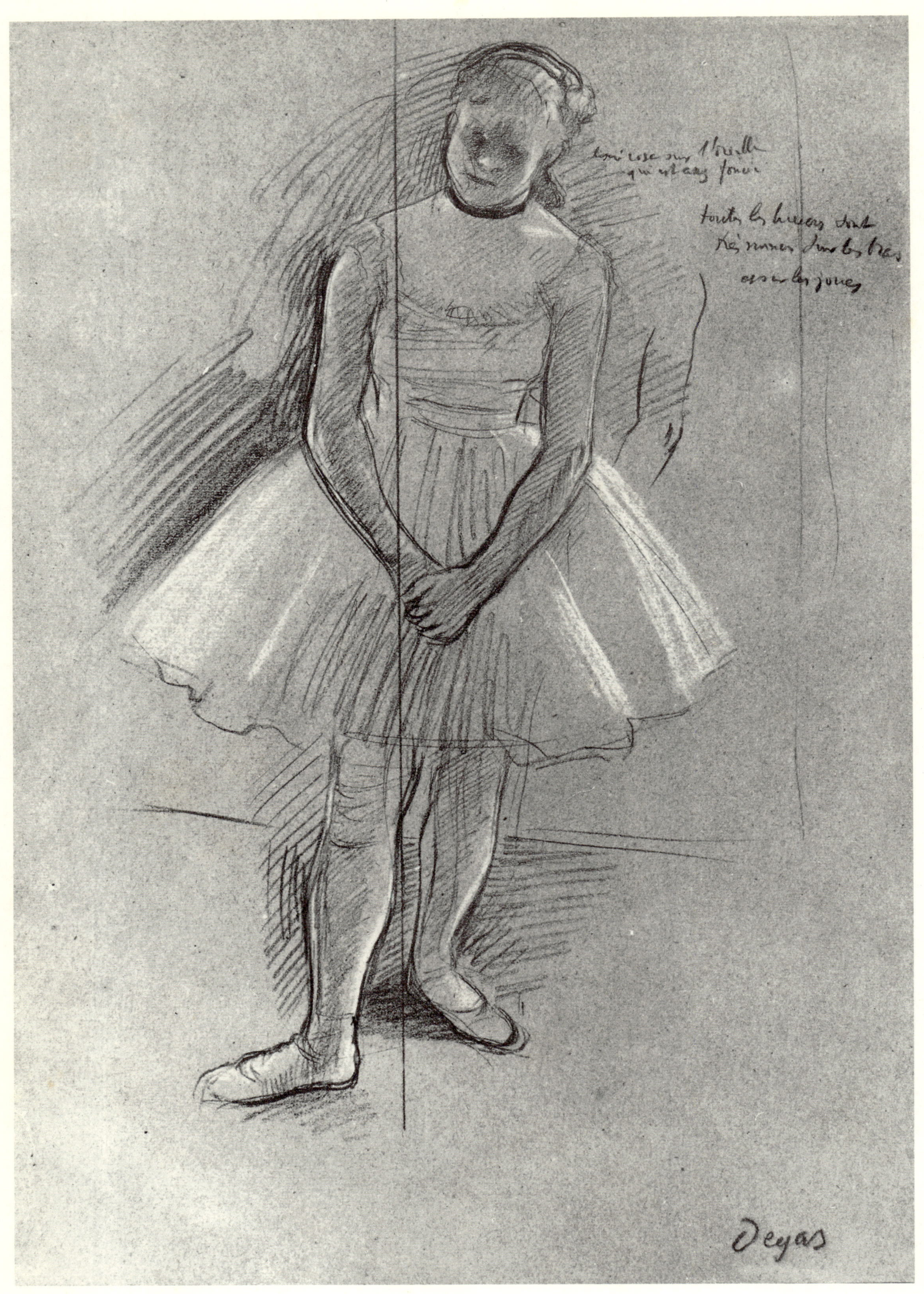
Degas

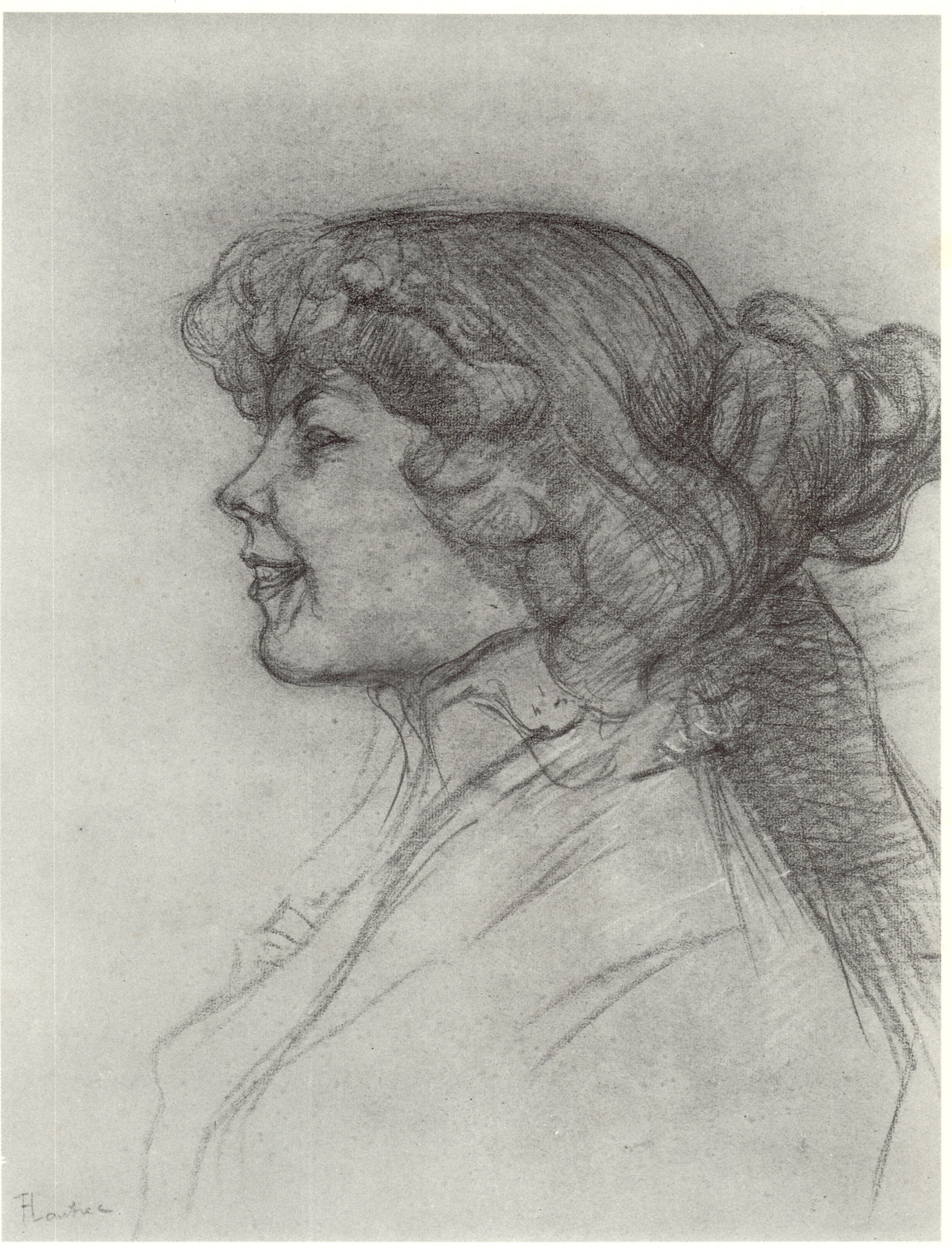

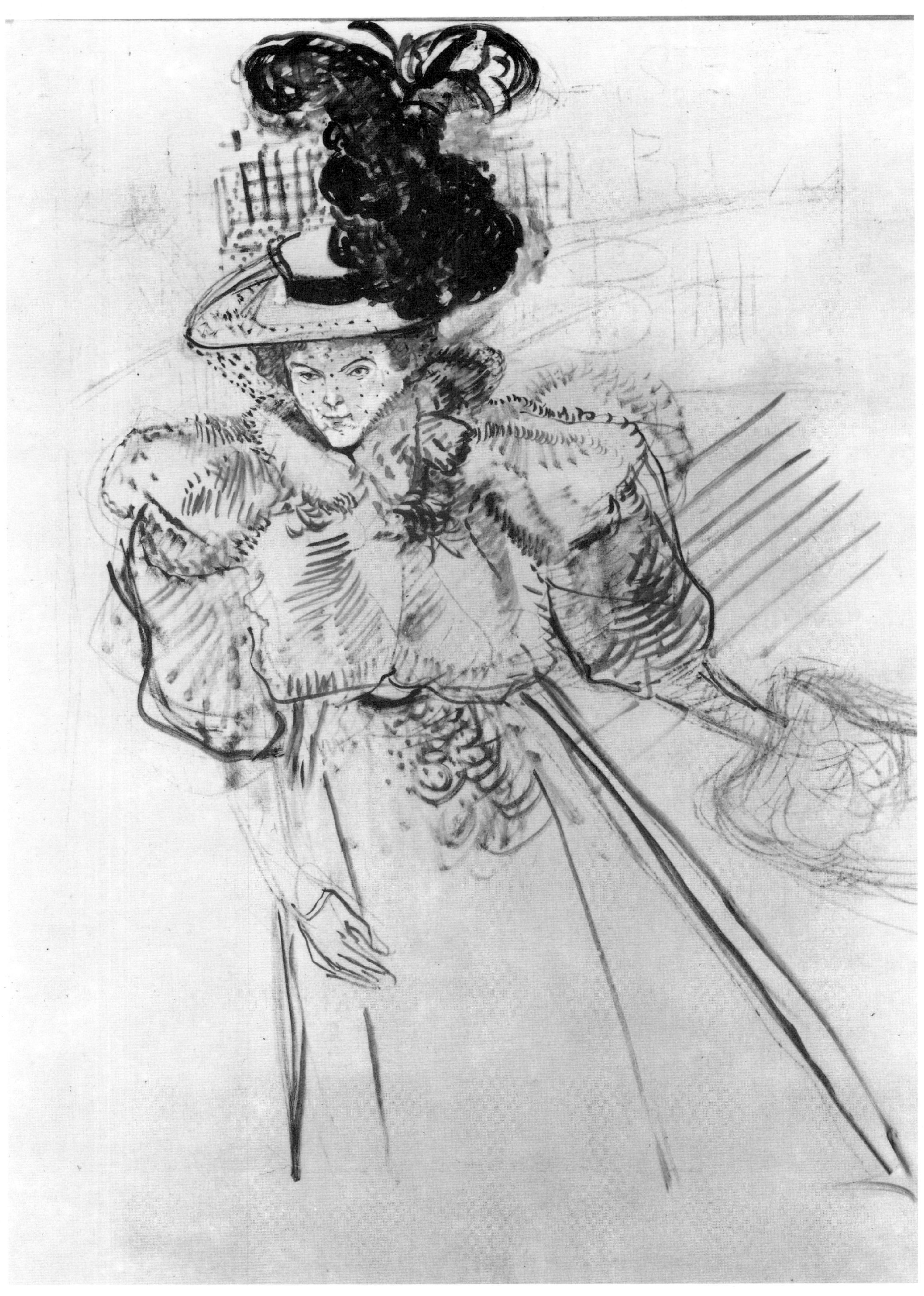

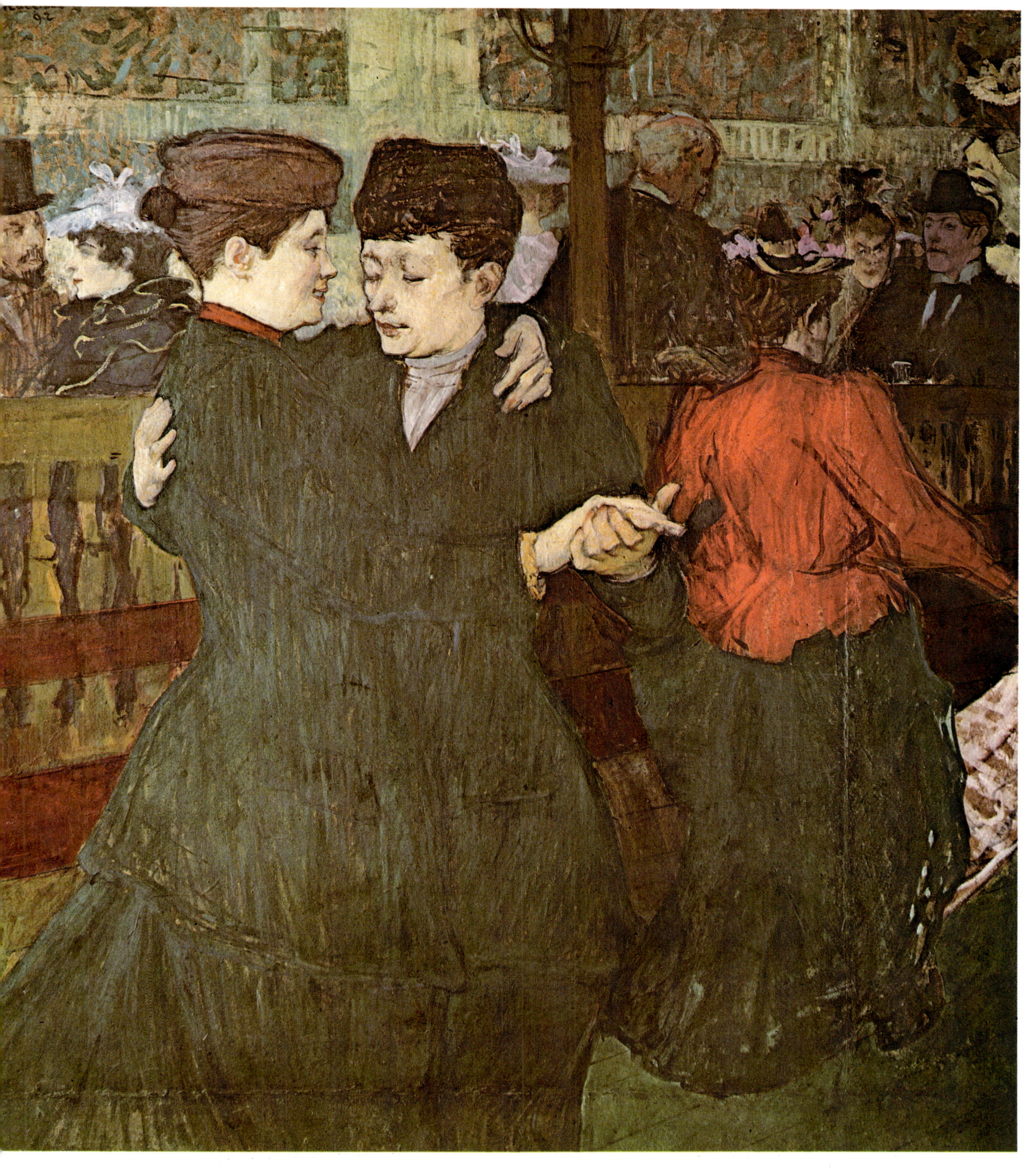

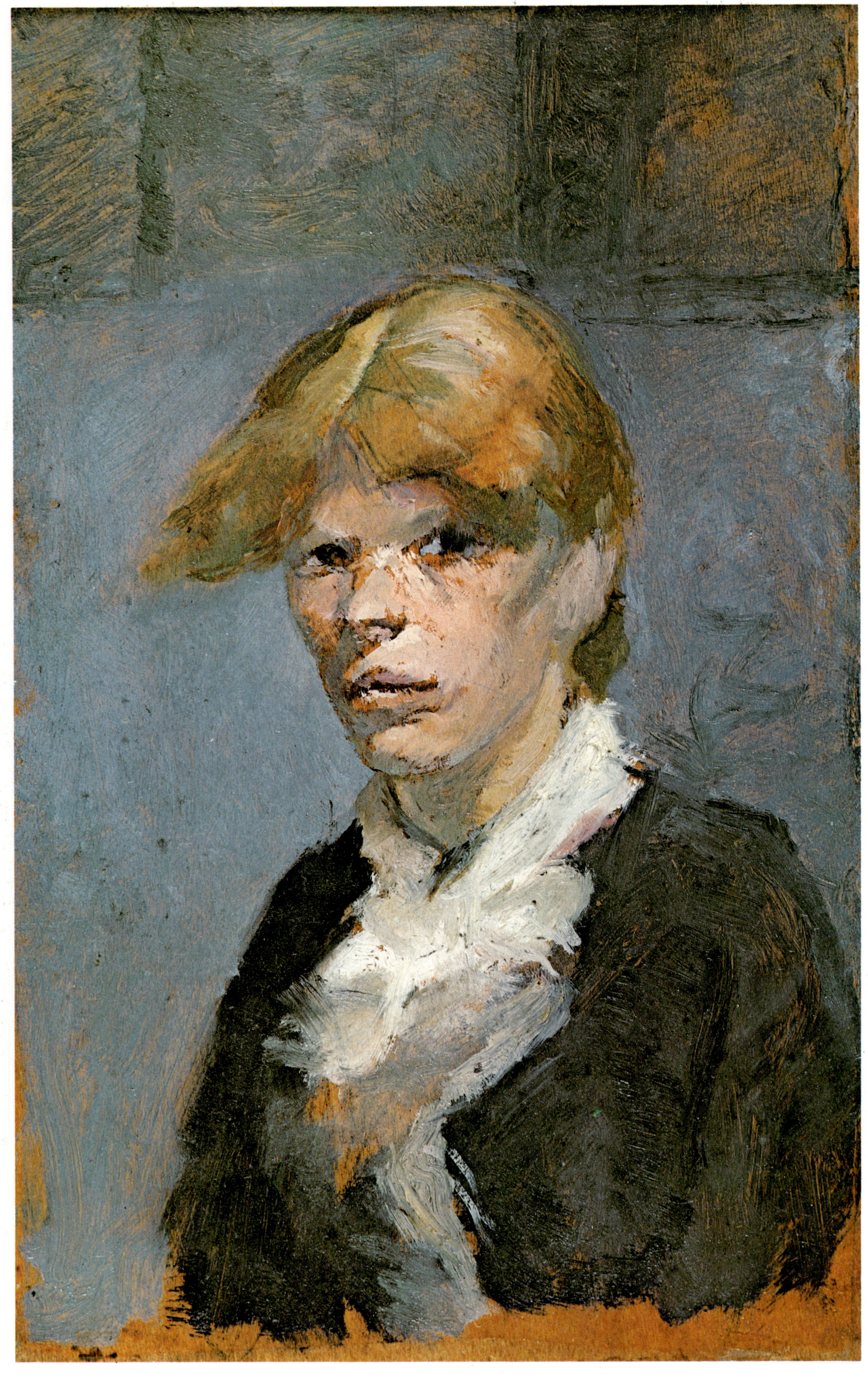

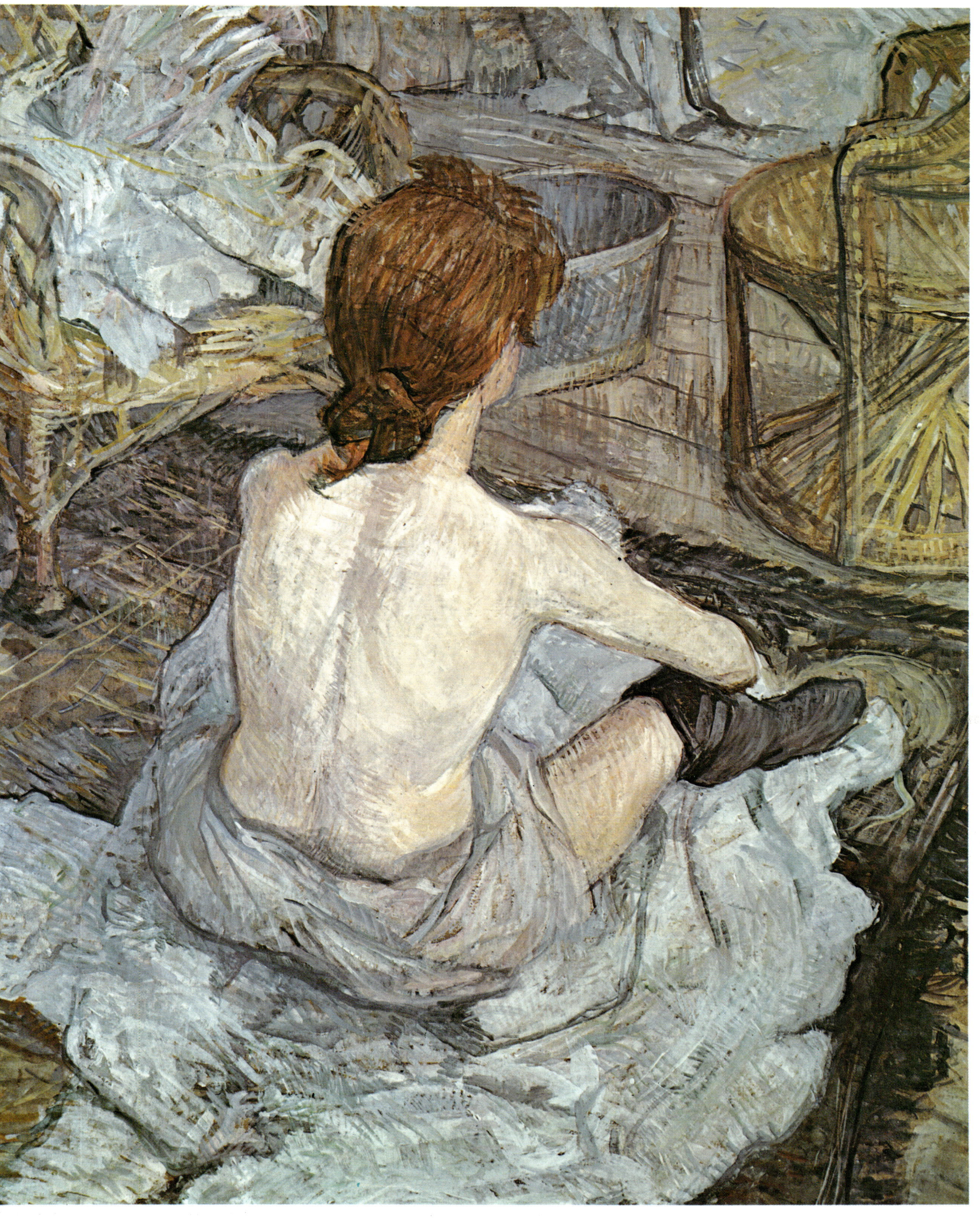

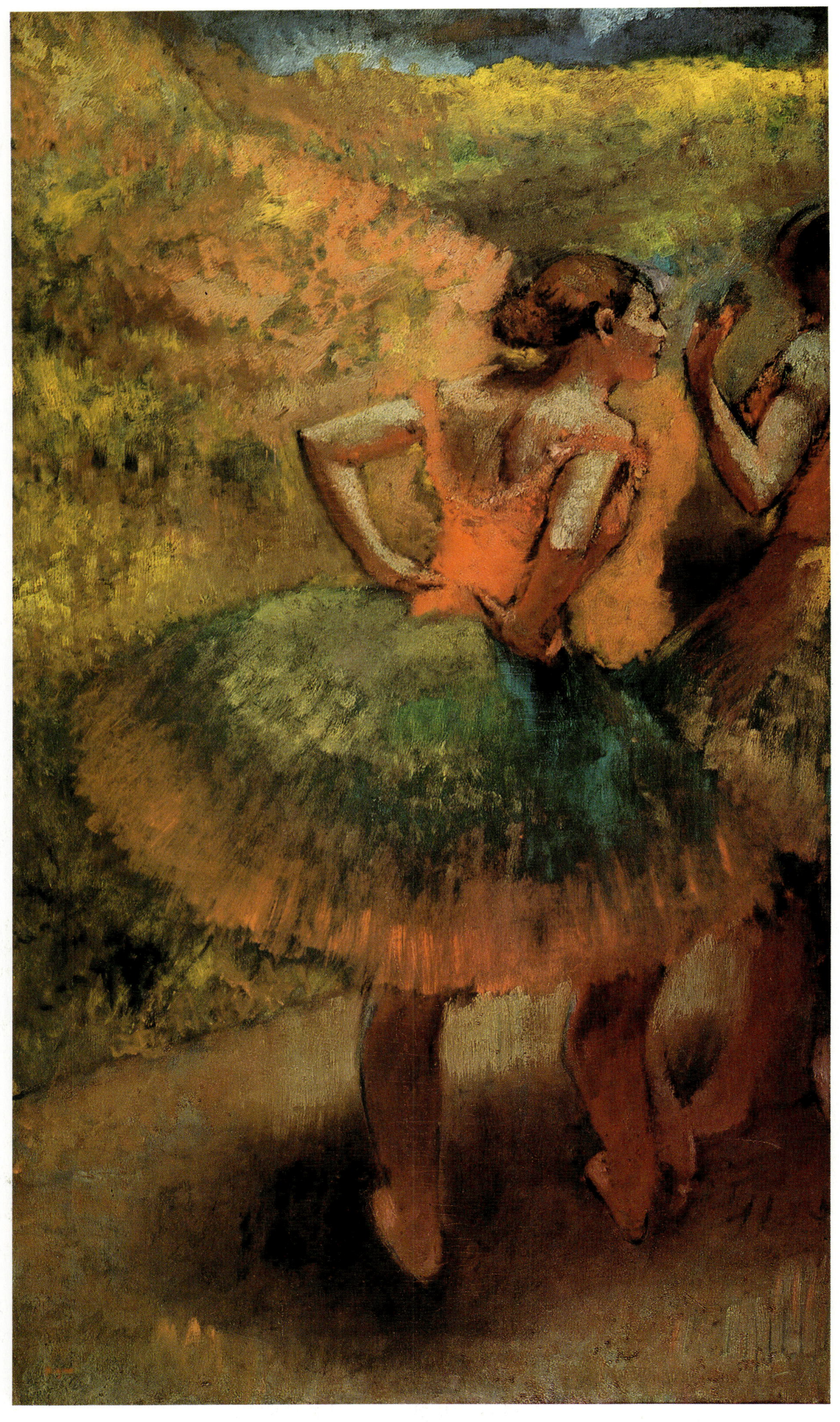

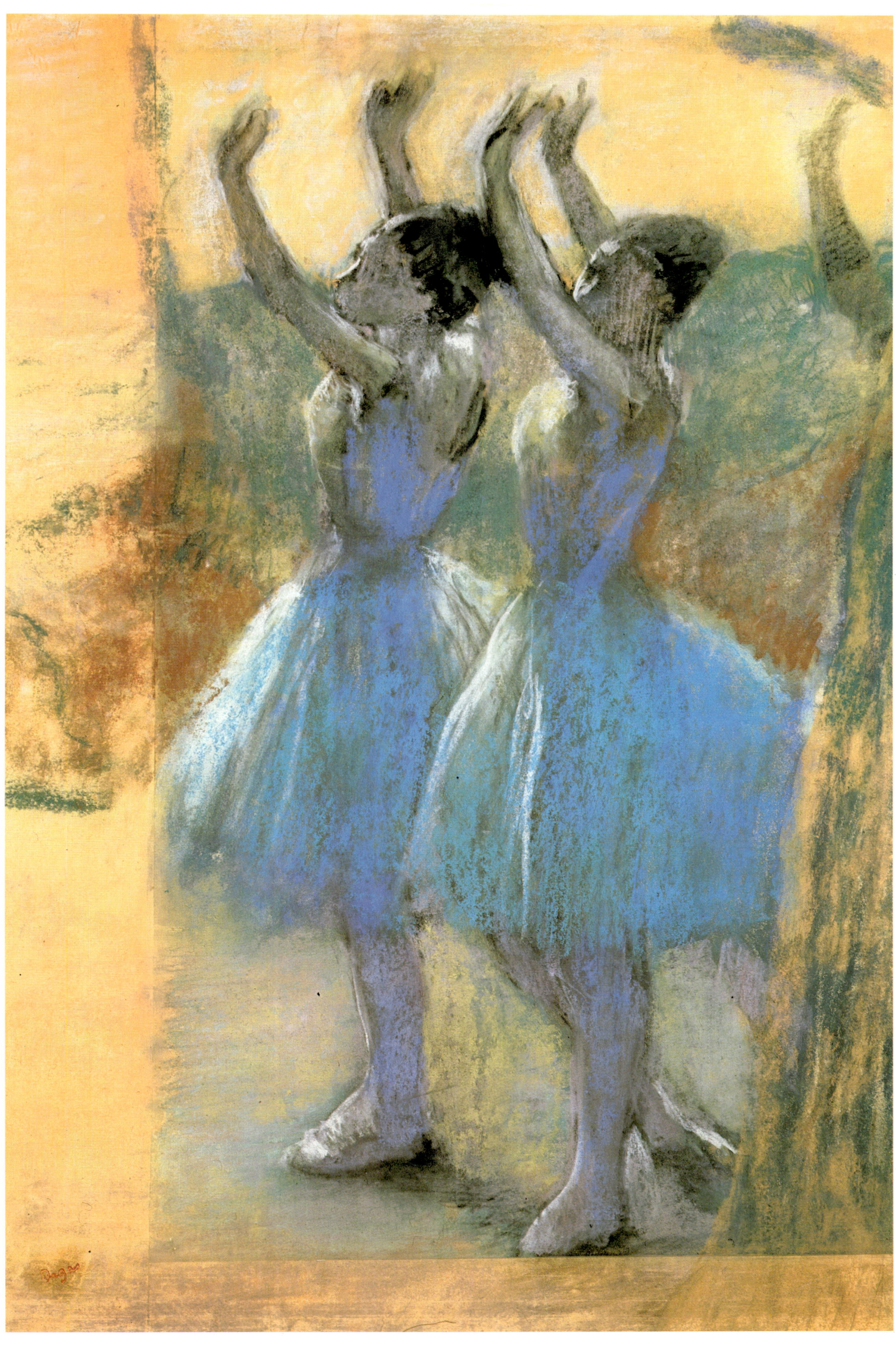

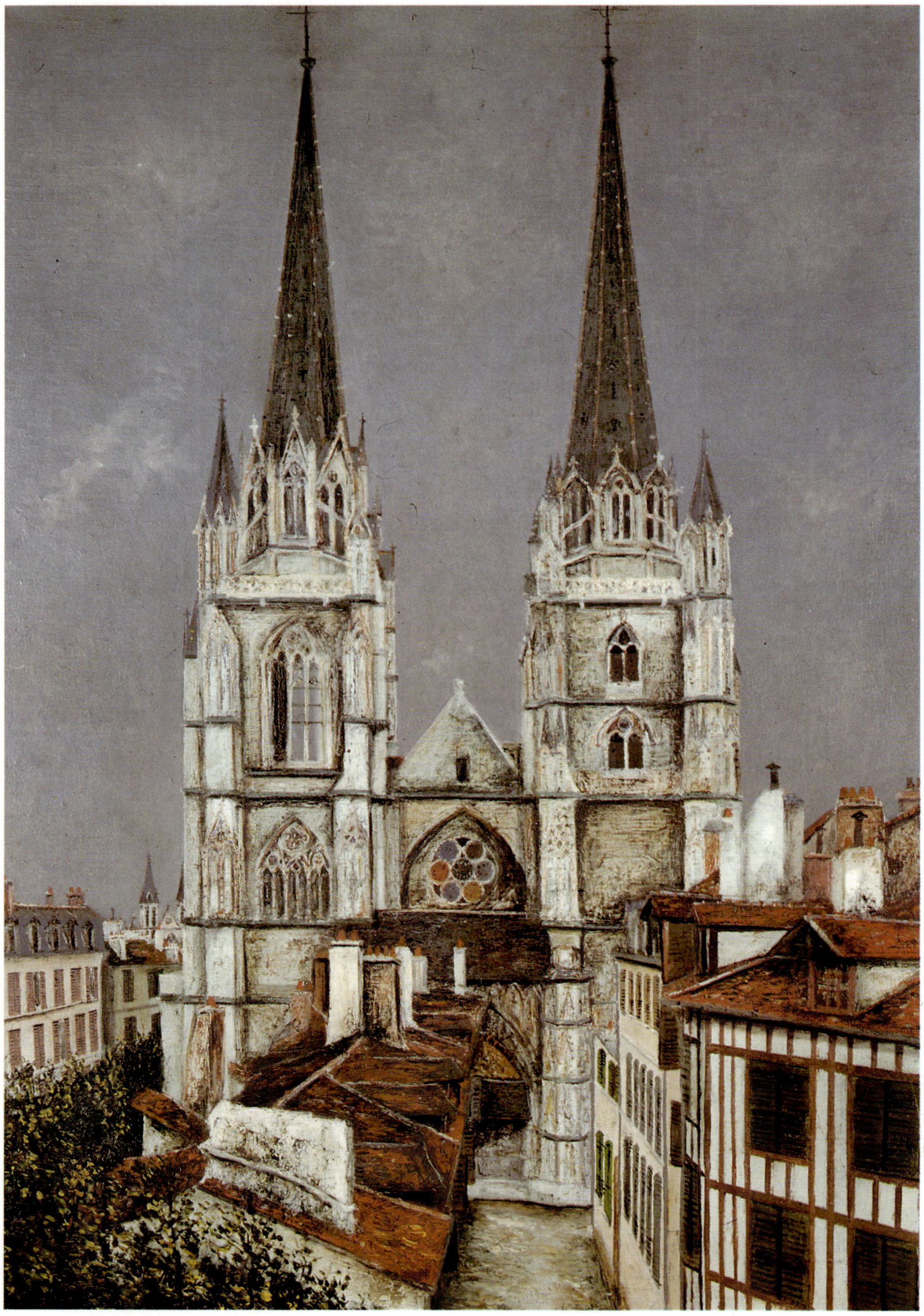

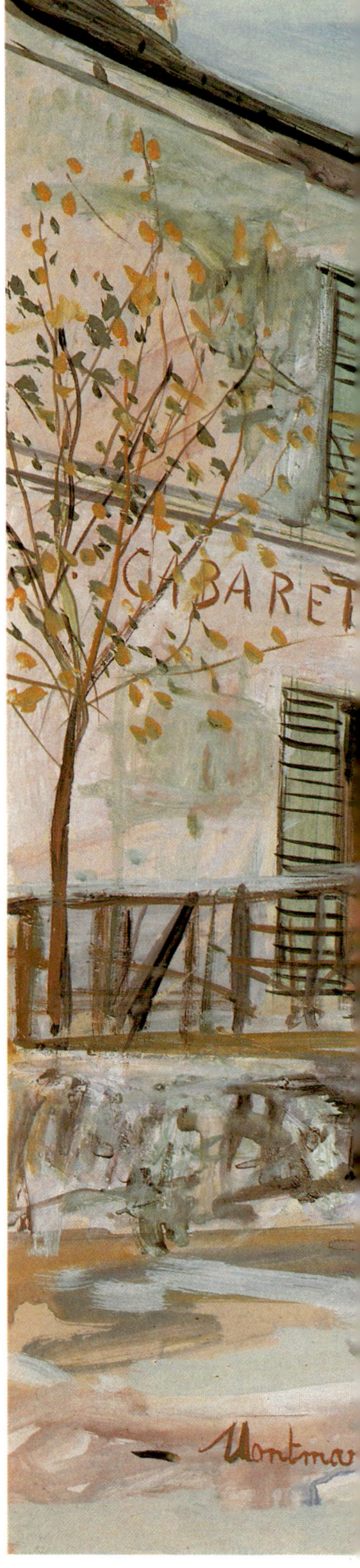

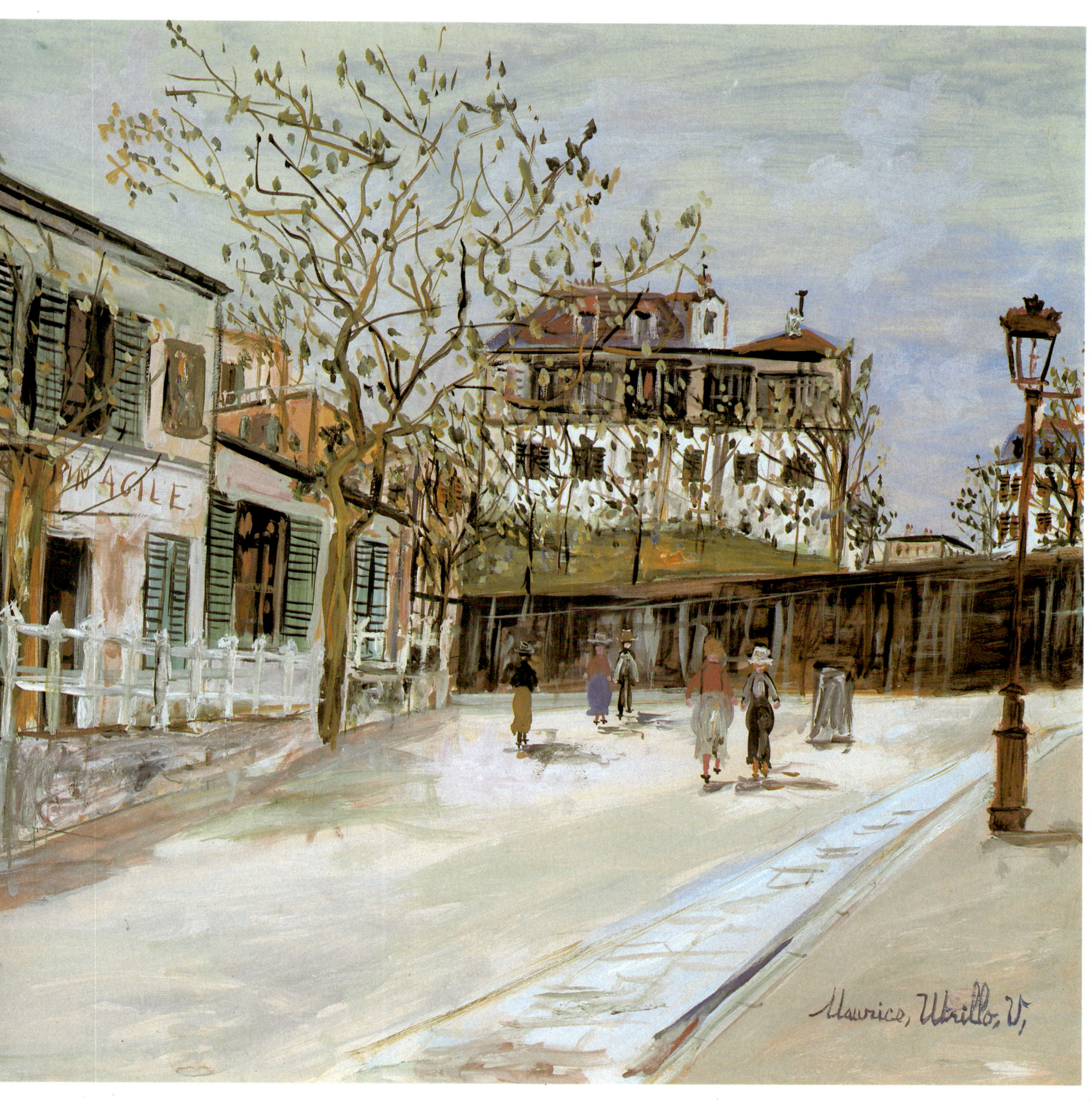
AGILE
Maurice, Utrillo, V,

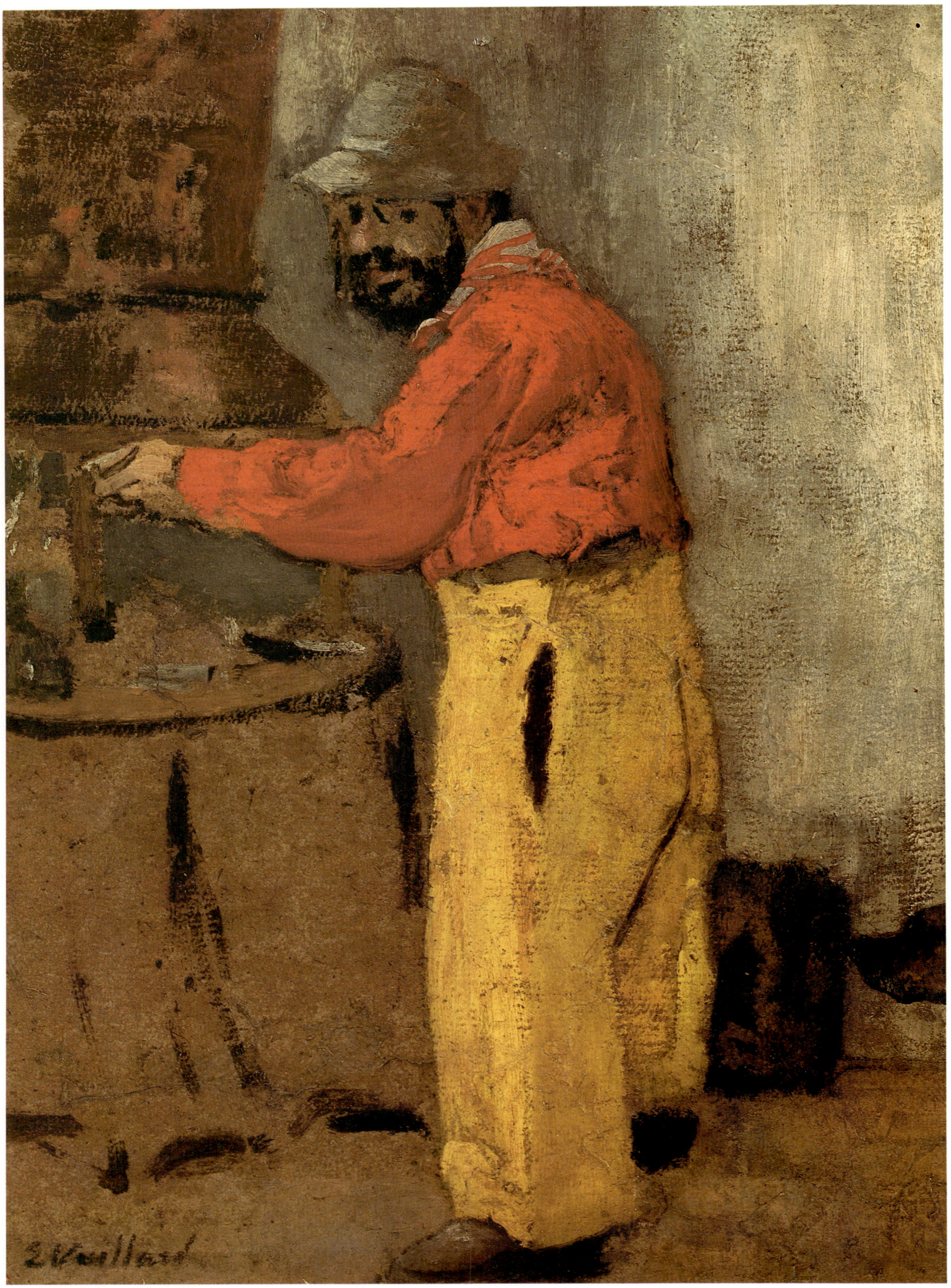
E Vuillard

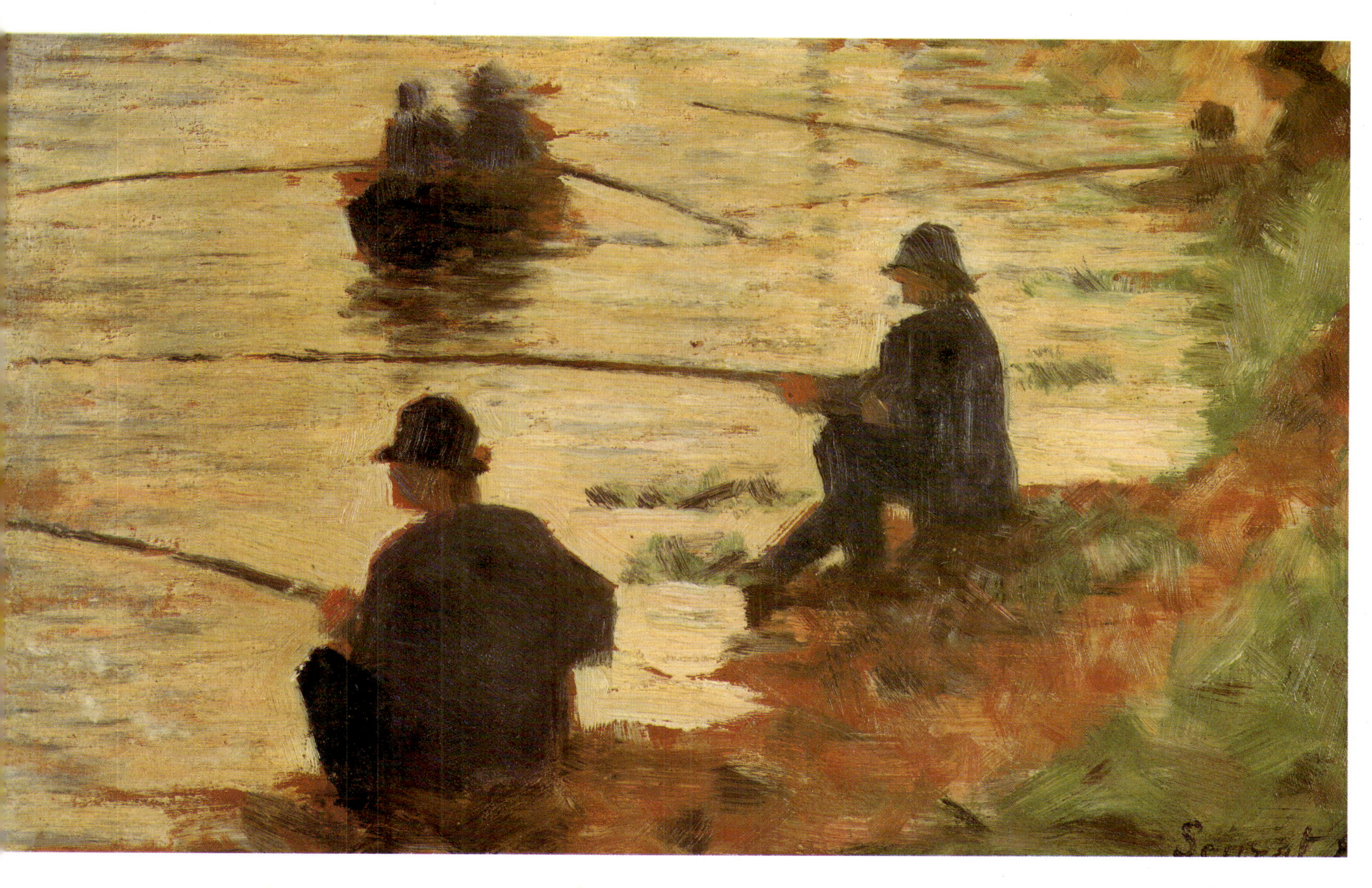

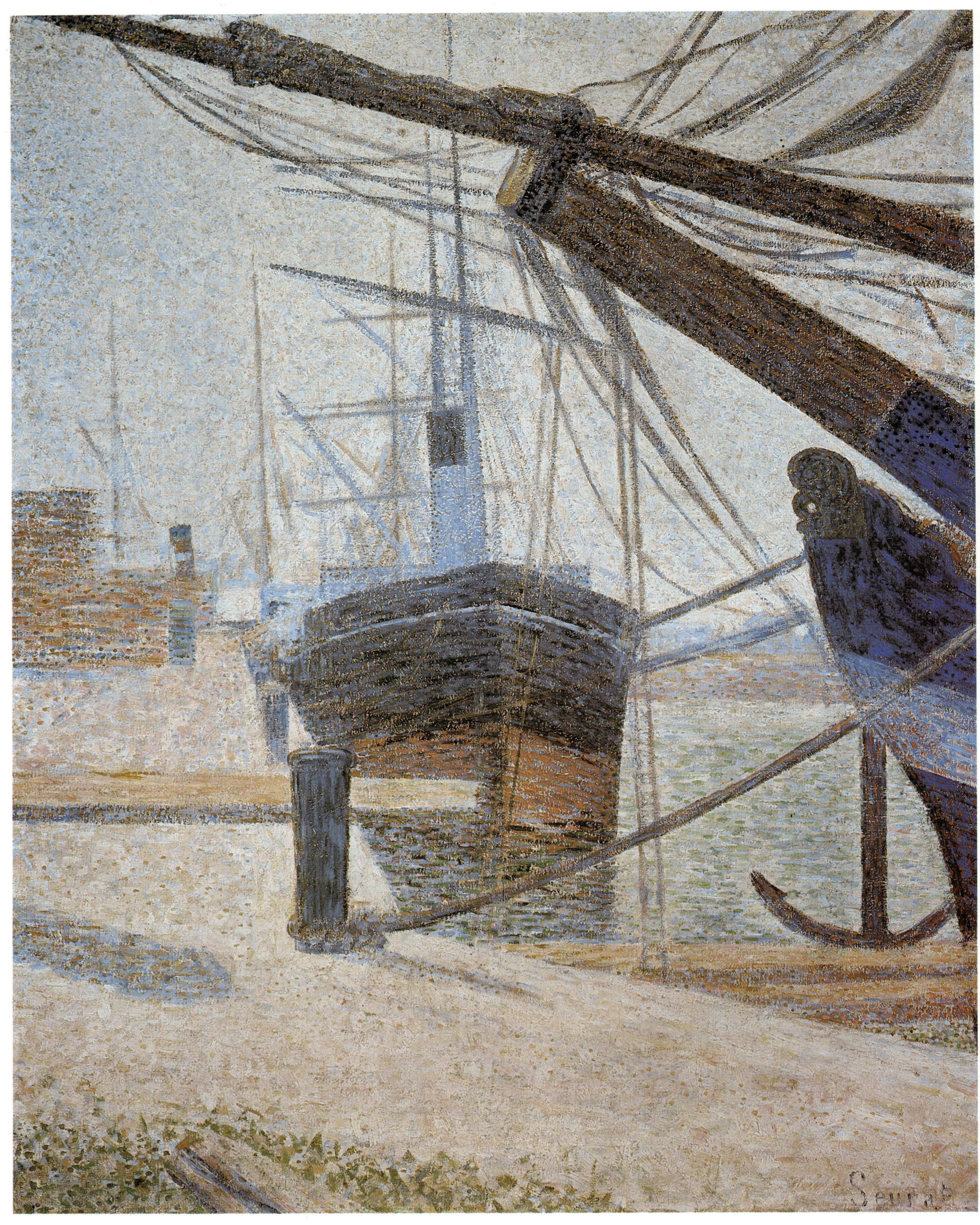

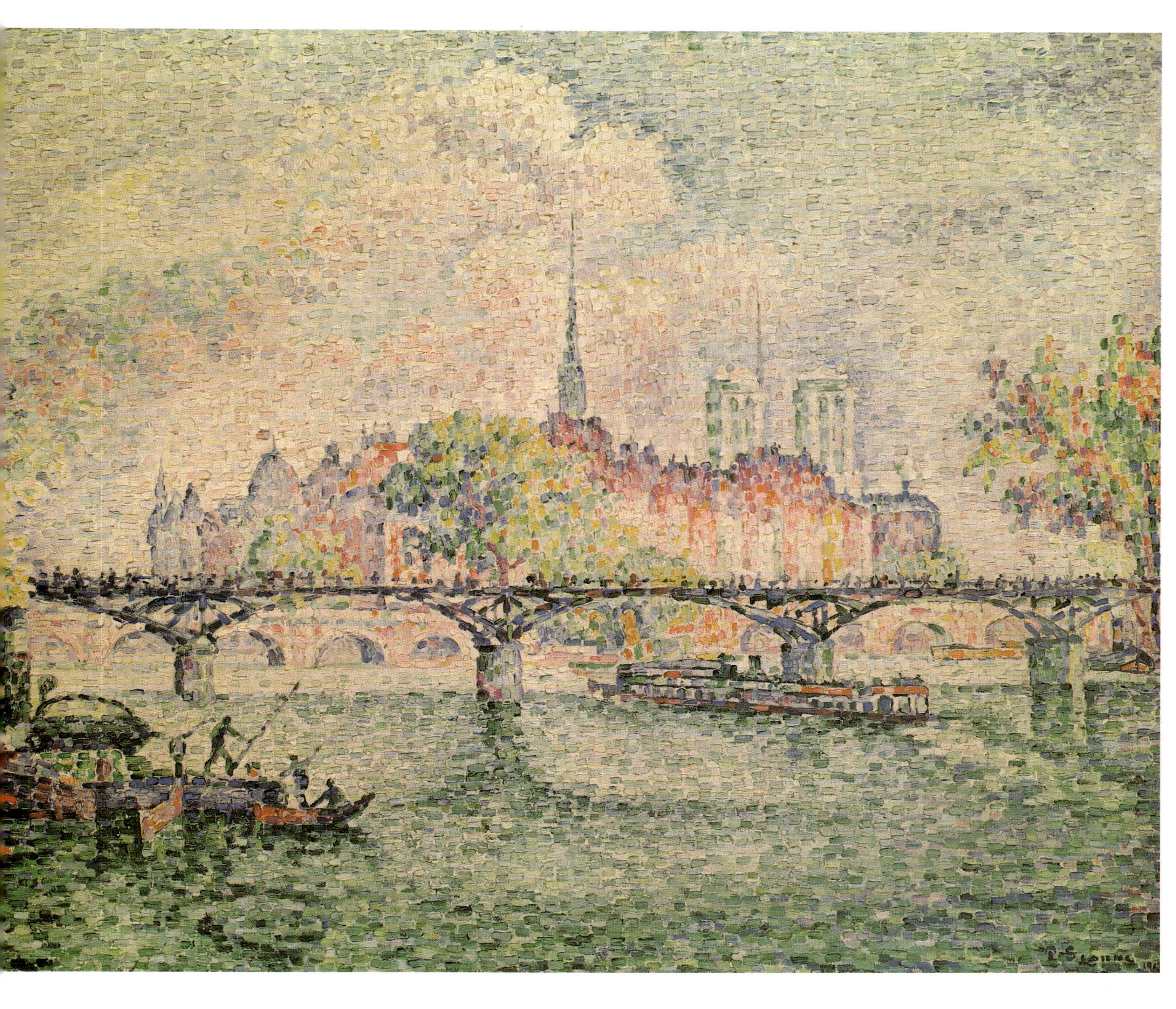

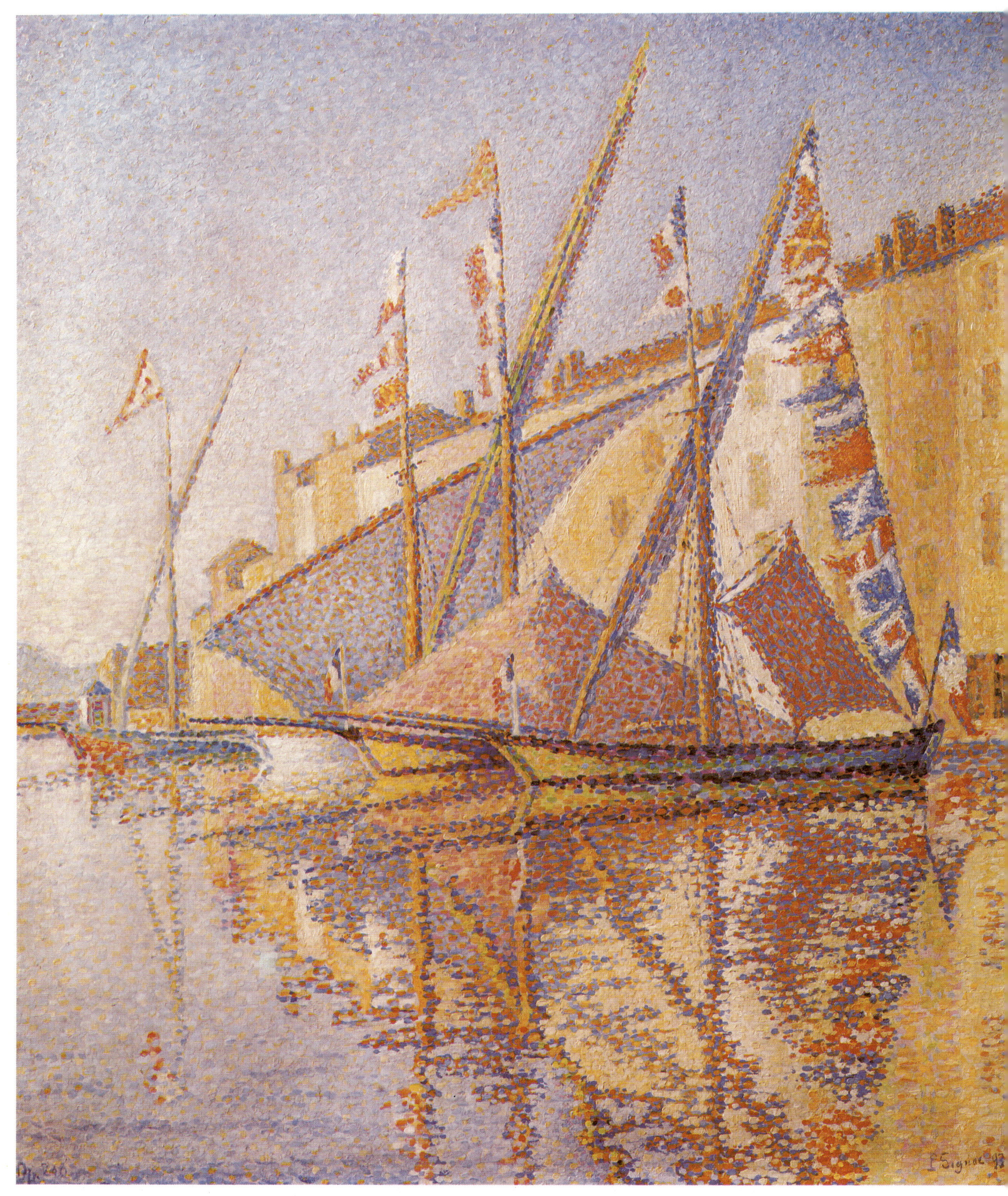

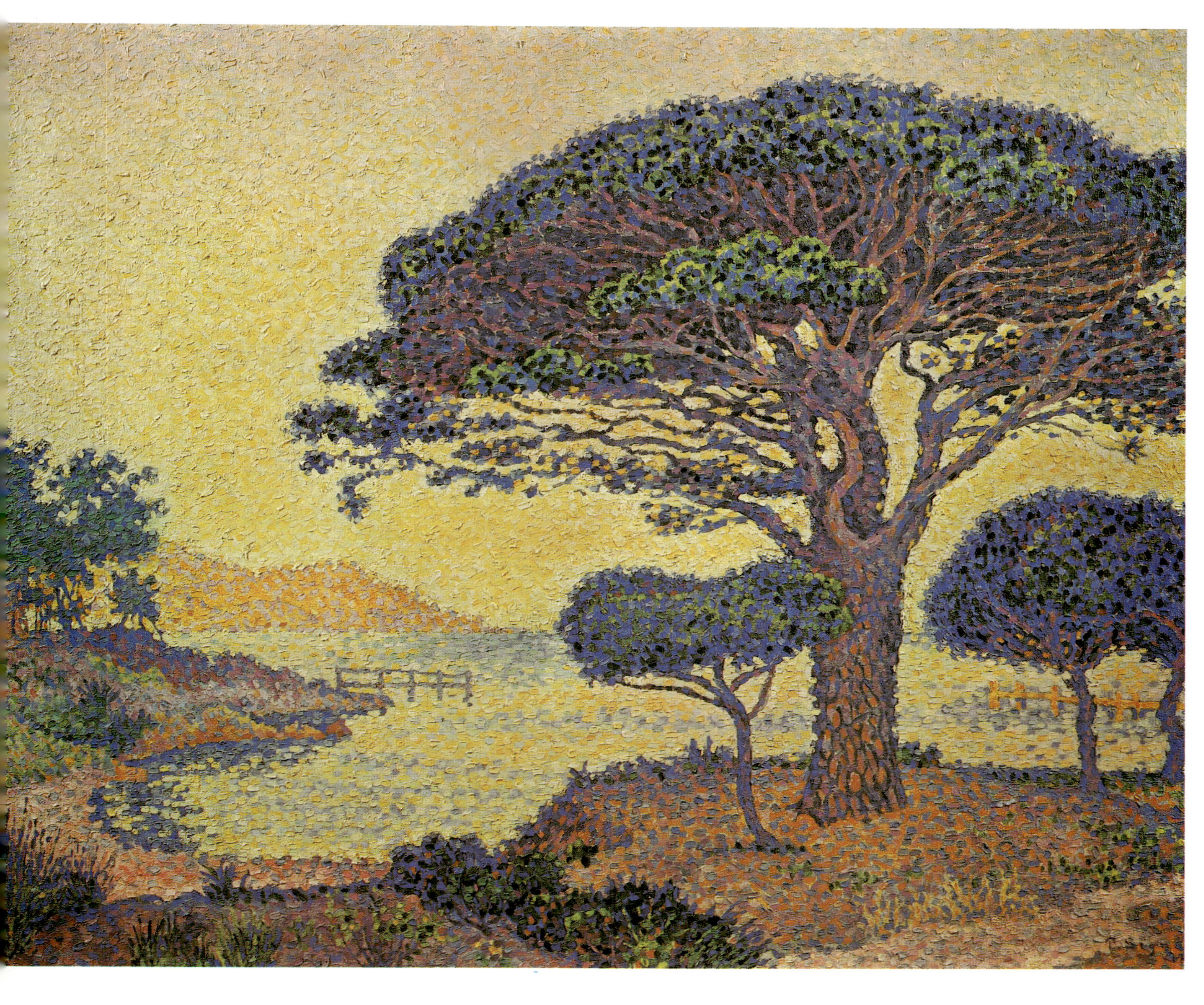

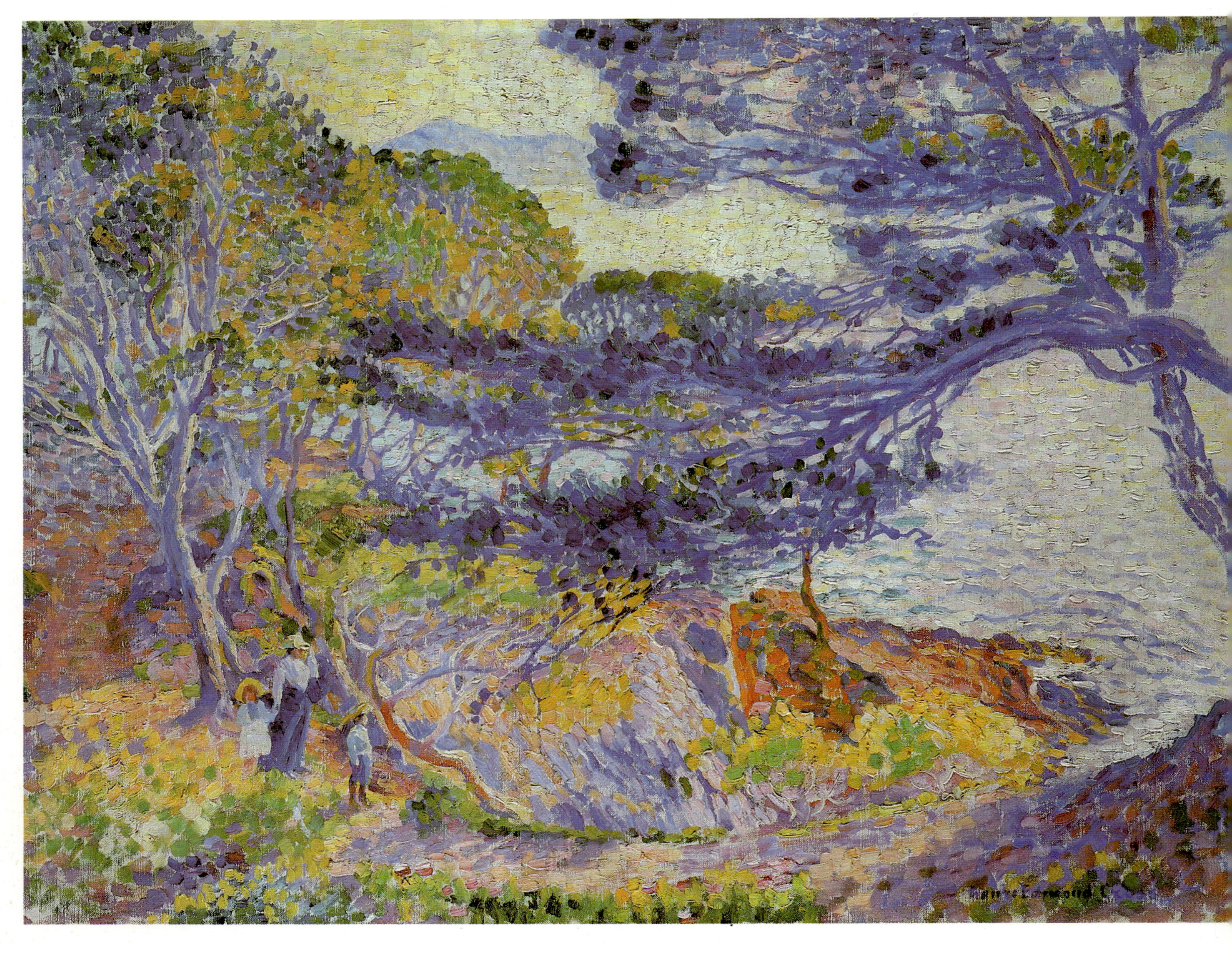

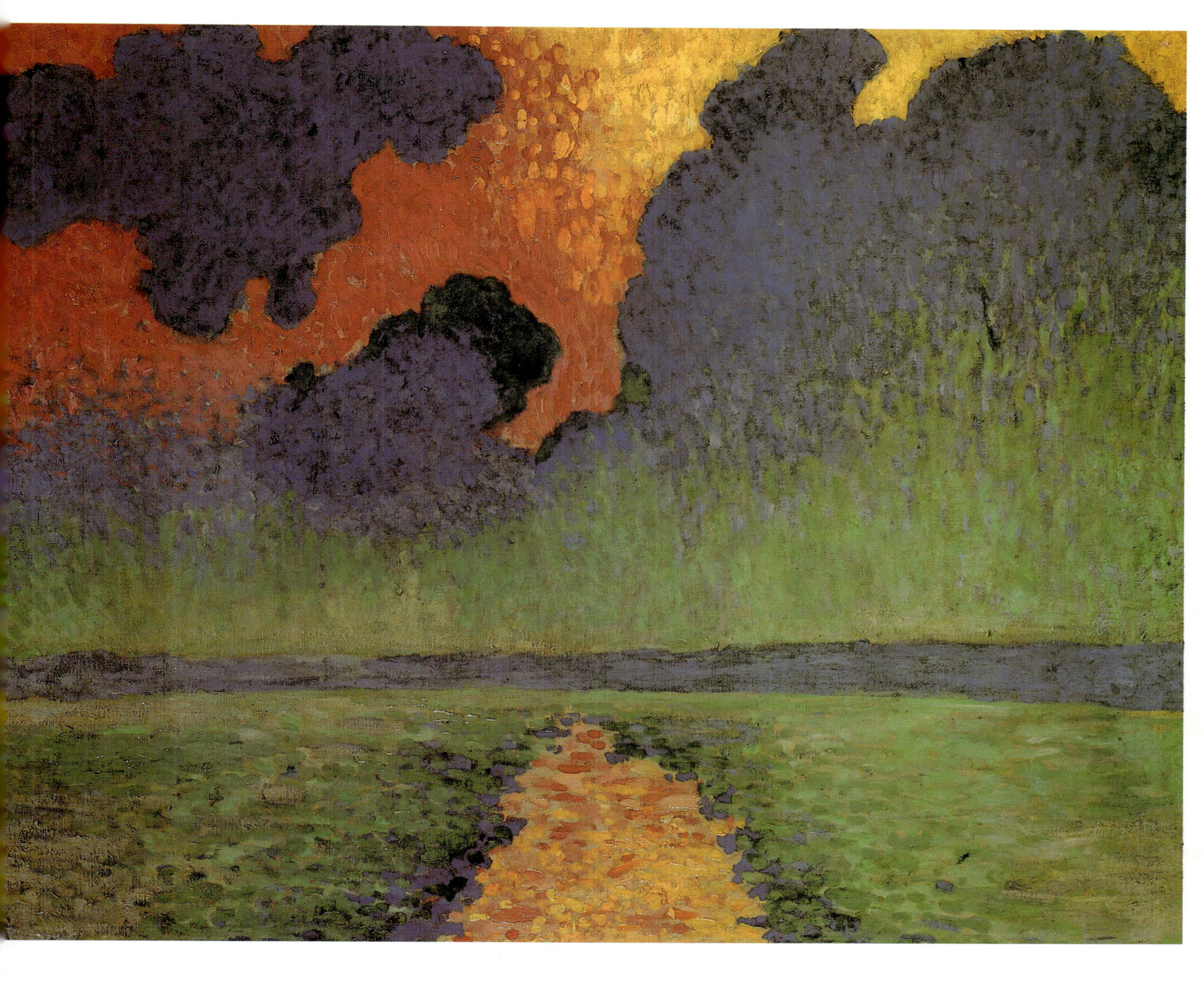

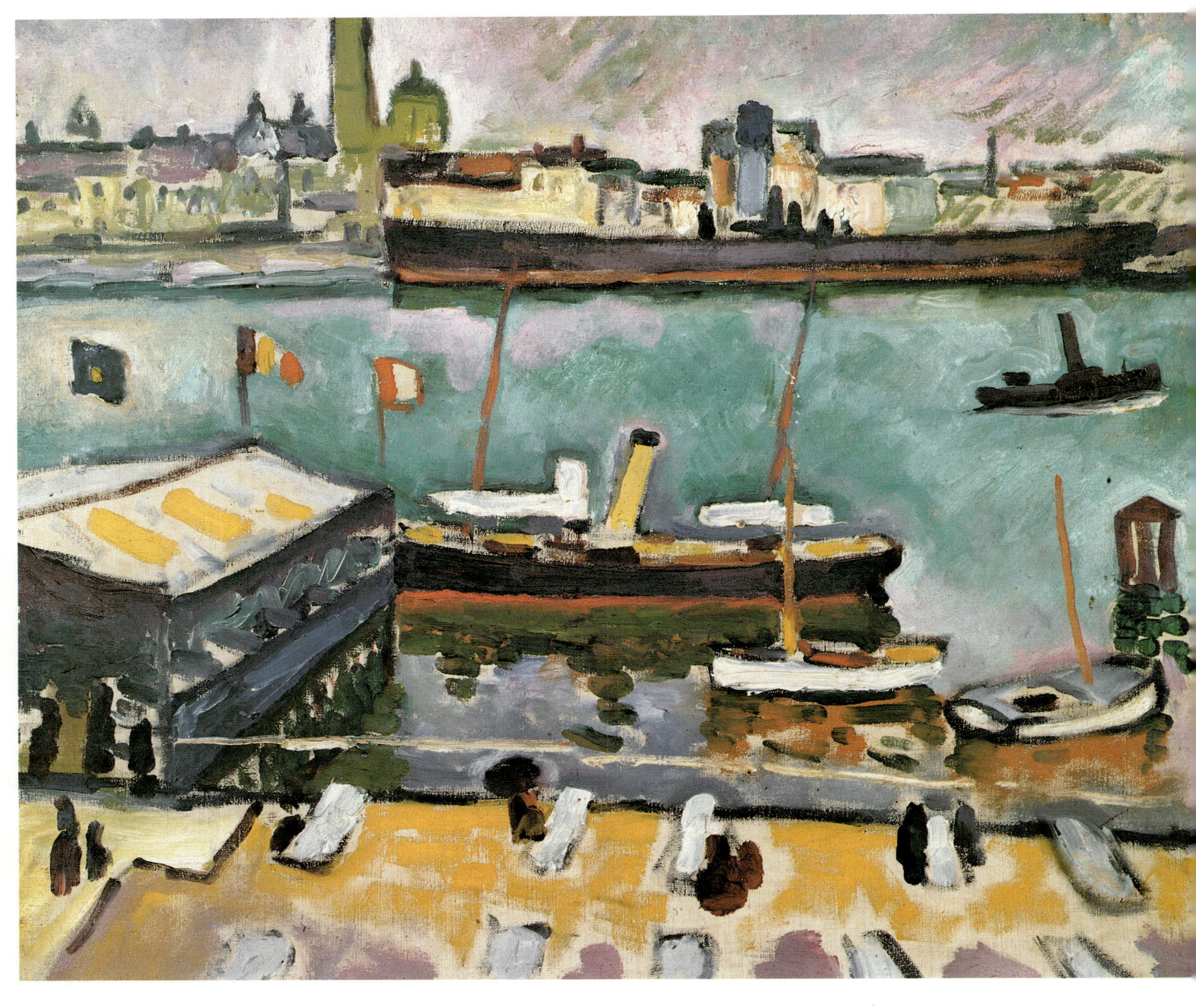

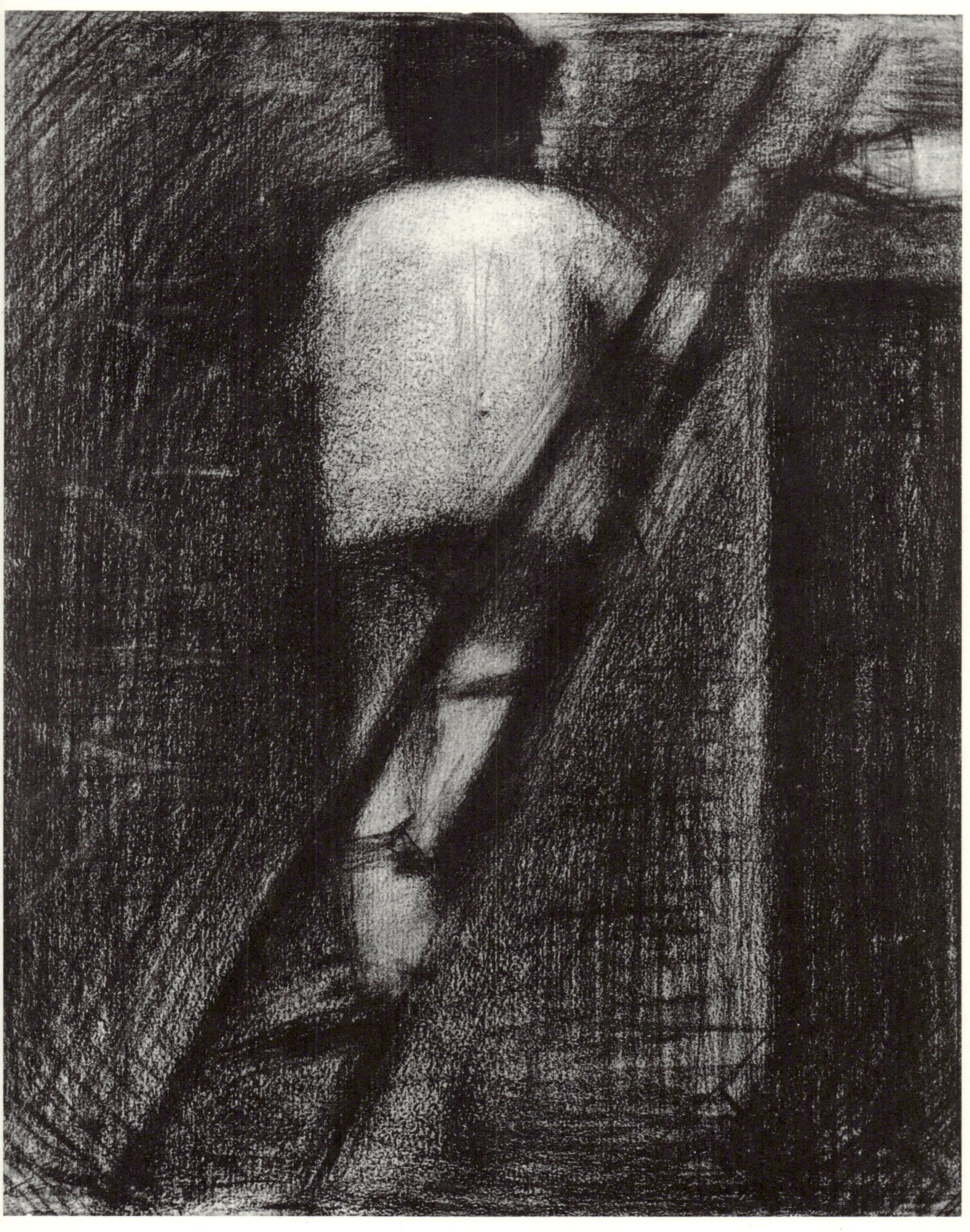

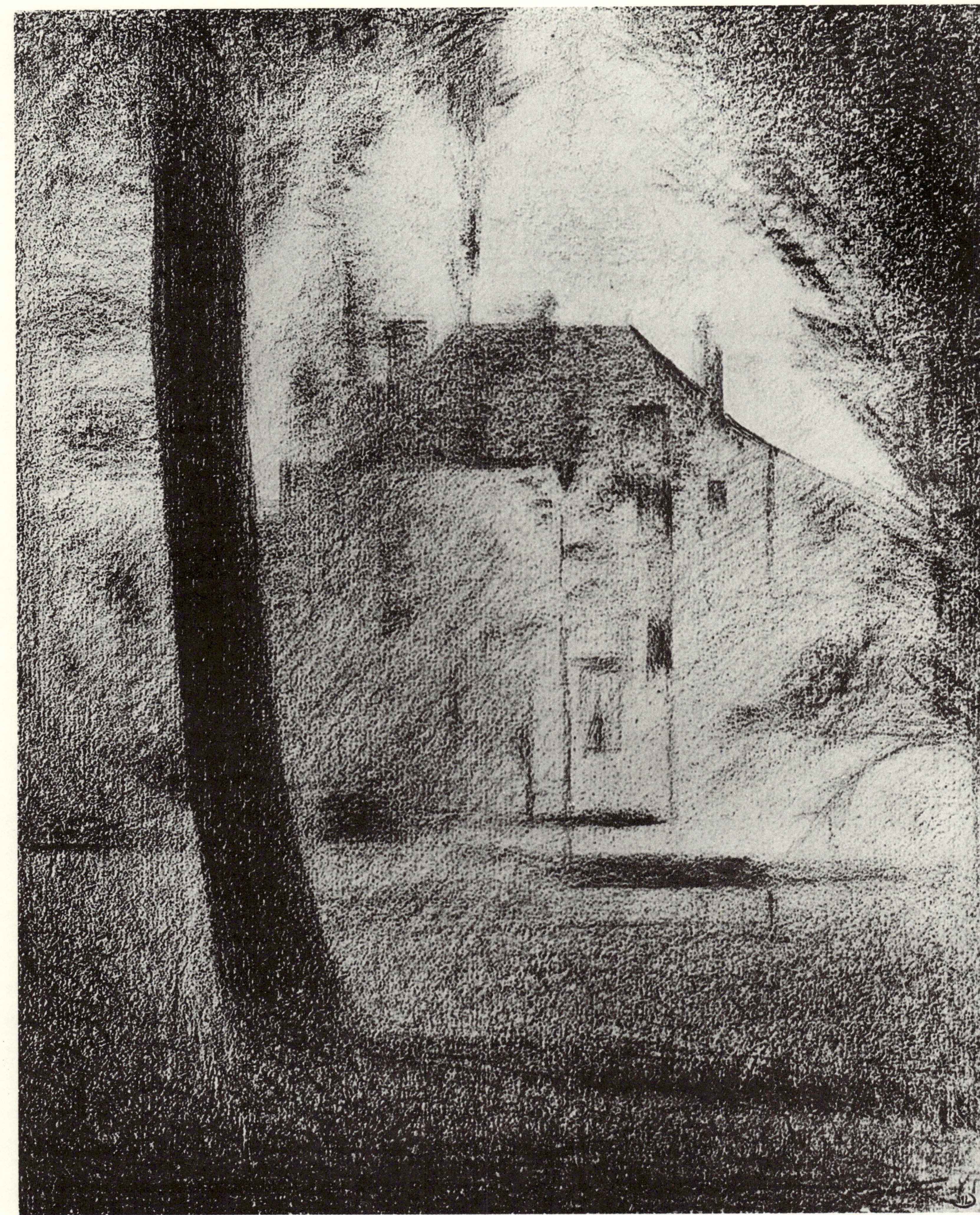

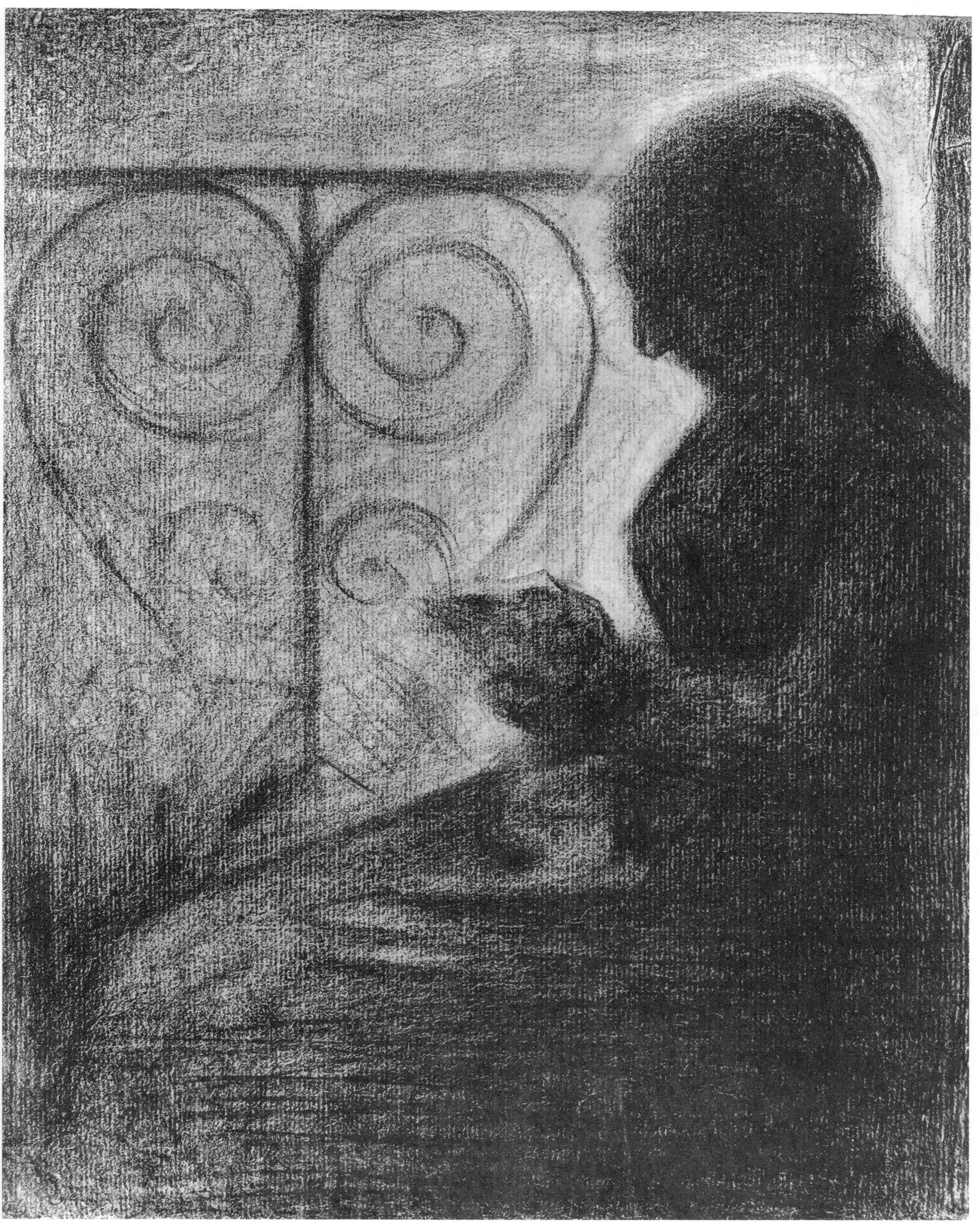

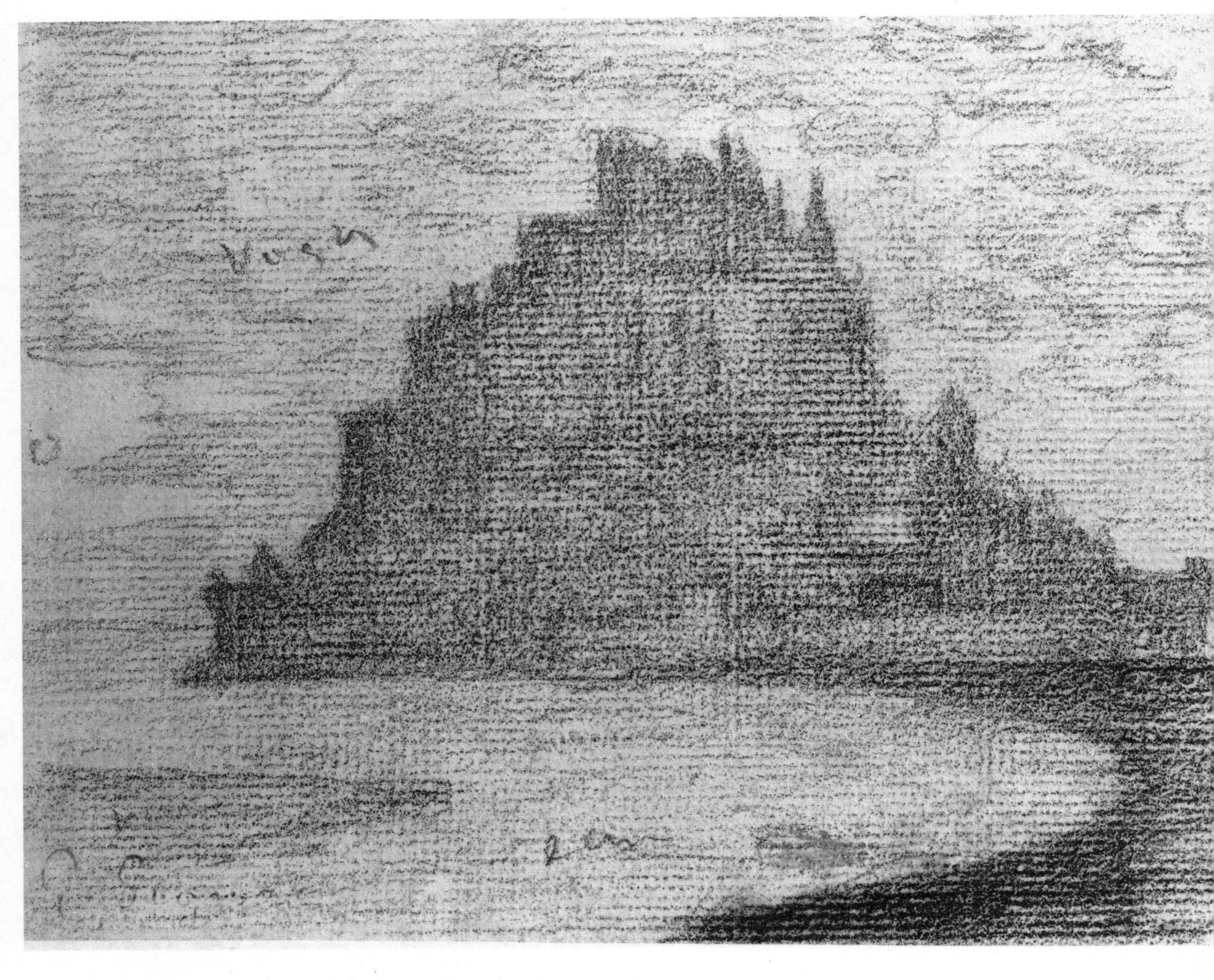

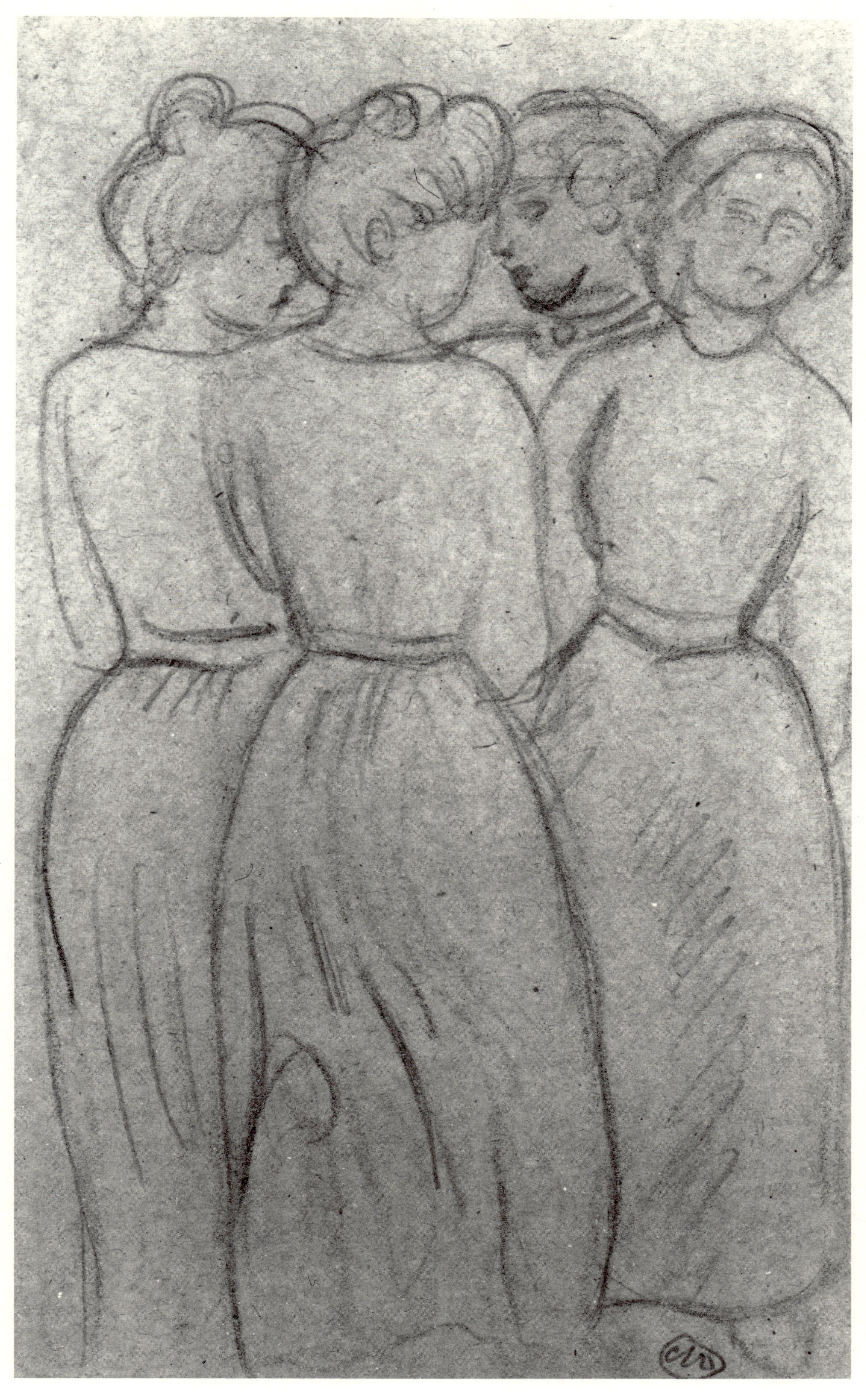

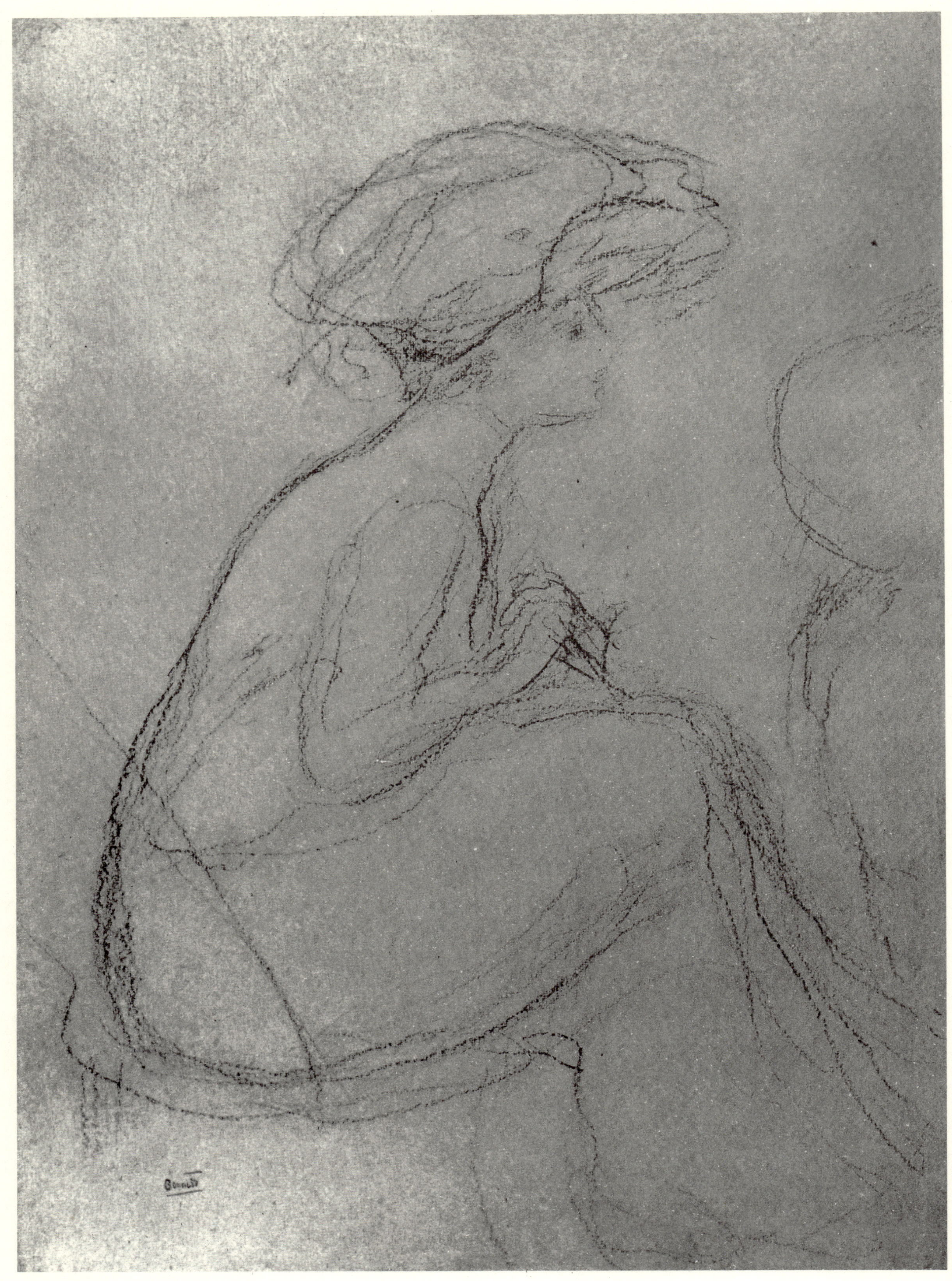

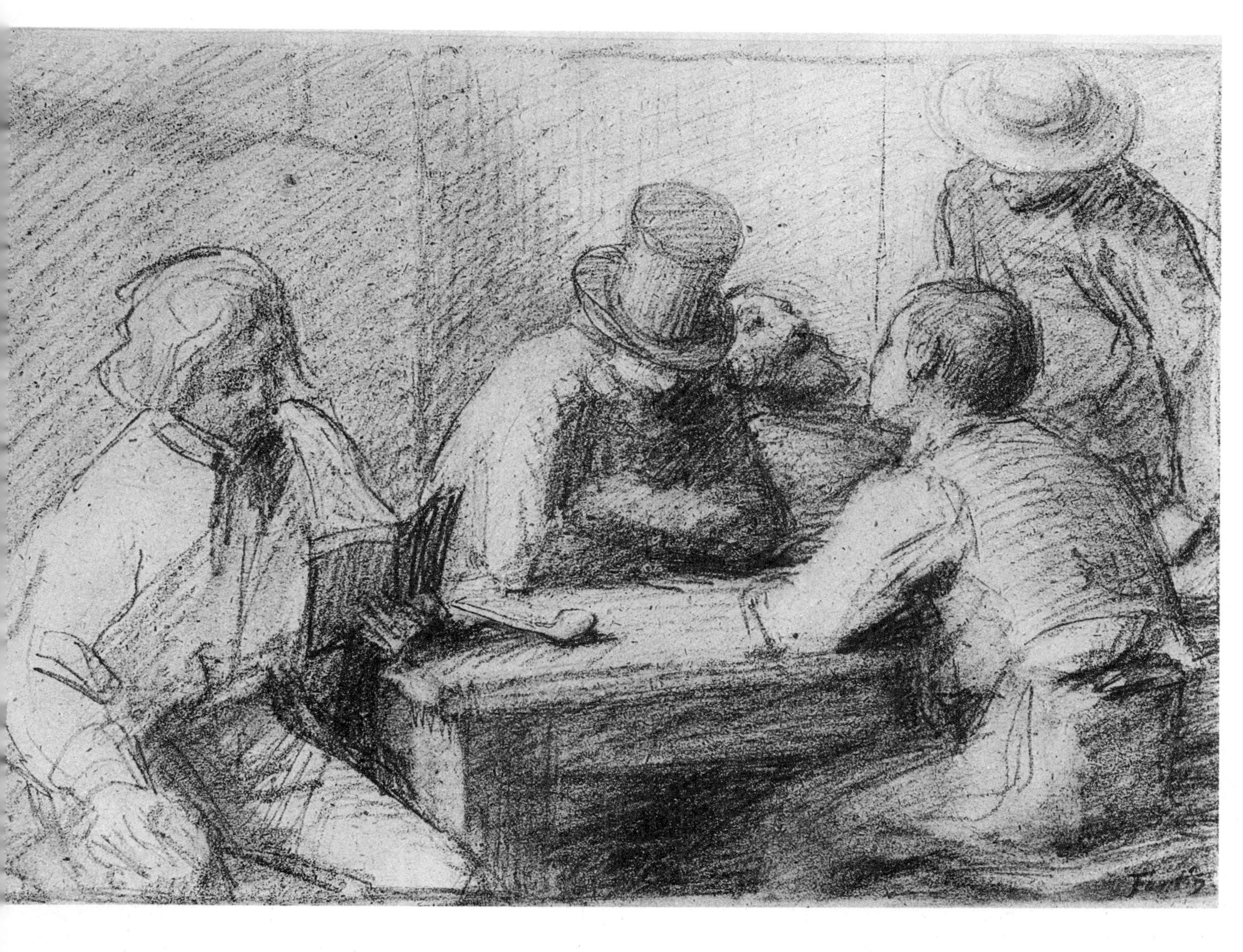

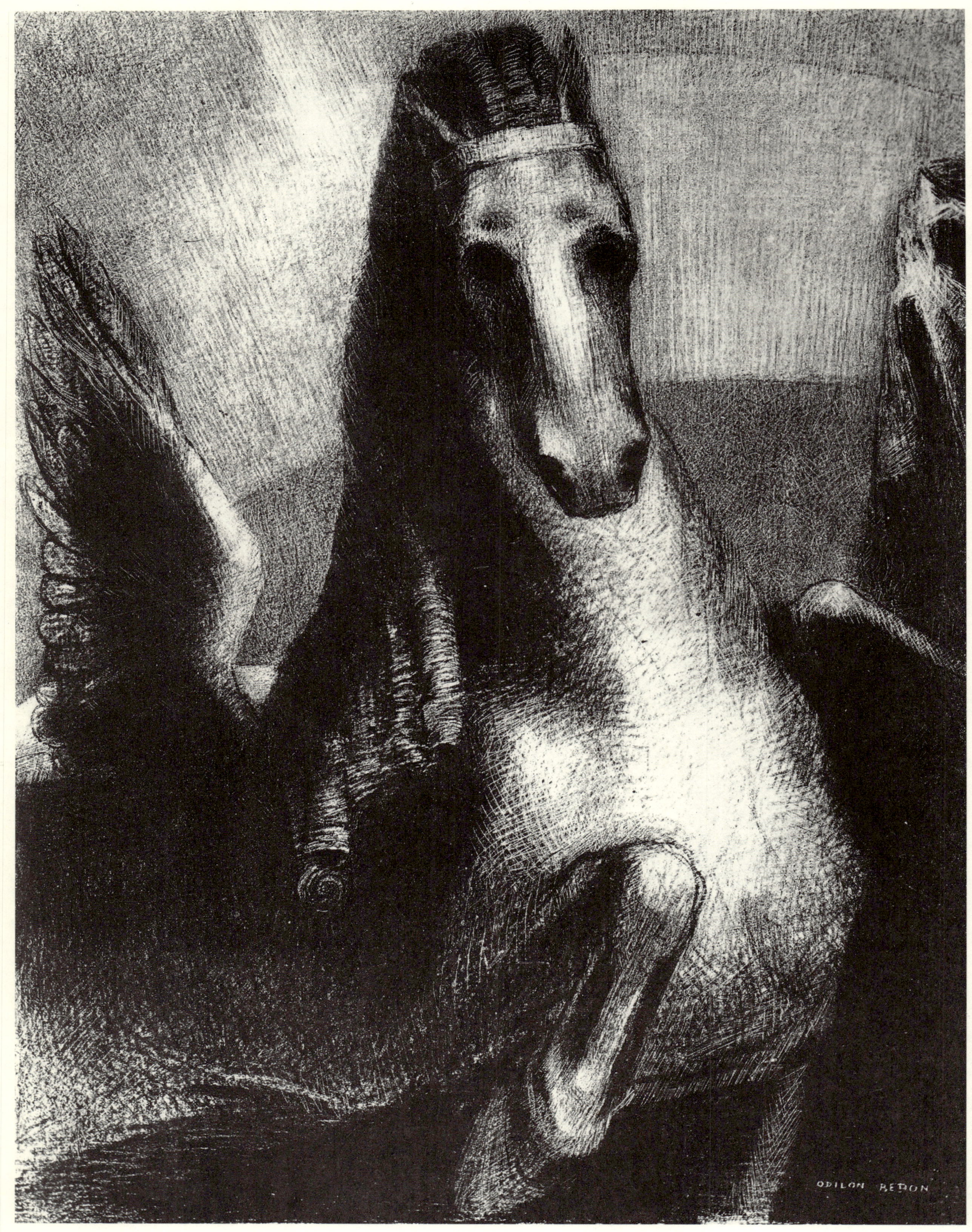
ODILON REDON

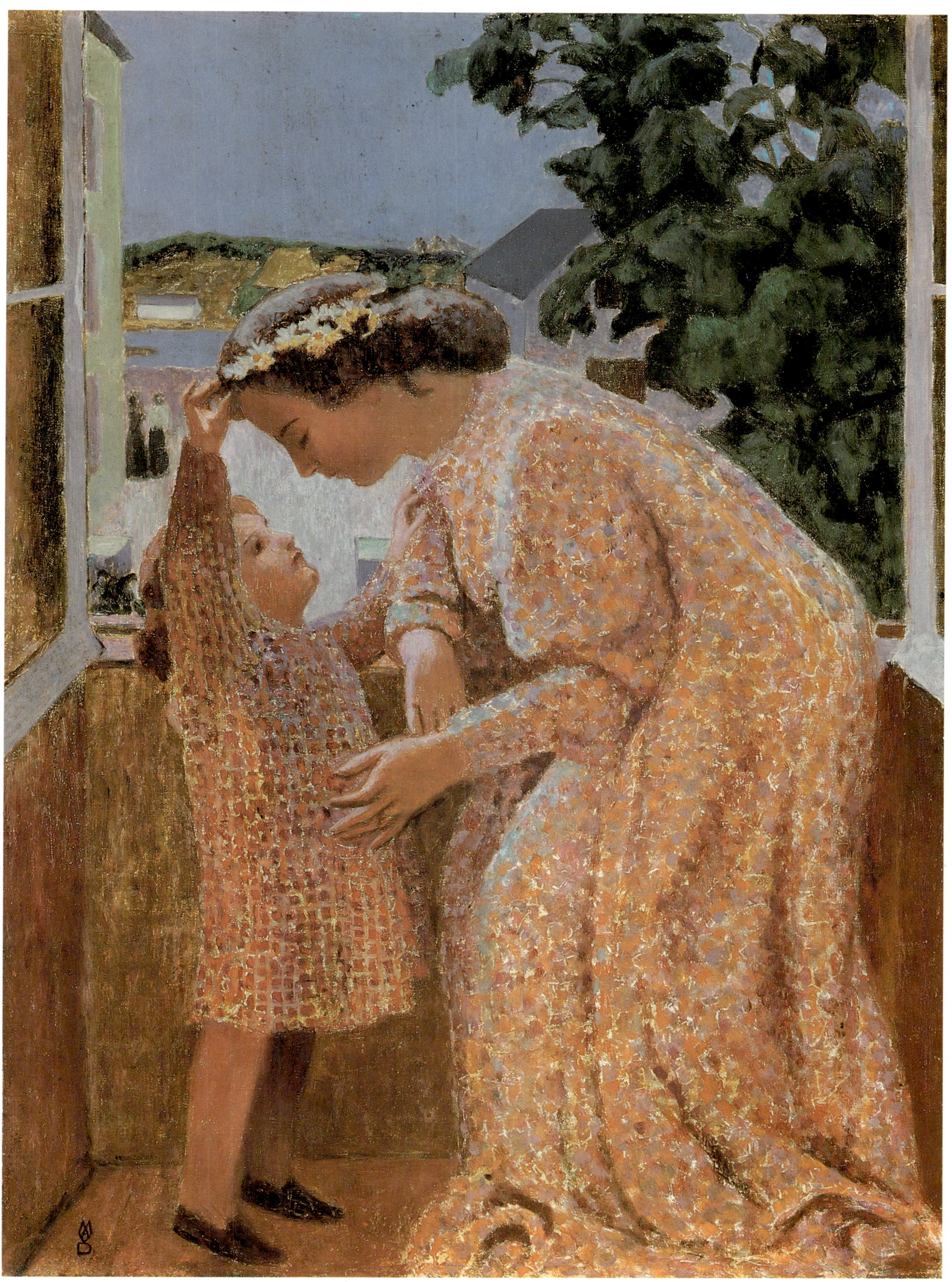

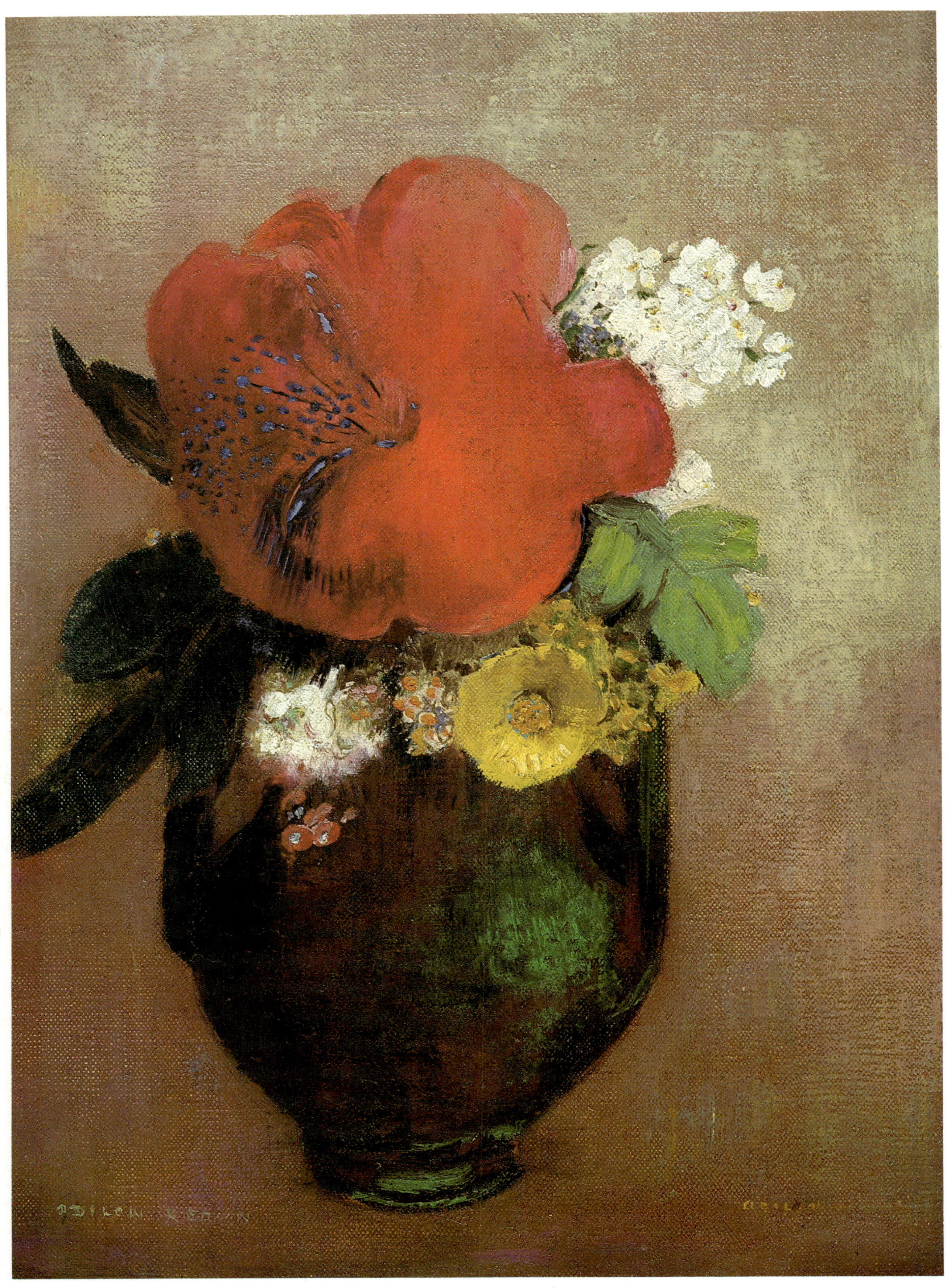

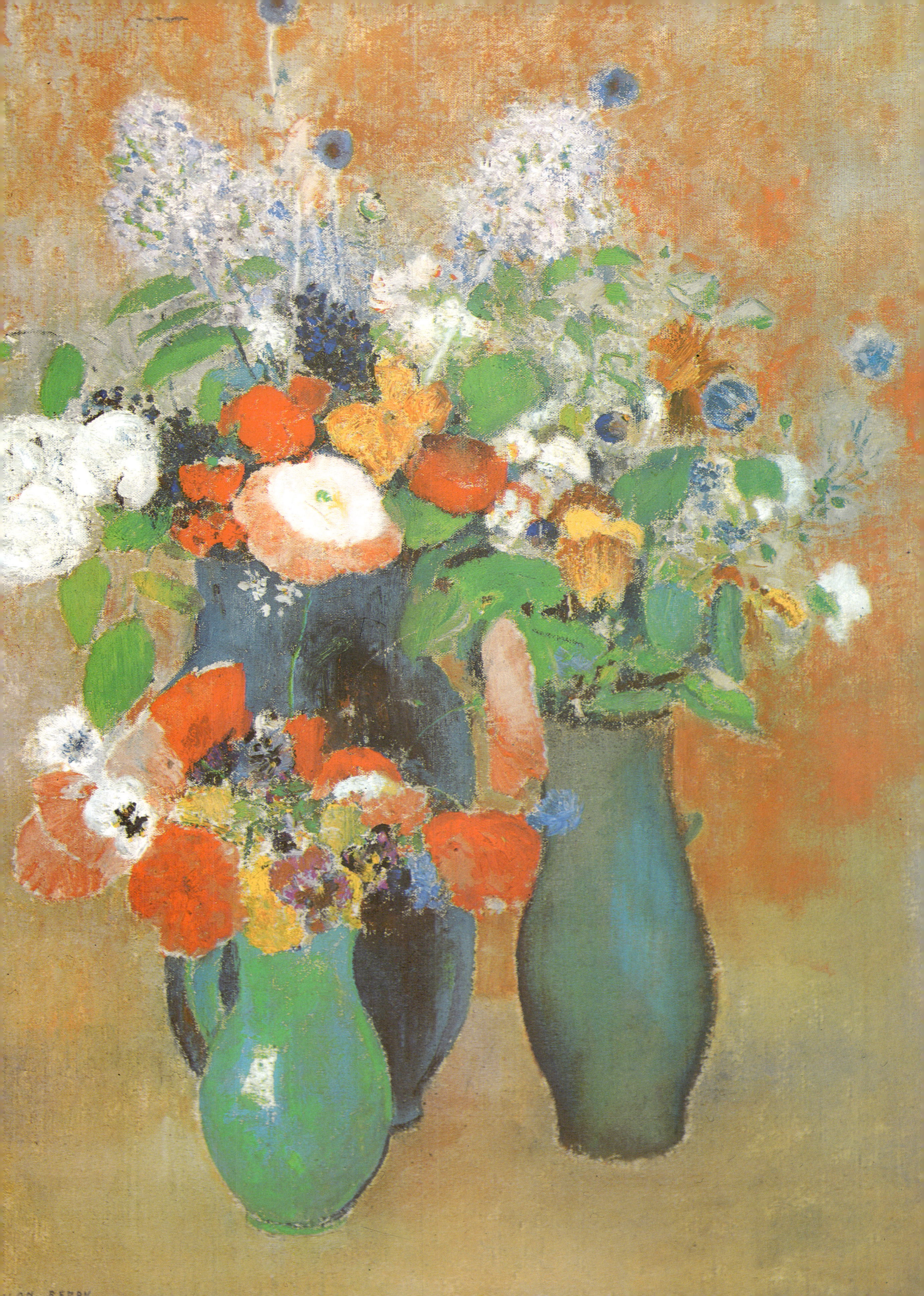

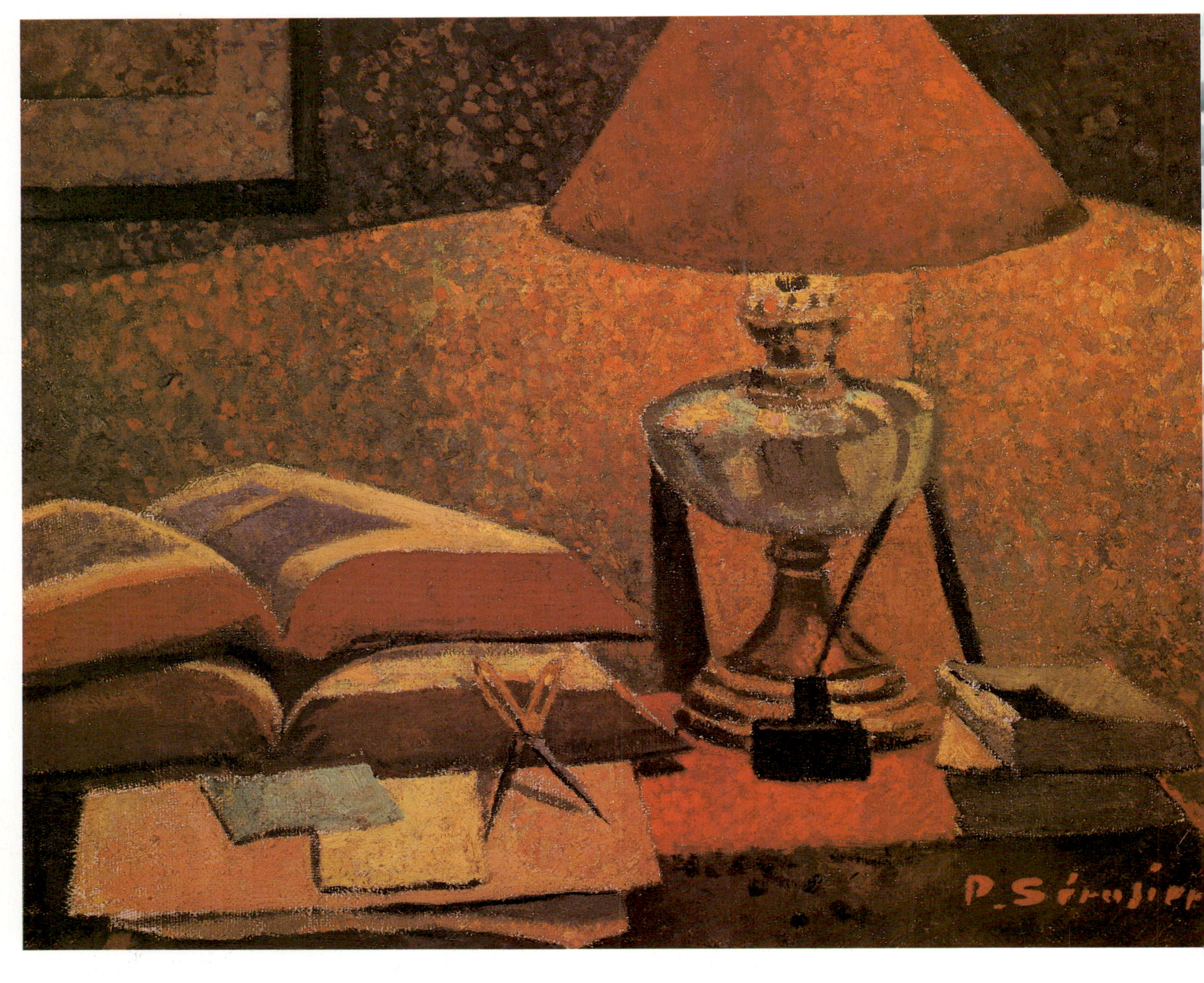
P. Sérusier

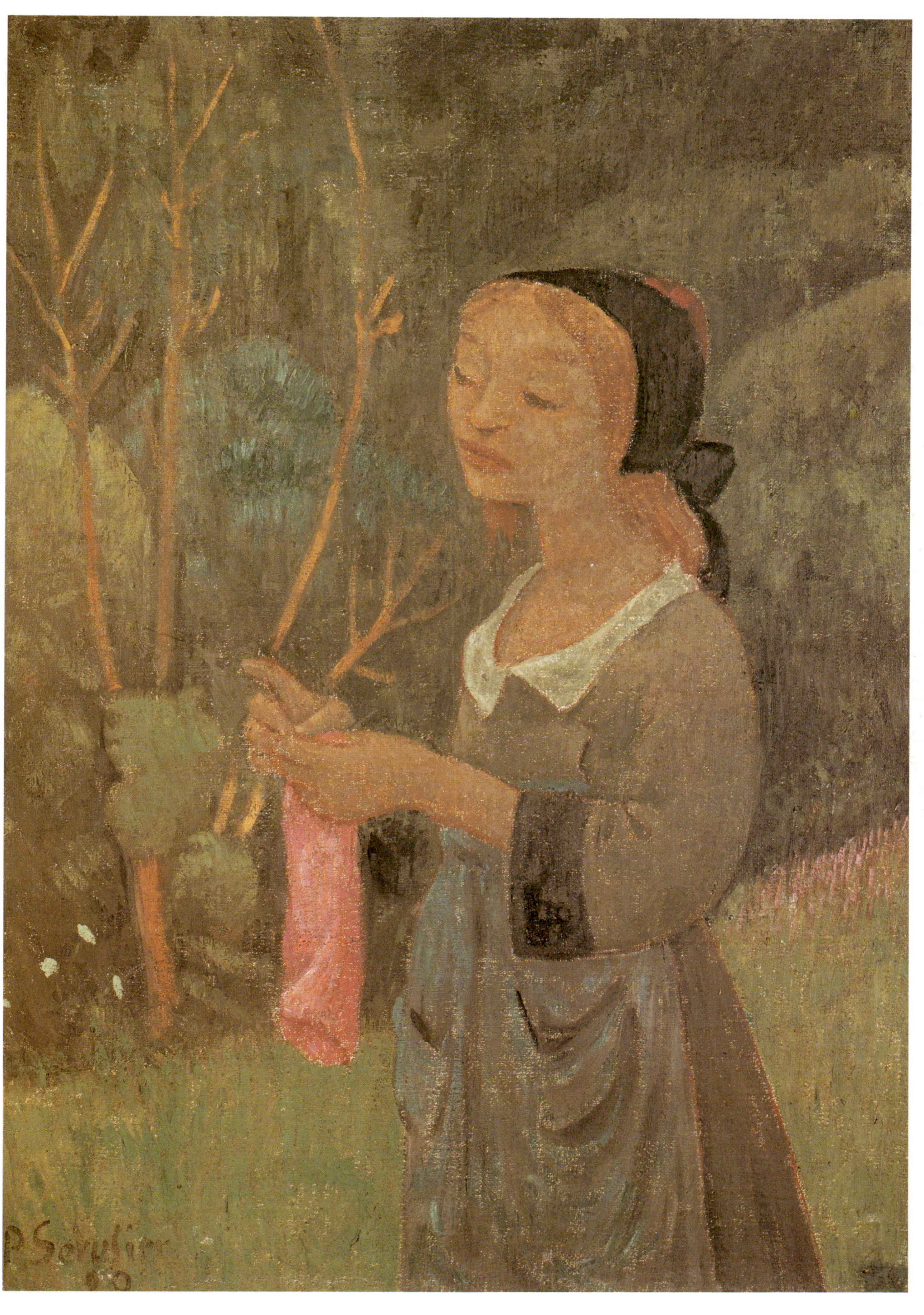

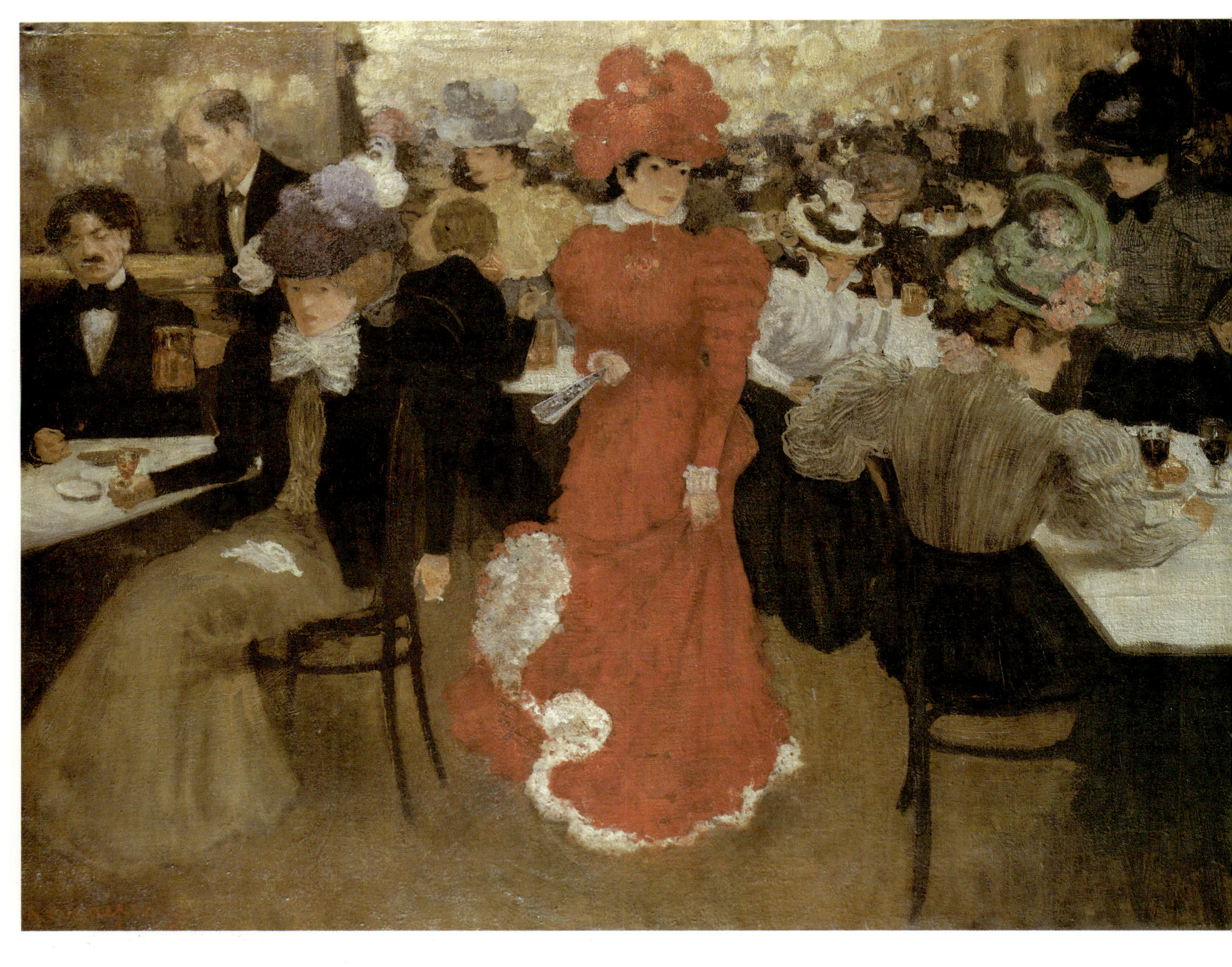

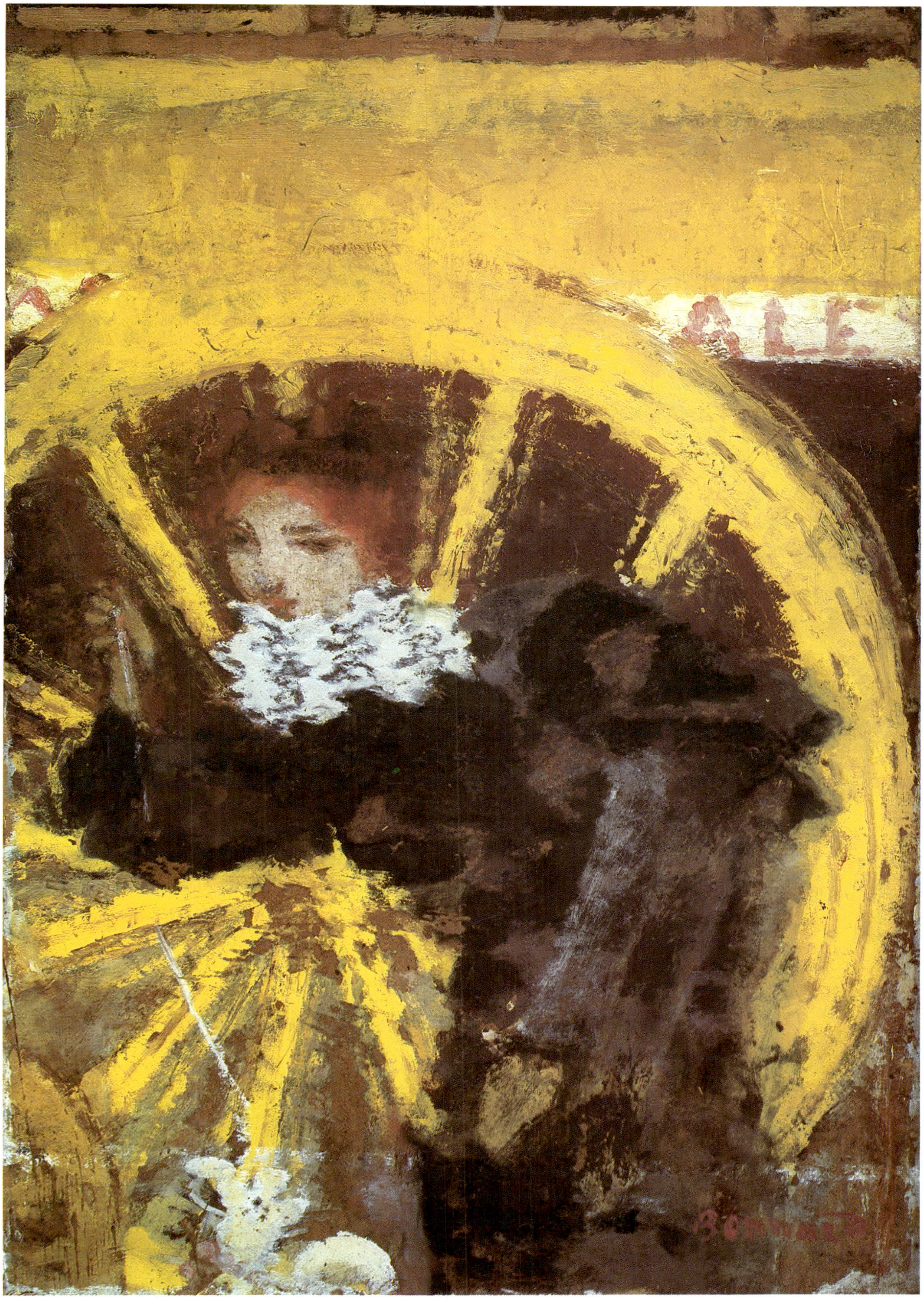

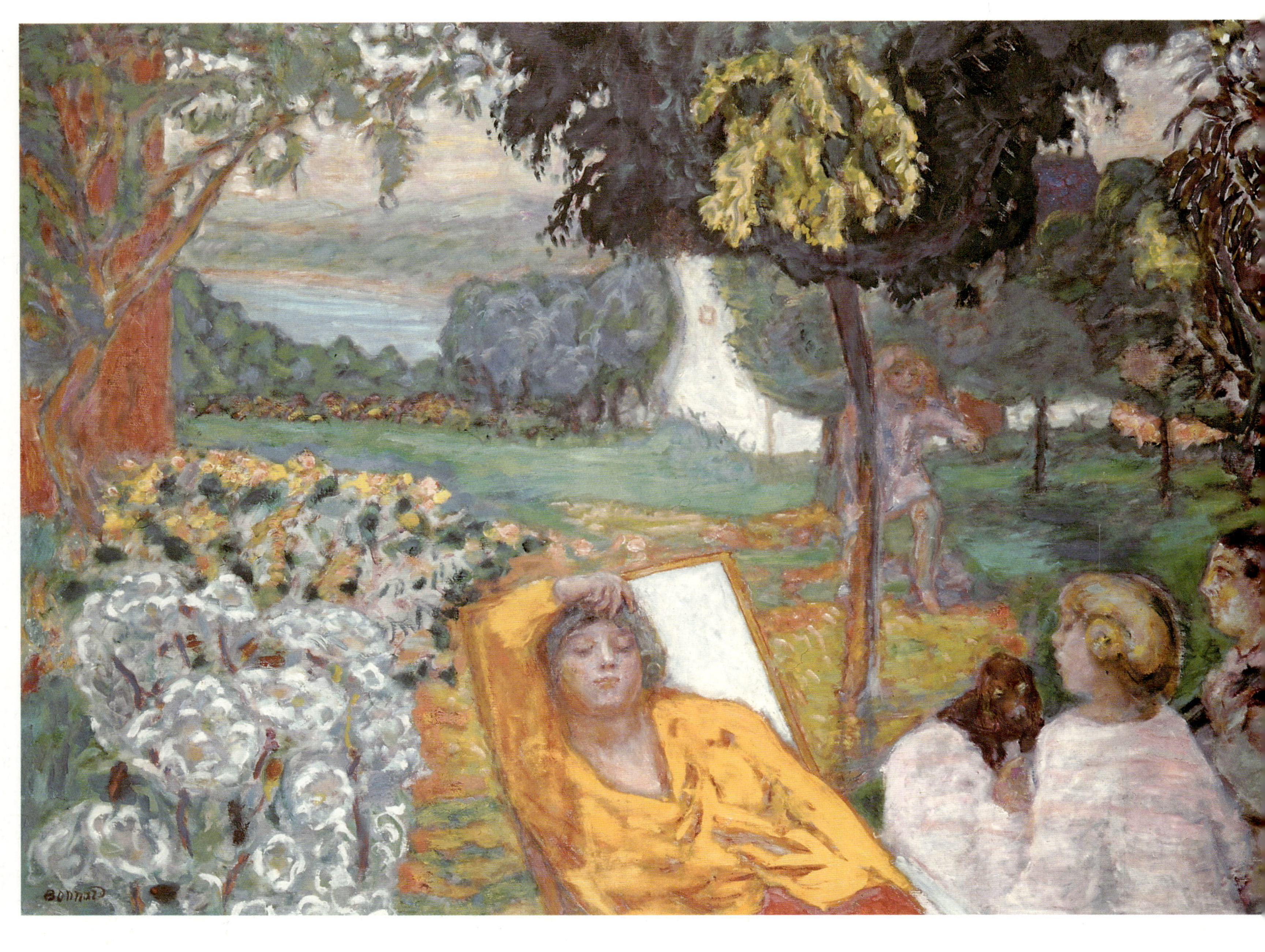

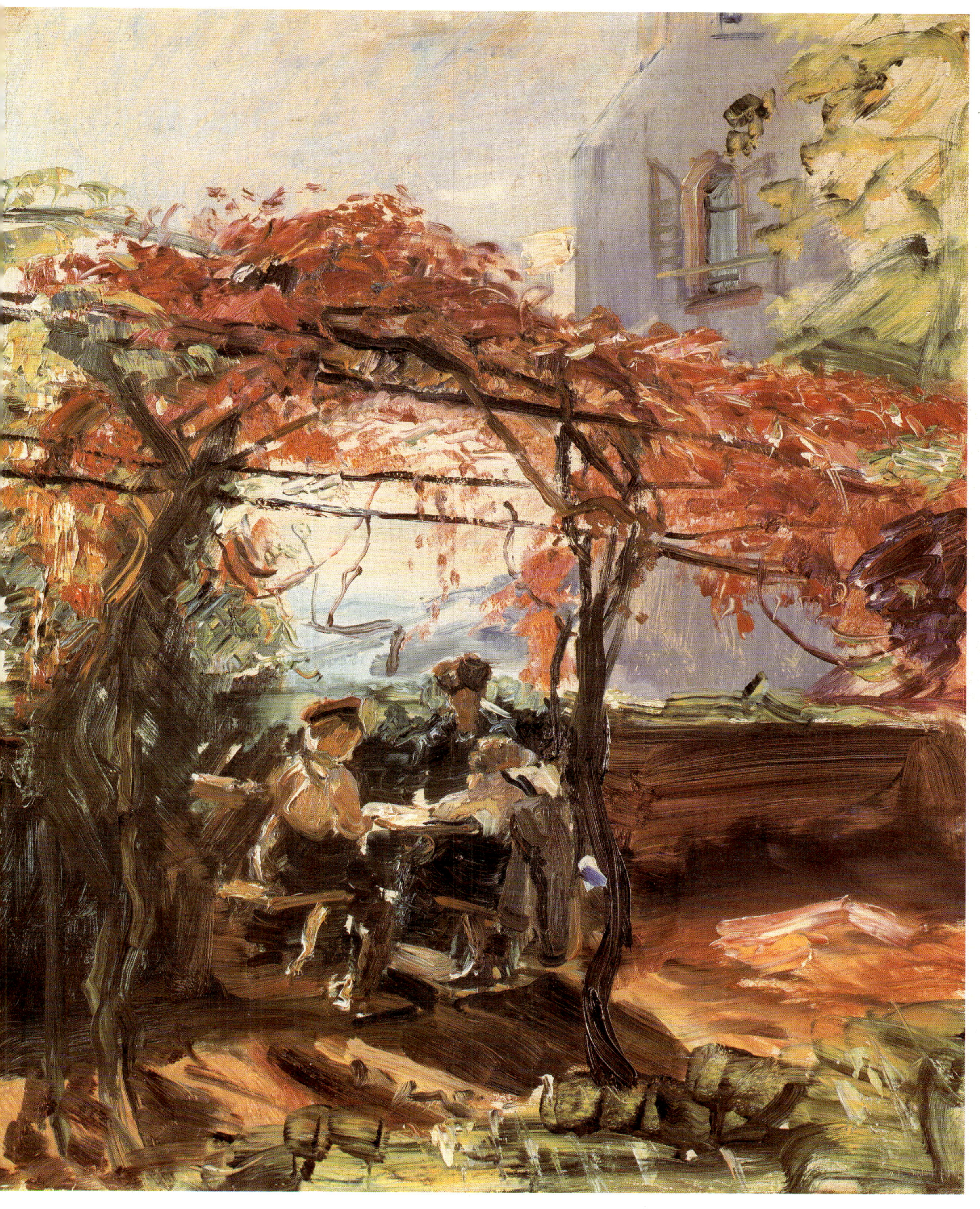

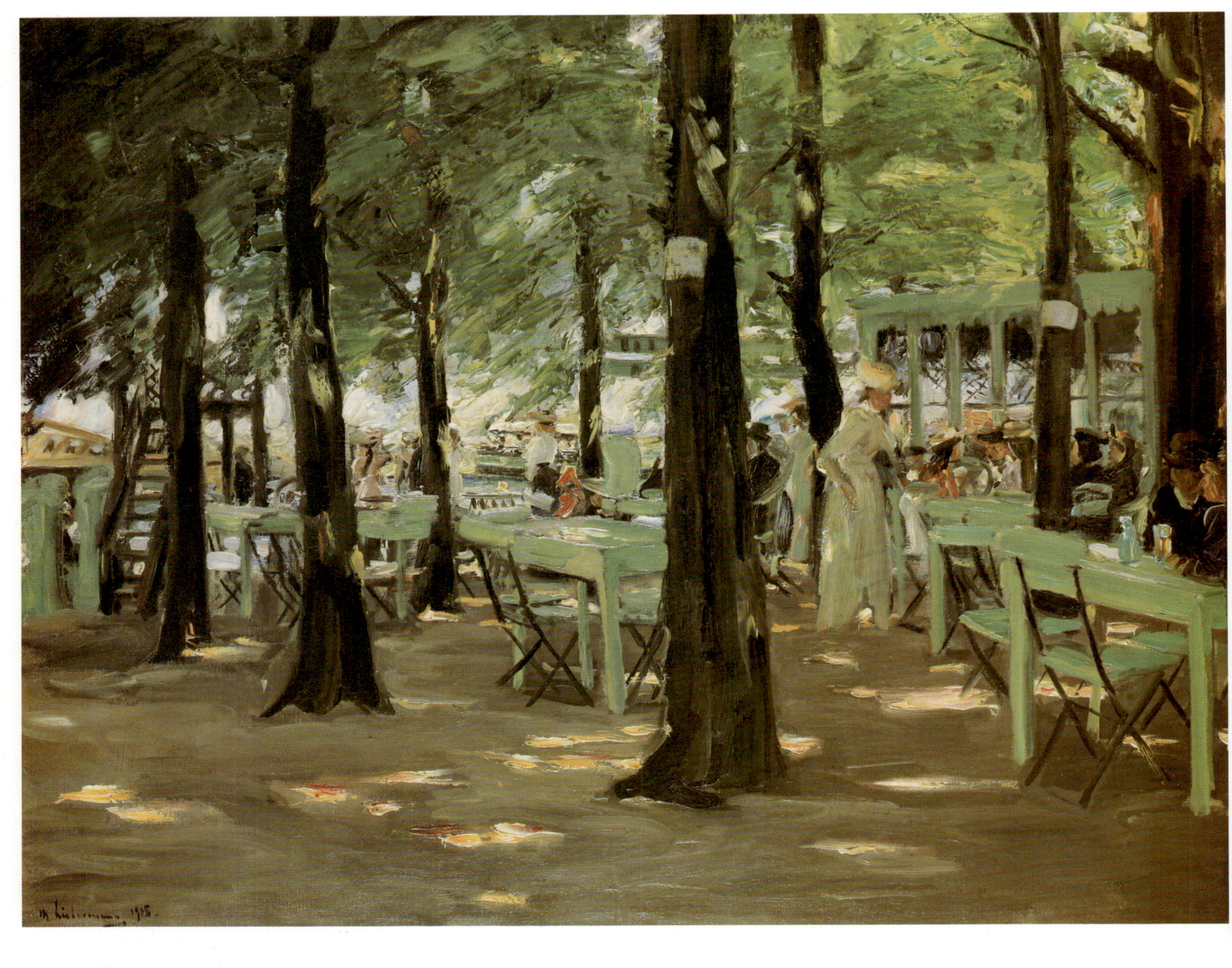

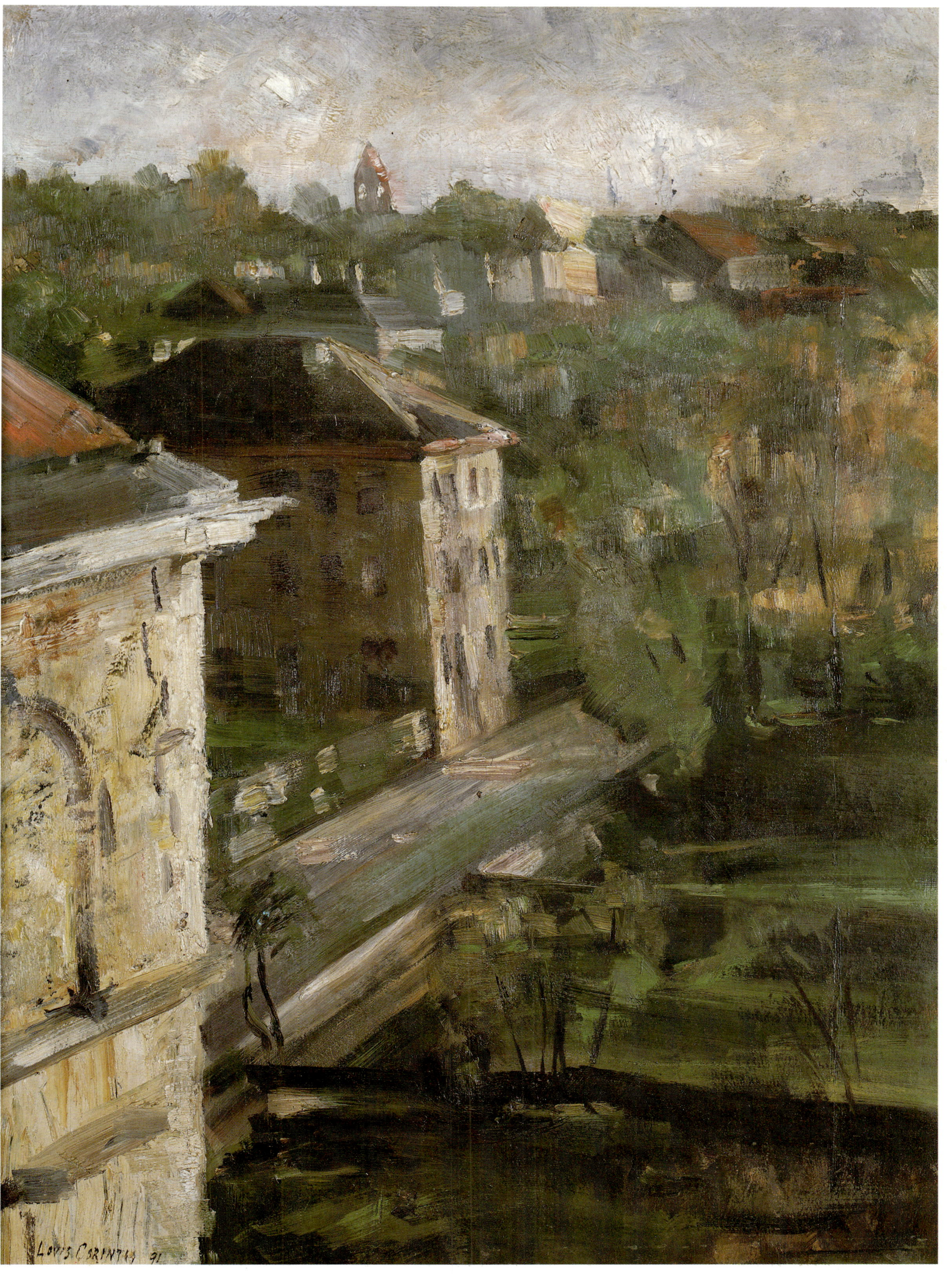
LOVIS CORINTH 91

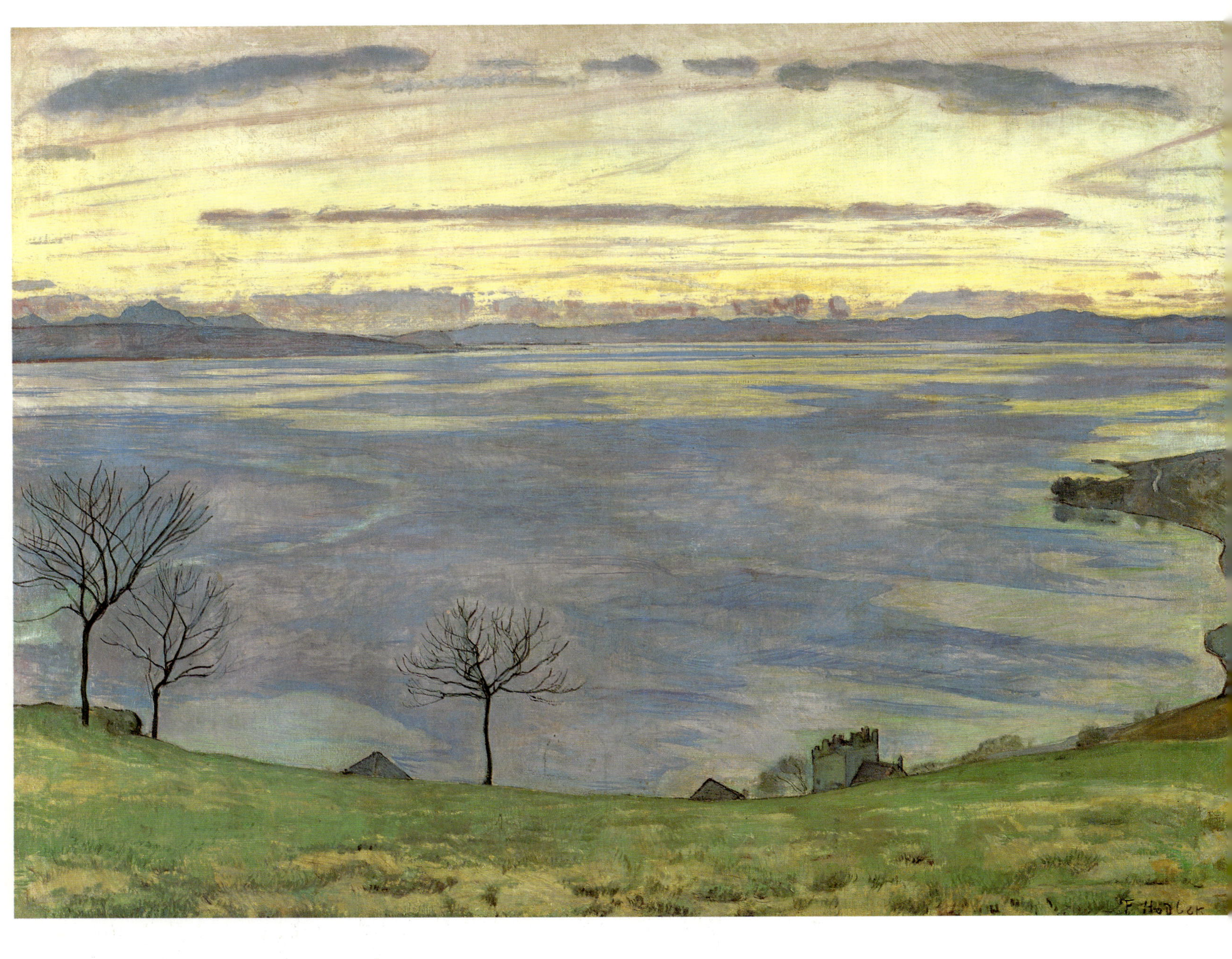
F. Hodler

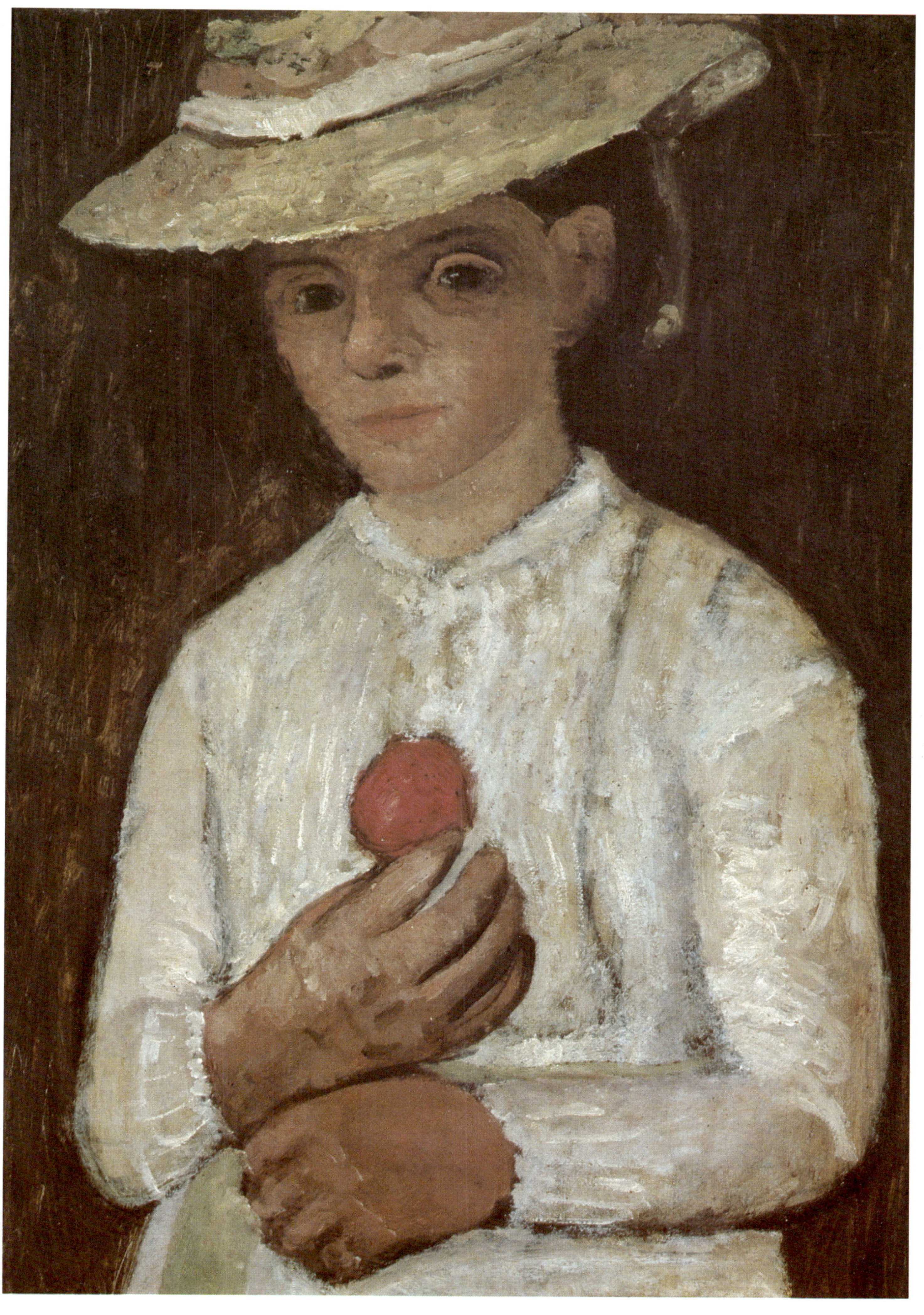

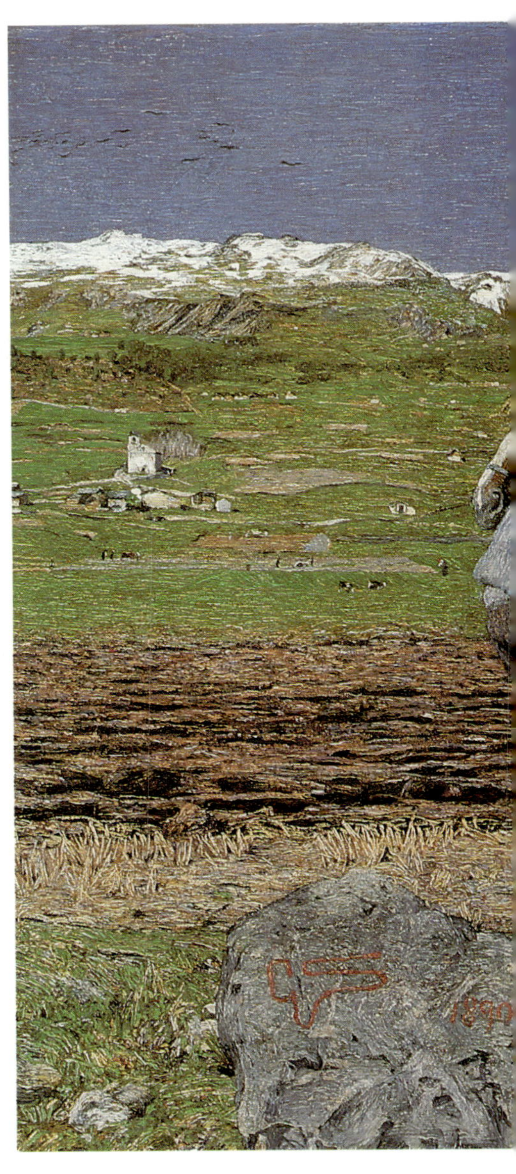

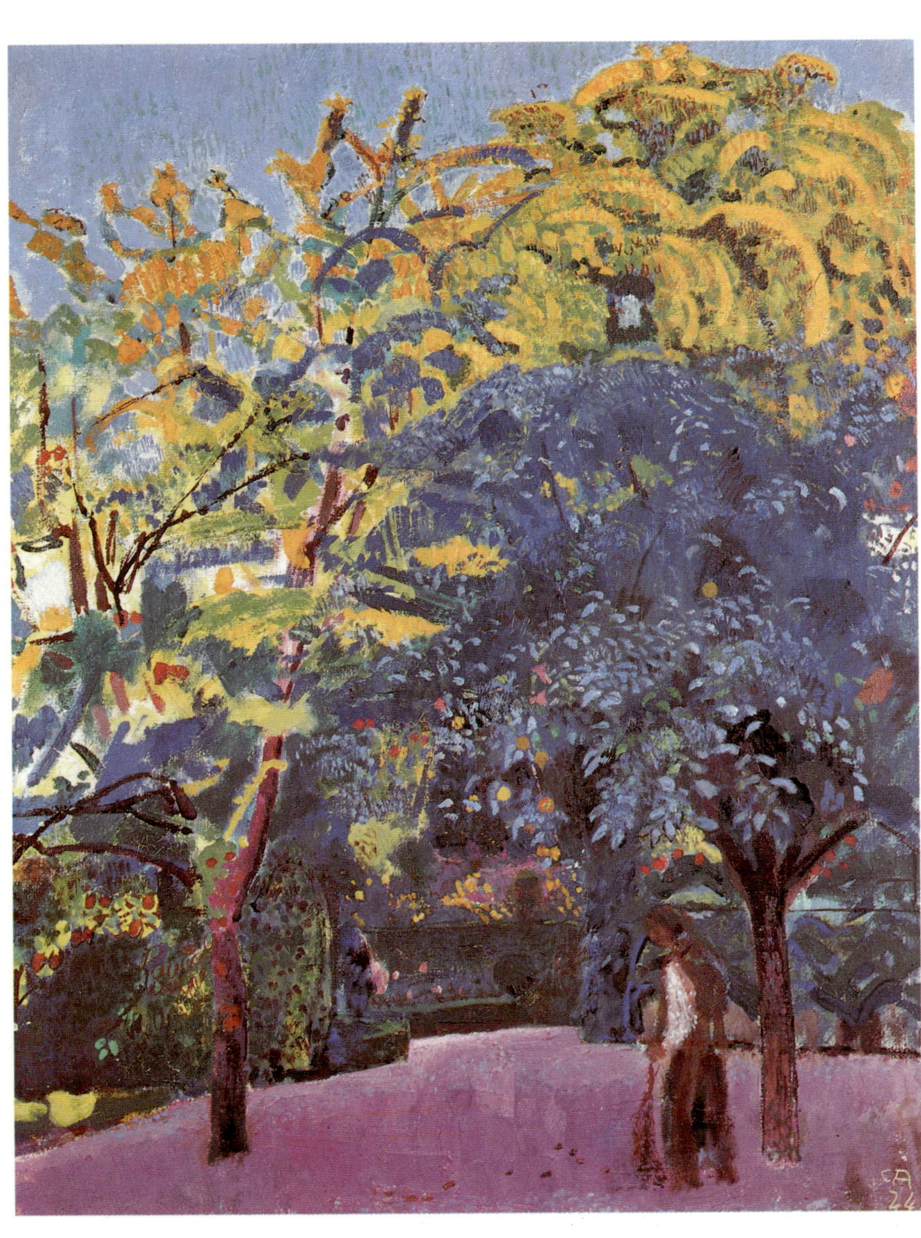

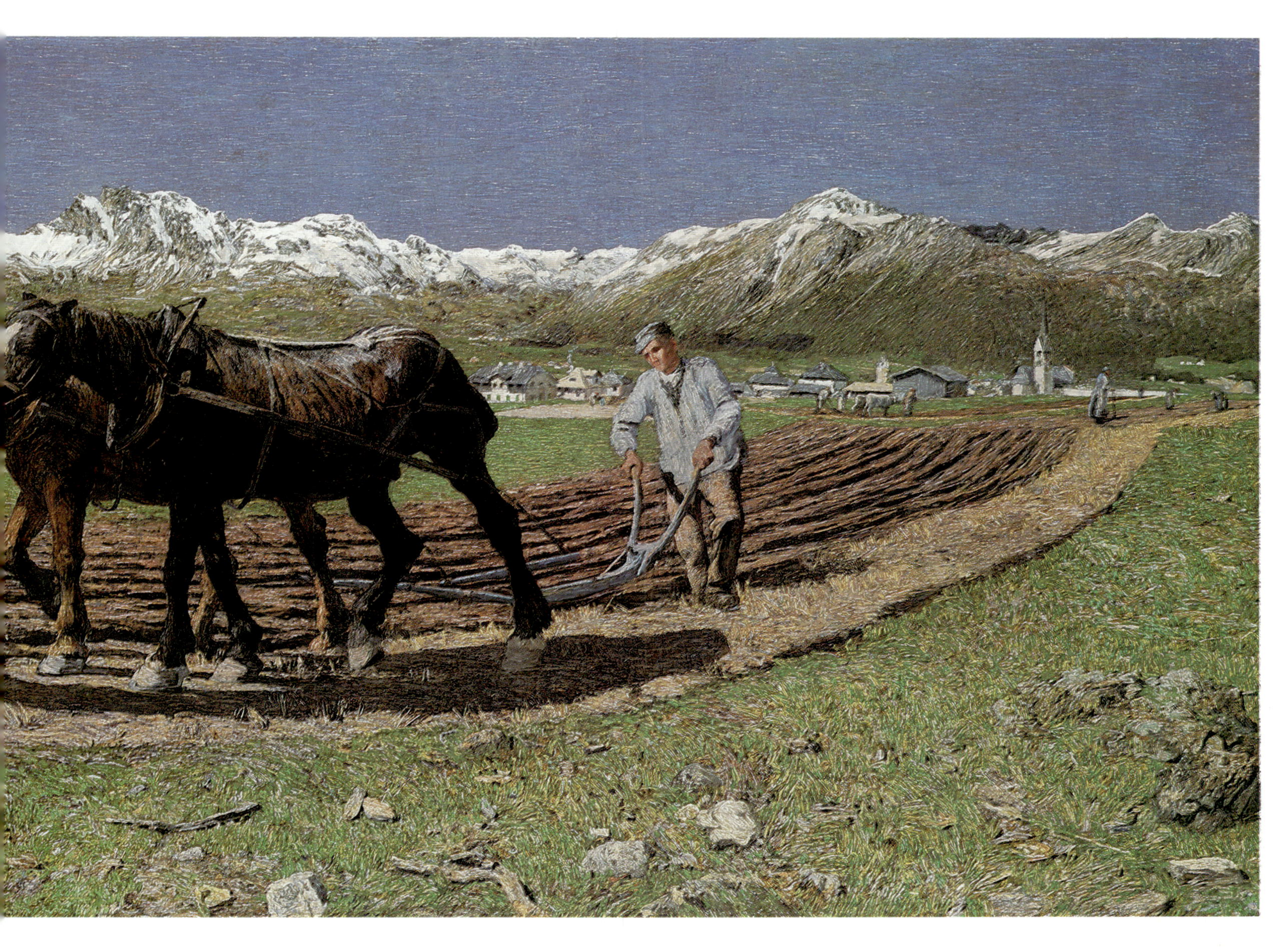

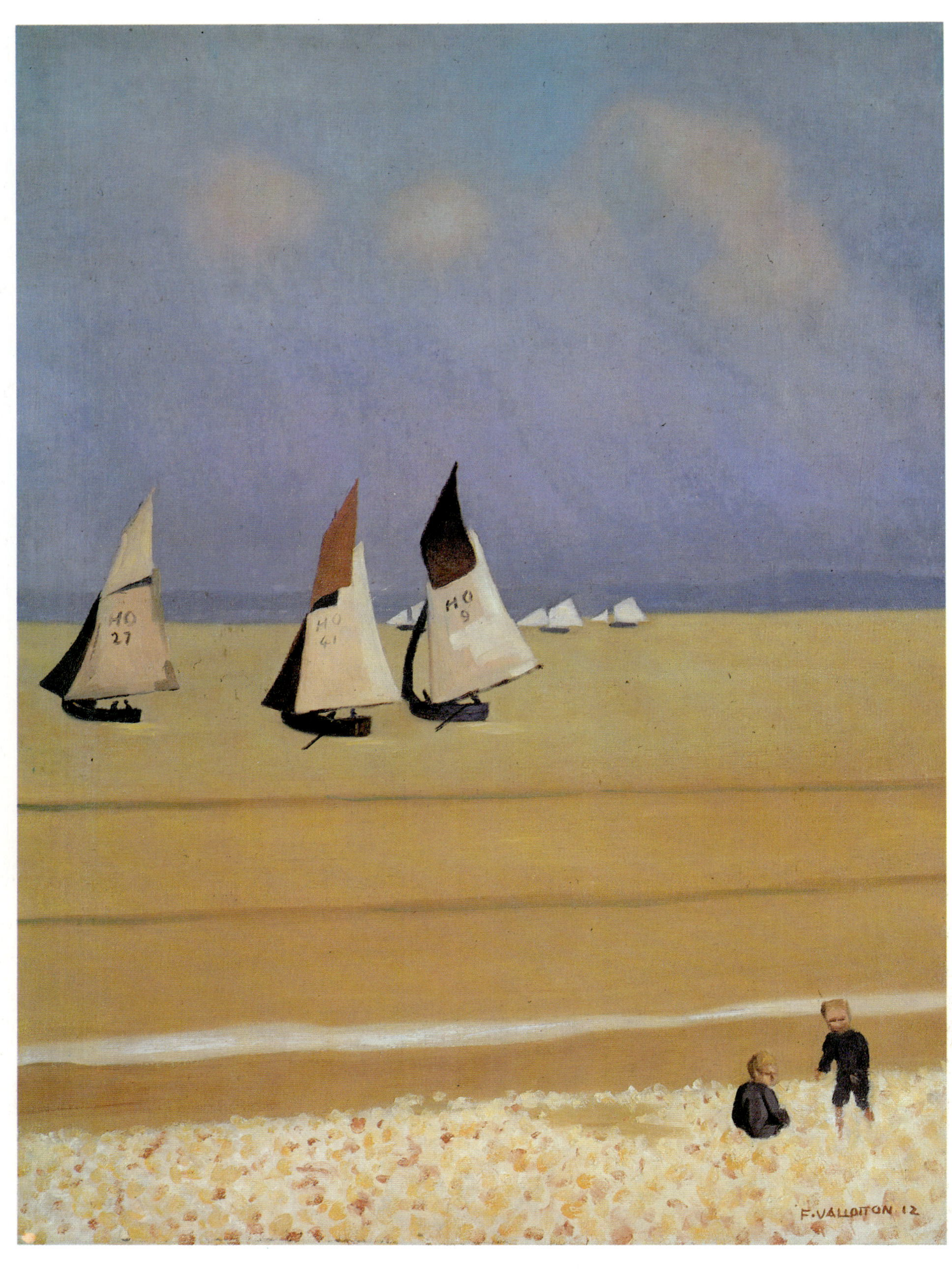
HO
27
HO
41
HO
9
F.VALLOTON 12

BIOGRAPHICAL NOTES

AMIET, Cuno
Solothurn 1868–1961 Oschwand

Amiet got to know Pointillism through the Segantini pupil Giacometti. Like many young painters at that time he went to Pont Aven, was very impressed by the paintings by van Gogh and Gauguin which he saw there, and joined Sérusier and Bernard. When he eventually was offered the opportunity to work with Renoir, he very quickly found his own personal style. His contact to the Synthetists and Auguste Renoir remained obvious in his work, even after his return to Switzerland.

Ill. p. 118

ANQUETIN, Louis
Entrapagny/Eure 1861–1932 Paris

Born and raised in Normandy, Anquetin came to Paris in 1882 where he worked in the beginning in Cormon's studio. There he got to know Toulouse-Lautrec, Bernard and van Gogh. Later he worked intensively with Gauguin. It seems that Anquetin was the "inventor" of *Cloisonnism*, that stained-glass style, strongly coloured painting which was practised by the Pont Aven painters in their first years. After 1890 Anquetin turned more towards Lautrec's work which influenced him very strongly.

Ill. p. 62

BERNARD, Émile
Lille 1868–1941 Paris

Bernard began his studies in Studio Cormon when he was just sixteen years old. There he painted together with Anquetin, Toulouse-Lautrec and van Gogh when he was not being thrown out for disobedience. He worked with Gauguin from 1888 to 1891. He also had contact with Cézanne which was above all reflected in interesting correspondence. Bernard was not just successful as a painter, his numerous writings are no less important as he constantly analysed and commented on his friends' work.

Ill. p. 70

BONNARD, Pierre
Fondenay-aux-Roses 1867–1947 Le Cannet

He was a graduate of the Académie Julian where he learned together with Denis, Roussel, Vuillard and Sérusier. Sérusier's contact to Gauguin was responsible for the friends forming a group, calling themselves *Nabis*. Later, when the friends turned to a great degree to religious art, Bonnard left the group. His friendship with Thadée Natanson, the founder of the journal *Revue Blanche* was very significant. His work for this journal and for the art dealers Vollard and Bernheim-Jeune ensured him world fame and a sure income.

Ill. pp. 102, 111, 112

BRAQUE, Georges
Argenteuil 1882–1963 Paris

At the beginning of his career Braque was clearly influenced by Corot and he joined the Fauves before his friendship with Picasso led him to seek his artistic fulfillment in the style principles of Cubism of which he was a co-founder. Cézanne's world was decisive for this development. Following Cézanne's theories, Braque completely dispensed with pure colour in his landscapes in favour of a tectonic-geometric composition in the spirit of Cézanne.

Ill. p. 96

CARRIÈRE, Eugène
Gournay 1849–1906 Paris

Carrière, who was already well versed in the technique of graphic art began his artistic career in Jules Chéret's studio. Chéret was described as the "king of the poster" in Paris. As an independent artist, Carrière found early recognition due to the excellent portraits which he created. As a thoughtful theorist he wrote profound articles on art. In 1898 he opened a studio, the Académie Carrière, which soon became very popular. Matisse and Derain were just two of his many pupils.

Ill. p. 74

CÉZANNE, Paul
Aix 1839–1906 Aix

Cézanne is one of the leading Post-Impressionists. He received his first groundwork as an independent artist from Pissarro who took him to Auvers and introduced him to Impressionist plein air painting. Cézanne accepted the colourfulness but did not remain with Impressionism. He soon developed his own style and attempted a rhythmically constructed design in his compositions while not modelling with light and shadow but instead with fine contrasting colour values.

Ill. pp. 8, 33, 34, 35, 36, 37, 38, 39, 40, 52, 53

CORINTH, Lovis
Tapiau (East Prussia) 1858–1925 Zandvoort (Holland)

Corinth was one of the few representatives of Impressionism in Germany. After studying at the Königsberg Academy in Munich he went to Paris. There he discovered the essential impulses of Impressionist painting which he brought back with him to Germany. Although Impressionist in his palette, in his late work he approached a completely independent Expressionism, especially in his *Walchensee* paintings which he painted when he was seriously ill. From 1915 he was president of the Berlin Sezession, in 1918 he became professor.

Ill. p. 115

CROSS, Henri-Edmond
Douai 1856–1910 Saint-Clair

Cross first began his artistic career with realistic paintings, but soon joined the Impressionists. Through his association with Seurat and Signac he developed to become a Neo-Impressionist and practised the Pointillist style of splitting up colour with extreme resolution. From 1891 he lived mainly on the Mediterranean. In his late work, he worked with great freedom of colour and stood very close to Expressionism.

Ill. p. 94

DEGAS, Edgar
Paris 1834–1917 Paris

As a pupil of the Ecole des Beaux Arts he learned from Ingres and the Old Masters. Around 1885, he came into contact with Manet and the Impressionists and decided to join them. He loved movement and character studies into which he placed a large quantity of psychological observation. He was unique in his ability to capture and contain fleeting movements in the lives of the people around him. Most of his paintings were produced in his studio and were carried out with the greatest conscientiousness. As opposed to this there is his enormous œuvre of sketches which were made in the best Impressionist technique.

Ill. pp. 17, 19, 76, 77, 84, 85

DENIS, Maurice
Grandville 1870–1943 St.-Germain-en-Laye

Maurice Denis belonged to the circle of young painters who as graduates of the Académie Julian together with Sérusier formed the Nabis. He was strongly influenced by Gauguin's work and Japanese woodcuts. Through Symbolism he found a way to a revival of religious art which soon separated him from his friends. Denis was an excellent author who wrote convincing theories on Post-Impressionist art.

Ill. p. 105

DERAIN, André
Chatou, near Paris 1880–1954 Chambourcy

His friendship and work together with Vlaminck was very important for his artistic development. Derain was one of the co-founders of Fauvism where he clearly took over elements from van Gogh's technique of painting. Taking elements from Cézanne he came close to Cubism later in his life. Art dealers were interested in him from early on in his career. He worked for Vollard from 1907 and from 1909 also for Kahnweiler.

Ill. p. 95

EVENEPOEL, Henri Jacques Edouard
Nice 1872–1899 Paris

A Belgian painter. He settled in Paris in 1892 and belonged to the artists who took up the great final stage of Impressionism, trained himself on its perceptions and carried the style further. An early phase of Impressionist views and techniques was followed by a phase of rejection and turning towards Expressionism. However, his membership of the Fauves was also a transitory stage, as was a short phase of Art Nouveau. His excellent observational talent enabled him to compose exciting paintings combined with an unerring sense for colour and delicate hues.

Ill. p. 110

FANTIN-LATOUR, Henri
Grenoble 1836–1904 Buré (Orne)

Fantin-Latour worked in Paris as a painter and graphic artist. Although he was a friend and contemporary of the Impressionists he did not count himself among their circle and did not exhibit together with them. His painting is more conventional and traditional, his style is close to Degas'. His great work is in portraits and graphic art. Posterity can thank him for his many portraits of the Impressionists and their famous contemporaries.

Ill. p. 103

FORAIN, Jean-Louis
Rheims 1852–1931 Paris

Forain's contemporaries regarded him above all as a caricaturist who was critical of contemporary issues. Several paintings with socio-critical content also brought him a certain amount of fame because the works had a strongly erotic slant. In this area of his work he was close to Toulouse-Lautrec and Daumier. In his paintings he was the youngest of the Impressionists; although in this part of his work his friendship with Degas can be seen.

Ill. p. 73

GAUGUIN, Paul
Paris 1848–1903 Fatu-Iwa (Marquesas Islands)

Gauguin began his artistic career late in his life. Before this he had been a successful banker. He worked at first with the Impressionists and in 1887 he went to Martinique where he discovered his own style. Back in France he moved to Brittany where, after several experiments, he confronted the form-disintegrating *Pointillism* with *Cloissonism*, the style of painting with flat colours and dark contours. His uncontrollable urge to live a simple life in tropical naturalness, a life which was to be completely dedicated to his natural, though artistically notable art led to him spending his last years in the South Sea. Besides Cézanne and van Gogh, Gauguin is the third artist who made a decisive impact on Post-Impressionism.

Ill. pp. 28, 65, 66, 67, 68, 69

GOGH, Vincent van
Groot Zundert 1853–1890 Auvers sur Oise

He was one of the most significant pioneers of 20th century art. He was self-taught and learned from Mauve and Israels, although his main interest was for Millet. After he had got to know the Impressionists' work in Paris he quickly absorbed their perceptions but just as quickly changed to his own individual expressive style. Van Gogh's life was one single fight against himself in his endeavour to capture what he saw on the canvas. During his lifetime he was completely unsuccessful, however, his œuvre was excellent and no other painter has had such an effect on following generations as this master of Post-Impressionism.

Ill. pp. 56, 57, 58, 59, 60, 61, 63, 64

HELLEU, Paul César
Vannes 1859–1927 Paris

Helleu was a painter and graphic artist with an especially talented hand for etching. His main area of work was people and portraits. In the circle around Boudin he painted and sketched a lot at the coast, as he was also interested in landscape. However, it was his portraits which brought him fame. He painted and sketched many of the Impressionists and the artists who came after them.

Ill. opposite title page, p. 13

HODLER, Ferdinand
Berne 1853–1918 Geneva

Developing from naturalism, Hodler quickly developed his own characteristic style. His pictures are defined by well-balanced symmetry, large areas of colour, strangely expressive poses and a use of extreme tension of movement. Especially in his landscapes he is a Post-Impressionist at the beginning of Expressionism, while his figural pictures tend more towards Symbolism. Hodler was a highly regarded artist from Paris to Vienna who had much influence on younger artists.

Ill. p. 116

LIEBERMANN, Max
Berlin 1847–1935 Berlin

Liebermann is regarded as the main representative of German Impressionism. As a pupil of the Art School in Weimar, he trained further in Paris between 1873 and 1878, influenced by Israels, Courbet and Millet. He travelled a lot to collect impressions and to study other masters. He was very impressed by Holland and the people there. The influence of French Impressionism can first be recognized in his style from the 90s. From 1910, he altered his work to colourful, brilliant paintings in a more free and easy style.

Ill. p. 114

MAILLOL, Aristide
Banyuls-sur-Mer 1861–1944 Banyuls-sur-Mer

As a graduate of the Ecole des Beaux Arts he first painted like the Barbizon artists before turning to Impressionism. He came into contact with Gauguin through Daniel de Monfreid; soon after he joined the Nabis. Eye problems forced him to turn more towards sculpture shortly before the turn of the century. His graphic work was made famous by the art dealer Vollard who provided for its propagation. But as a sculptor he found world fame with his incomparable nudes.

Ill. p. 101

MANET, Edouard
Paris 1832–1883 Paris

He was a pupil of Couture, later influenced by the Realists, especially Courbet. His first effect on the public was a scandal which was caused by the exhibition of his picture *Déjeuner sur l'herbe*. He was an innovator in art and as such the central figure among the Impressionists. Although his thoughts and considerations were responsible for the Impressionist style, he himself preferred more conservative contents in the theme of his paintings.

Ill. p. 49

MODERSOHN-BECKER, Paula
Dresden 1876–1907 Worpswede

She cultivated the simplicity of the large form and representation of the unpretentious. The wide moorlands of Worpswede and the work together with the Worpswede painters were important for her paintings. A stay in Paris was decisive for her work; she was impressed by van Gogh, Cézanne and Gauguin and herself arrived at a style of painting using large areas of colour with thick layers of earthy paints. She had contact to the Nabis. She was often ahead of her idols in the mastering of compositional problems.

Ill. p. 117

MONET, Claude
Paris 1840–1926 Giverny

In his early days he was influenced by Courbet, Jongkind and Manet. While studying at the Studio Gleyre, he got to know Pissarro, Renoir and Sisley. They discovered plein air painting together. This group became the core of the Impressionist movement. Monet mainly dedicated himself to landscape painting. He painted the same view again and again at different times of the day, with different lighting and at different times of the year. Monet was the leader of the Impressionists and – involuntarily – its name giver.

Ill. p. 48

PISSARRO, Camille
St. Thomas (West Indies) 1830–1903 Paris

Pissarro arrived in Paris in 1855 where he joined Corot and the painters from the Barbizon, as his whole attention was given to landscape painting. Later he got to know Manet and Monet and became their companion in discovering Impressionism. In the middle of the 80s, he joined up with Seurat in a common attempt to "free painting of fixed forms to a decomposition in a moving atmosphere" – Pointillism. His later work makes him one of the most important Post-Impressionist painters.

Ill. pp. 28, 32, 46, 47, 54, 55

REDON, Odilon
Bordeaux 1840–1916 Paris

In 1868 he got to know Courbet, Manet, Pissarro and Corot at an exhibition and recognized that the Impressionism of that time was the only living art form. Unter Fantin-Latour's guidance he occupied himself a lot with lithography and became an excellent graphic artist. He exhibited along with the Impressionists, however, he did not regard himself as one of them. As a Symbolist he was one of the most significant Post-Impressionist artists.

Ill. pp. 104, 106, 107

RENOIR, Auguste
Limoges 1841–1919 Cagnes

Renoir studied in Gleyre's studio where he got to know Monet and Sisley. Together with them he began to paint from nature. However, Renoir was not, like his friends, a pure landscape painter, he much preferred the human form, the portrait, figure painting. After 1880 he turned away from painting out of doors and returned to the studio as he found that the rash painting of motifs under changing light conditions had a deforming effect on the form and composition which were his main interests.

Ill. pp. 22, 41, 42, 43, 44, 45, 50, 51

SEGANTINI, Giovanni
Arco (Prov. Trento) 1858–1899 Pontresina

In the 19th century there were only a very few artists who managed to find financial success after turning to revolutionary new aims. Segantini was one of those exceptions; early contact to a capable art dealer in Milan soon made the very talented artist internationally famous. He became the main representative of Post-Impressionism in Italy, was a Pointillist and important Symbolist. His work had a great influence also in France and Belgium, Vienna and Munich.

Ill. p. 119

SÉRUSIER, Paul
Paris 1863–1927 Morlaix

His work is on the one hand a bond between the Impressionists and Gauguin's style of painting (they were together in Pont Aven) and on the other hand his painter friends from the Académie Julian: Denis, Bonnard and Vuillard. Together with these friends he formed the *Nabis* who carried the art of Gauguin and van Gogh further. He became one of the leading Symbolists, taught at the Académie Ranson and was one of the Nabis who tended towards religious art which led him to seek contact to the School of Beuron.
Ill. pp. 24, 108, 109

SEURAT, Georges
Paris 1859–1891 Paris

Even during his studies at the Ecole des Beaux Arts, Seurat was very interested in the theoretical elements of painting and especially for all questions relating to the theory of colours, including pure physical laws. He had a great talent for painting and endeavoured from very early on in his career to compose careful, well thought out pictures with well-balanced colours and a harmony between construction and colour. Seurat was the greatest theorist among the *Neo-Impressionists* and the founder of *Pointillism* (although he strictly rejected this term). Many of his friends, including van Gogh, can thank him for much of their basic knowledge.
Ill. pp. 89, 90, 97, 98, 99

SIGNAC, Paul
Paris 1863–1935 Paris

Signac began as an Impressionist and changed with Seurat, who was a good friend, to Pointillism. He was an excellent author on art and in many publications he precisely formulated Seurat's ideas and conveyed them to his colleagues. He was especially interested in sailing ships and in harbour life, but also in landscapes. His preference for these themes was probably responsible for his moving to the Mediterranean after the death of his friend Seurat.
Ill. pp. 91, 92, 93, 100

SLEVOGT, Max
Landshut 1868–1932 Neukastel (Palatinate)

He was a master of Impressionism in Germany along with Liebermann and Corinth. He attended the academy in Munich and during travels between 1890 and 1900 in Paris and Italy he came into contact with the Impressionists and adjusted their perceptions to fit in with his own ideas. His enormous versatility in technique and theme makes it difficult to see him as an Impressionist all the time. He regarded himself as one but formed his own interpretation of the description.
Ill. p. 113

TOULOUSE-LAUTREC, Henri de
Albi 1864–1901 Castle Malromé (Gironde)

Toulouse was a pupil of the academy in Paris and lived at Montmartre. In spite of close contact to the Impressionists he was less influenced by them than the artistic personalities Manet, Renoir and especially Degas. These three artists, like Toulouse-Lautrec, are counted among the Impressionists, but in their personal work they were somewhat removed from the group. Toulouse-Lautrec discovered Parisian life for his art. He captured life around him in a realistic, easy-going Impressionist style. His outstanding technique and ironic spirit made him an incomparable portrayer of the milieu in Paris.
Ill. pp. 78, 79, 80, 81, 82, 83

UTRILLO, Maurice
Paris 1883–1955 Paris

Suzanne Valadon, a favourite model of the Impressionists and later also a painter of outstanding quality was Maurice Utrillo's mother. Utrillo had serious problems with alcohol in his youth. His mother persuaded him to paint for therapeutical reasons and soon a great talent developed. Without obvious instruction from the other painters he discovered his own style which reached from Impressionism to strongly expressive compositions.
Ill. pp. 86, 87

VALLOTTON, Félix
Lausanne 1865–1925 Paris

Vallotton was, above all, an outstanding graphic artist. He quickly achieved international recognition with a novel distribution of colour and ingenious black and white effects. In his painting he orientated himself towards Courbet and Manet, however, he placed special emphasis on strong contours and on exaggerated graphic quality of the figures. He joined the *Nabis* in 1892. He was also a valued member of *La Revue Blanche*.
Ill. p. 120

VLAMINCK, Maurice de
Paris 1876–1958 Reuil-la-Gadelière

In his early work Vlaminck was very much under van Gogh's influence. He painted with strong colours and mainly painted landscapes. In 1900 he got to know André Derain and common interests led to them becoming friends. Fauvism is regarded as having its basis in the work of these two artists. After 1907 he was more influenced by Cézanne's work. He again reduced his colours and discovered a very unique style of landscape which clearly placed him in the circle of Post-Impressionists.
Ill. pp. 71, 72

VUILLARD, Edouard
Cuiseaux 1868–1940 La Baule

Vuillard was closely associated with the Impressionists, joined the *Nabis* and belonged to the central circle of Symbolists. As an excellent graphic artist he produced outstanding lithographs. Some of the best prints in the journal *La Revue Blanche* came from Vuillard. He developed especially matt and transparent colours for his oil paintings. He was a main representative of Post-Impressionism.

Ill. pp. 75, 88

WHISTLER, James
Lowell (Massachusetts) 1834–1903 London

An American/English painter and graphic artist. He studied at Gleyre's studio in Paris. Although he lived mainly in England, he furnished a permanent studio in Paris so that he could learn from the masters from the Barbizon School and from the Impressionists. This knowledge, combined with an exact study of the Dutch masters made him a very successful painter in his own country – even during his lifetime. His participation in the *Les Vingts* exhibition in Brussels also brought him success.

Ill. p. 10

Auguste Renoir 43
Morning Toilet. 1910
Painting, 55 x 46 cm
Musée Jeu de Paume, Paris

Auguste Renoir 44
Coastal Landscape. After 1900
Oil on canvas, 22 x 33 cm
Niedersächsisches Landesmuseum, Hannover

Auguste Renoir 45
Bunch of Chrysanthemums. Ca. 1885
Painting, 82 x 66 cm
Musée des Beaux-Arts, Rouen

Camille Pissarro 46
Avenue along the Canal of the Loing. 1902
Painting, 65 x 81,5 cm
Musée Jeu de Paume, Paris

Camille Pissarro 47
Peasant Girl with Switch. 1881
Painting, 81 x 64,7 cm
Musée Jeu de Paume, Paris

Claude Monet 48
Pond of Water Lilies with Bridge. 1899
Painting, 89 x 93,5 cm
Musée Jeu de Paume, Paris

Edouard Manet 49
Girl Making Her Toilet. 1862
Chalk drawing, 28 x 20 cm
Courtauld Institute, London

Auguste Renoir 50
Woman Sewing. Ca. 1895
Chalk drawing
Private collection

Auguste Renoir 51
Dancing Couple. 1880
Etching

Paul Cézanne 52
Four Bathers. 1879–92
Pencil and black chalk, 20,3 x 22,3 cm
Museum Boymans van Beuningen, Rotterdam

Paul Signac 93
Parasol Pine. 1898
Painting
Musée de l'Annonciade, St. Tropez

Henri Edmond Cross 94
Coastal Landscape. Ca. 1904
Oil on canvas, 48 x 64 cm
Neue Pinakothek, Munich

André Derain 95
Reflections of Light on the Water. 1905
Oil on canvas, 81 x 100 cm
Musée de l'Annonciade, St. Tropez

Georges Braque 96
Antwerp Harbour. 1906
Oil on canvas, 38 x 46 cm
Von der Heydt-Museum, Wuppertal

Georges Seurat 97
Decorator. 1883
Charcoal drawing, 31 x 24 cm
Cabinet des Dessins, Louvre, Paris

Georges Seurat 98
Castle in the Park. 1883
Charcoal drawing, 31,5 x 24 cm
Cabinet des Dessins, Louvre, Paris

Georges Seurat 99
Woman Sitting on the Balcony. 1883
Charcoal drawing, 31 x 24 cm
Cabinet des Dessins, Louvre, Paris

Paul Signac 100
Mont Saint Michel
Charcoal drawing
Cabinet des Dessins, Louvre, Paris

Aristide Maillol 101
Four Girls Standing Together
Pencil and charcoal drawing
Petit Palais, Paris

Pierre Bonnard 102
Sitting Lady with Hat
Pencil drawing
Cabinet des Dessins, Louvre, Paris

Henri Fantin-Latour 103
Group of Men around the Table
Charcoal drawing
Cabinet des Dessins, Louvre, Paris

Odilon Redon 104
The Wings (Pegasus). 1892
Lithograph, 13,9 x 24,5 cm

Maurice Denis 105
Mother and Child. Ca. 1900
Oil on carton, 35,5 x 25,7 cm
Neue Pinakothek, Munich

Odilon Redon 106
Still Life with Flowers. After 1895
Painting, 27 x 19 cm
Musée du Louvre, Paris

Odilon Redon 107
Still Life with Flowers. Ca. 1910
Oil on canvas, 73 x 54 cm
Von der Heydt-Museum, Wuppertal

Paul Sérusier 108
Under the Lamp. 1906
Painting, 60 x 73 cm
Art Museum Atheneum, Helsinki

Paul Sérusier 109
Young Breton Woman Knitting. 1920
Painting, 57 x 39 cm
Musée des Beaux Arts, Orleans

Henri J. E. Evenepoel 110
Café d'Harcourt, Paris. 1897
Oil on canvas, 114 x 148 cm
Städelsches Kunstinstitut, Frankfurt

Pierre Bonnard 111
The Omnibus. Ca. 1895
Oil on canvas, 59 x 41 cm
Private collection, Paris

Pierre Bonnard 112
In a Southern Garden. Ca. 1914
Oil on canvas, 84 x 113 cm
Kunstmuseum, Bern

Max Slevogt 113
The Artist's Children in the Vine Arbour of Neukastel. 1917
Oil on canvas, 61 x 49 cm
Wallraf-Richartz-Museum, Cologne

Max Liebermann 114
Restaurant 'De oude Vink' in Leiden. 1905
Oil on canvas, 71 x 88 cm
Kunsthaus, Zurich

Lovis Corinth 115
Schwabing. 1891
Oil on canvas, 64,5 x 50 cm
Neue Galerie, Linz

Ferdinand Hodler 116
Evening on Lake Geneva. 1898
Oil on canvas, 100 x 130 cm
Kunsthaus, Zurich

Paula Modersohn-Becker 117
Self-Portrait with Red Rose. Ca. 1905
Painting, 65 x 45 cm
Private collection

Cuno Amiet 118
Morning Sun. 1924
Oil on canvas, 86 x 66 cm
Kunstmuseum, Berne

Giovanni Segantini 119
Ploughing. 1887/90
Oil on canvas, 116 x 227 cm
Neue Pinakothek, Munich

Felix Vallotton 120
Sailing Boats at Honfleur. 1912
Oil on canvas, 73 x 54,5 cm
Musée d'Art et Histoire, Neuchâtel

Photographic acknowledgements:
Artothek J. Hinrichs, Planegg: pp. 62, 69, 94, 105, 117
Colorphoto Hinz SWB, Allschwil: p. 59
If not mentioned otherwise, the photos were kindly supplied by museums and collections or come from the Berghaus Archive.